OUR THEATRE TODAY

Our Theatre Today

*A Composite Handbook on the Art, Craft, and
Management of the Contemporary Theatre*

BY

Arthur Hopkins, Brock Pemberton, Alfred Harding,
Irving Pichel, Priestly Morrison, Melville Burke,
Barrett H. Clark, Aline Bernstein, Cleon
Throckmorton, Stanley R. McCandless,
Bertram Harrison, Louis Erhardt,
and Tamara Daykarkhanova

EDITED BY

HERSCHEL L. BRICKER

Essay Index Reprint Series

 BOOKS FOR LIBRARIES PRESS
FREEPORT, NEW YORK

INTERNATIONAL STANDARD BOOK NUMBER:

0-8369-1823-1

LIBRARY OF CONGRESS CATALOG CARD NUMBER:

79-128213

PRINTED IN THE UNITED STATES OF AMERICA

To

MARY ELLA BRICKER

My Mother

ACKNOWLEDGMENTS

Our Theatre Today, begun three years ago, has received the good will of dozens of theatre people. Working with the authors of the several chapters has been pleasant, and I deeply appreciate their keen interest, their willing coöperation, their patience, and their encouragement. Among the many others to whom I am indebted, I should not wish to forego mention of Mr. Melville Burke, for his kindly advice; of Dr. Ronald B. Levinson, Professor of Philosophy, University of Maine, for his helpful suggestions; and of Mr. Harold H. McKeen, for checking the bibliography and quotations. I am especially indebted to my good friend, Dr. Ruth Crosby, Assistant Professor of English, University of Maine, for her constant encouragement, and for the many hours she has spent with me in going over the manuscripts and in reading proof.

H. L. B.

Orono, Maine

CONTENTS

INTRODUCTION..............*Herschel L. Bricker* xv

INTRODUCTION FOR STUDENTS............. xix
Herschel L. Bricker

PART ONE: HISTORY

THE THEATRE'S FIRST THREE THOUSAND
YEARS..................*Alfred Harding* 3

I. GREECE AND ROME.................... 5
The Great Greeks—Two on the aisle in Athens—
Borrowed plumage: the Roman Theatre.

II. THE CONTINENTAL THEATRE.......... 29
In Cassock and Cotta—Italy: from the classics to
grand opera—Spain: the drama of cloak and sword
—France: drafting the "classic" formula—The
theatre meets the Revolution—Through romance
and realism to the present—Germany: from Hans
Wurst to Hitler.

III. ENGLAND 75
In Good Queen Bess's Glorious Days—Reformation and Restoration—A theatre of actor-managers.

IV. AMERICA 98
A Theatre from Abroad—The stars in their courses
discover the road—The Empire and the Syndicate
—And there were Shuberts—The road that went
down hill—Shadows on a roll of celluloid—Enter
the Actors' Equity Association—The theatre in
temporary eclipse.

CONTENTS

x

THE PRESENT DAY THEATRE......*Irving Pichel* 143

A change takes place in the theatre—Waiting for younger men to push forward—The influence of the talking pictures—The condition of the theatre today differs greatly from that of two decades ago —The university theatre is the most hopeful place to look for a new wave of creativeness.

PART TWO: PLAYS AND PRODUCTION

PLAYWRIGHT AND THEATRE...*Barrett H. Clark* 157

The playwright's excuses—Managers buy and produce the best plays they can find—No one method of classification is properly applicable to managers as a class—No fixed way of buying or selling plays —Circumstances favor the newcomer—Broadway does not give us everything that we want in the theatre—We must move into the country—Our problem is to find some means of reaching an immense playgoing public.

PRODUCER AND PLAY...........*Arthur Hopkins* 177

It is imperative that the producer should find and believe in the author's intent—A producer should not tamper with a work which he has found to have authenticity.

PART THREE: STAGE DIRECTION

THE DIRECTOR................*Brock Pemberton* 185

The director's task is at once one of the most difficult and important assignments in the theatre— There are two general schools of directing: those who visualize every detail in advance and those who let the performance develop itself—The former discloses the full activities of a good director.

MY METHOD OF DIRECTING.....*Melville Burke* 197
> Mastery of mechanical skill is the structural basis of stage direction—A director must guide rather than propel his actors through a performance—A director should be sympathetic to the play—Approaching the play prior to rehearsal—The rehearsals—The director's qualifications—Actors are of two kinds.

MY METHOD OF DIRECTING...*Bertram Harrison* 215
> The reader accompanies the director through a production period—Study of the script—The dressing of a stage setting—Different methods of directing for different plays—The rehearsal period—The by-products of stage direction.

MY METHOD OF DIRECTING...*Priestly Morrison* 237
> Staging a play involves an unbelievable amount of careful planning and painstaking effort—The director's first reading of a play—Understanding between author and director—A page of play manuscript—Drawing the ground plans—The property plot—Casting the play—The grind of daily rehearsal—Hints to aspiring young stage directors.

PART FOUR: STAGECRAFT

SCENIC ART................*Cleon Throckmorton* 269
> Scenic art has not become important until within the last twenty-five years—European influence—The fresh vision of new men—A designer's qualifications—Designs upon paper and their realization on the stage—This country's artists—New and damaging roads—Scenic art should be an art and not a traditional procedure.

TECHNICAL METHODS......*Cleon Throckmorton* 279

Many methods of producing scenery—The creative idea comes first—Arriving at the attack to be made on a given play—Drawings—Scale model—Keep lighting in mind—Material—Interior and exterior settings—Water paint—Shifting sets—Stages—New methods are born with each artist that enters the field.

THE PROCEDURE FOR LIGHTING A PRODUCTION...*Louis Erhardt* and *S. R. McCandless* 287

Lighting should be more closely coördinated with the traditional means of expression—Plans for lighting as indicated in the manuscript—The type of play: tragedy, comedy—The style of production: classicism, romanticism, realism, expressionism—The interpretation of the mental picture in terms of lighting: visibility, intensity, color, form, movement, locale, composition, mood—Summary: analysis of two plays.

THE APPLICATION OF LIGHTING TO THE STAGE....*S. R. McCandless* and *Louis Erhardt* 313

The use of instruments: the acting area, blending the acting areas, background lighting, special instruments for lighting definite objects, *etc.*—Procedure —Steps and precautions.

COSTUME.....................*Aline Bernstein* 331

Careful study of text of play—The dress must be suitable—Four things to be considered in designing a costume—Designing costumes for period plays—Material used—Color—The dye pot—Cutting and fitting—Finished product is thing that counts.

MAKE-UP FOR THE STAGE *Tamara Daykarkhanova* 339

Make-up in the past—Stage make-up in the American theatre—Make-up and stage lighting—Analysis of make-up—The technique of make-up—The sucessions of operations in make-up.

APPENDIX I 363

APPENDIX II 368

APPENDIX III 378

APPENDIX IV 385

APPENDIX V 402

BIBLIOGRAPHY 409

INDEX 417

INTRODUCTION

by

Herschel L. Bricker

This is the first book of its kind, a composite reflection by a dozen specialists on several important aspects of the theatre. The authors of the various chapters—producers, directors, scene designers, critics, actors, lighting experts, and writers of books and articles on the theatre—have been invited to speak each from his own standpoint with the utmost freedom. Their remarks are directed to the play-going public as a whole as well as to the students of the theatre in colleges, little theatres, and dramatic schools.

If the reader has no contact with the theatre other than enjoying the performances he sees from across the footlights, he may be interested and possibly surprised to note the many steps involved in preparing a single production. This book will reveal the hundreds of detailed problems that confront the producer prior to and during the period of rehearsals. In fact, the preliminary activity centered about putting a play on the stage might be viewed by lookers-on as a drama in itself. The authors give one a peek behind the proscenium, a chance to envisage the drama that goes into action there during the weeks previous to the opening night, with its many varied comic and tragic scenes played by scores of "actors" and "actresses."

The emphasis on this aspect of the theatre is made necessary by the essential nature of theatre art. A painter or a sculptor is not directly concerned with anyone in his work; the final product, be it good or bad, is credited entirely to him. A single artistic stage production, however, involves dozens of individuals, each working directly toward the final goal—the playwright, the actors, the director, the scene designer and his staff of experts and technicians, the costume designer and costume makers, and the make-up artist. The phases represented by all these persons, as discussed by the authors of this book, will give one an idea of the fascination and the romance of the theatre.

Alfred Harding, in charge of the editorial work for the Actors' Equity Association, and for many years an active theatre worker, outlines the history of dramatic art, while Irving Pichel, actor and director of screen and stage plays, discusses the present day theatre and its problems. Following these chapters, Barrett H. Clark, an international authority on drama, gives us a few sidelights on the playwright and producer; and Arthur Hopkins, the director whose long list of successful productions has won for him the status of New York's most noted producer-director, tells us what attitude the producer should take toward a play which he is about to stage. Four directors of wide experience, who have guided the destinies of many Broadway successes, Brock Pemberton, Melville Burke, Bertram Harrison, and Priestly Morrison, talk informally about types and methods of directing. Cleon Throckmorton, noted designer and builder of stage scenery, devotes two chapters to scenic art. These are followed by chapters on stage lighting written by Stanley R. McCandless, Associate Professor of Lighting, Yale University, who has had a tremendous influence on the development of lighting, and by Louis Erhardt, recently an Assistant to Professor McCandless and now lighting expert for Donald Oenslager. America's foremost woman scenic and costume designer, Aline

Bernstein, writes about the art and methods of costuming. The last chapter, on make-up, is written by Tamara Daykarkhanova, known to the theatre publics of Europe and America, and at the present time, the director of the Studio of Stage Make-Up, New York.

An excellent presentation of a fine play might be thought of as a symbol standing for all the dramatic performances that have been given down through the three thousand years of theatre history. It is a symbol of struggle and development. It is a symbol of artistic achievement. It silently expresses a hope of future artistic fulfillment. But in actuality it means more than this. The presentation of a play represents much effort by untiring and enthusiastic men and women, working to satisfy themselves, and to add another significant contribution to the pages of dramatic history, for only through this means, as every true artist of the theatre knows, can real progress be made.

This is the spirit of the men and women who have written *Our Theatre Today*. Their exposition embodies a living art and craft.

INTRODUCTION FOR STUDENTS

by

HERSCHEL L. BRICKER

THIS book is written for two groups of students: those who are sincerely interested in coming into actual contact with play production through practical experience in order to gain a deeper appreciation of acted drama; and those who feel that they have sufficient artistic ability to warrant the more exacting study of the several phases of production for the purpose of finding a work upon which to expend their boundless energy, and from which they may derive their joys in compensation. If the reader considers himself a member of either one or the other of the two divisions, then let us ponder over a few thoughts together before delving into the body of the book.

Twenty years from now—perhaps even ten years from now, I believe the legitimate theatre will play not only to much larger and more enthusiastic audiences than it does to-day, but also to audiences that will be much more intelligently critical.[1] I make that statement, be it right or wrong, on the

---

[1] Although the following from Kenneth Macgowan's *Footlights Across America* (Harcourt, Brace and Company 1929, p. 12) is now out of date, the statistics will give the reader some knowledge regarding the number of people who participate in dramatic art in one way or another.
"The extent of the local theater in America cannot be estimated at all accurately. George Pierce Baker of Yale has listed 1800 names of producing organizations. *Theatre Arts Monthly* has been in correspondence with 1000 groups. *The Drama Monthly* has 1000 on its list, and during the past two years it has printed the names of plays produced by almost 500. The Pasadena Community Theater sent out a questionnaire to 600,

supposition that the majority of people attending the theatre ten or twenty years from now will be those who are today studying production in our many little theatre groups, and in our colleges and universities.

Those studying drama by taking an active part in producing plays—and there are thousands doing that very thing—are developing a lasting appreciation for, and a better understanding of, acted drama.

On this assumption, every person interested in this apparently very popular art owes it to himself to attempt to study theatre in an effort to cultivate a keener sense about it, even if

and found more than a tenth of them dead and gone. I should estimate that there are 100 organizations of laymen making from 4 to 25 productions a year, and 100 universities doing about the same amount of work. There are at least 1000 groups that give one or two plays each season, 6000 high schools that produce as part of their class work anywhere from one bill of short plays to 25 bills of long and short, and 6000 more high schools with dramatic clubs that give at least one play a year.

	200 local theatres	1,000 sporadic groups	6,000 high school classes	6,000 high school clubs	Total
Average number of bills produced	5	1.5	2	1.5	.....
Average number of performances per bill	3	1	1	1	.....
Average number of performances per season	15	1.5	2	1.5	.....
Total number of plays produced .	1,000	1,500	12,000	9,000	23,500
Total number of performances .	3,000	1,500	12,000	9,000	25,500
Number of theatrical workers	10,000	25,000	180,000	120,000	335,000
Total number of admissions	1,500,000	500,000	6,000,000	4,500,000	12,500,000"

he wishes to use his knowledge only to the extent of enjoying plays. However, there is another factor which I can best set forth by a remark I overheard upon coming from the theatre one evening. Without intending to eavesdrop, I could not help hearing a young lady say to her escort: "She continues studying music; but it seems to me, if she studies a hundred years she will never be an artist." That very statement could be made of many people pursuing some phase of the theatre, and the pity of it—many people who intend to make some phase of it their profession.

My point is this: It is desirable for a student to study dramatic art for the sake of gaining cultural benefit; but he should not allow a spurt of undeveloped and undirected enthusiasm to lead him to believe that he has found his niche. In the latter event, the theatre would be far happier if the individual suddenly decided to dig gold in Alaska, plow corn in Iowa, or hoe potatoes in Aroostook.

A person who has studied piano has, undoubtedly, a finer appreciation of music than another person who does not know one note from another; but to have had piano lessons is no guarantee that one will become an Ignace Paderewski, is it? An individual who has had work at one of our best art schools will possess a deeper feeling for paintings than the individual who has studied only from observation; but how likely is the former to become a Henri Matisse? The same is true of dramatic art. Simply because one pursues the study of theatre —directing, acting, scene designing, stage lighting, costuming, make-up—is no assurance that one will become a Max Reinhardt.

Do not misunderstand. I am not saying that one either is, or is not, suited to follow the Dionysians regardless of effort, for it is absolutely necessary to do careful study, if one wishes to perfect one's dramatic technique. And I am not saying that a degree, the highest attainable, signifies the qualities—imagination, determination, comprehension, delicate feeling, understanding of emotions, vision, and love of humanity—that are vitally essential. As with any art, the aspirant must have what I choose to call an artistic sense; and that artistic sense comes largely from within. It is the basis from which a true artist derives his means of expression. It is the pivot from which he begins, and from which he must always revolve, even as he acquires more and more skill in the use of his medium—stagecraft. It is true talent, and as Constantin Stanislavsky says: "True talent is deeply hidden in the soul. It is not easy to lure it from its hiding place." [2]

Now the questions arise: How does one determine whether one has this artistic sense? What approach should one make in training for the theatre? Certainly there is no yardstick by which to measure accurately one's ability; but there are a few suggestions that may prove helpful.

It seems to me that the superior person who believes that he is gifted, and who has the determination to find out, should choose a capable and frank director to guide him in his early efforts. A man of no artistic ability can do much to set obstacles in the path of the neophyte—obstacles that will stand in the way throughout his career. The student of the theatre needs most of all a chance to express the ideas that will come from his fertile and vivid imagination, if he is worthy of the opportunity, under careful guidance.

After one has thus placed himself, there are, among many things, at least five of primary importance, to which he must always be keenly alert. To list them: (1) keep an open mind, (2) acquire a thorough historic background, (3) strive for a sympathetic working knowledge of stagecraft, (4) remember that the final goal is to translate abstract æsthetic values into

[2] *My Life in Art*, p. 89. Little, Brown.

concrete artistic terms, (5) gain adequate experience before beginning work of a professional nature.

AN OPEN MIND

If the theatre is to flourish, it is necessary for those participating within its pale to nurture, through a long and exacting course of study and practice, an individual and distinctive approach of their own. No student of dramatic technique should commit himself to the theories of one book, or one instructor. He should make it a policy during his period of preparation, to become acquainted with as many aspects as possible, keeping always an open mind. He should not be hasty in setting his mind on one theory, or on one group of methods, especially when it is based on the experiences of a limited few. He should not make a study of dramatic art, if he is not capable of approaching his subject with a mind willing to glean the best from every attainable source, and if he does not have the initiative to mould it, along with his own creative ideas, into a mature whole. It takes time to reach this goal, more time than most amateurs wish to spend. And therein lies a test that will reveal whether the student is superficially interested or genuinely sincere.

There are too many in the amateur and legitimate theatres today who have had insufficient training, and who have no artistic conceptions—no imagination upon which to depend. Thus, it should behoove the student of the theatre to approach his work with an open mind, and with a determination to listen wherever there is an opportunity, and then to choose wisely.

HISTORIC BACKGROUND

Acquiring a thorough historic background goes hand in hand with keeping an open mind. To have a thorough foundation—to know the history of the theatre since the days of the Greeks, to be able to visualize its developments and changes, and to be able to place it in relation to its contemporary society—will serve as an inspiration, and as a guide in itself.

KNOWLEDGE OF STAGECRAFT

Stagecraft is to the theatre what tools and a knowledge of the human physique are to the sculptor, or what the canvas and the palette are to the painter. Just as it is impossible for the sculptor, or the painter, to work without his mediums, so it is impossible for the producer of plays to work successfully without a comprehensive usable knowledge of the craft. It is through this means that the dramatic artist is able to create balanced, and significant stage scenes. He may be able to visualize his desired effects, but if he is unable to set them into a harmonious symphony—to make them reveal his visual images, he will be unable to maintain a high place in the theatrical realm.

ARTISTIC TERMS

Acted drama is an art translated through the means of stagecraft. To know stagecraft is one thing; and to use the knowledge of stagecraft as a means of conveying harmonious beauty, atmospheric correctness, and sympathetic picturization, is another. The attempt to translate abstract æsthetic values into concrete artistic terms is a touchstone, for it will invariably register the ambitious beginner as one having a distinct artistic sense, or as an utter failure.

ADEQUATE EXPERIENCE

As one traverses the theatre world from Broadway to the least of the little theatre groups, one hears more and more the complaint that too many people are rushing headlong into the theatre profession without adequate experience. It may be another footprint of our "rushing age"; I do not know. But I am pretty certain that, if it continues, it is going to check the healthy growth of our theatre. Our theatre aspirants should be encouraged to go through a much longer and a much more thorough period of study. Just how this can be managed for those who aspire to the empyreal heights, does not seem to be very well defined either by our amateur or our legitimate divisions.

It will have to be admitted, regrettable as it may seem, that the people bathing in the glory of our legitimate theatres today will not remain there forever. It will be necessary for a few, at least, of our ever increasing numbers, to carry on play production. And surely it is admitted that it is desirable for our younger generation to prepare for these offices. We have gone too long now on a hit or miss basis.

Some persons on the legitimate side of the fence declare that the little theatres, and especially courses in our colleges and universities, are doing much more harm than good toward training dramatic students; but I believe those persons are forgetting that many of our colleges and universities today are much better equipped, both in the way of instruction and in materials, to give work, than they were, say, fifteen years ago. Such critics are remembering only the amateur groups that are largely composed of a collection of individuals who will never be anything more than superficial enthusiasts, and who always stand in the way of desirable growth. It is true, I think, that dramatic art, more than any other, is impeded by the efforts of numerous willing but artless souls. It must break from this fetter before any true progress can be made. People must be educated to the fact that not every Tom, Dick, or Harry can stage plays.

At any rate, the high grade amateur training station seems to provide a place where the individual may test his genuine interest and ability. At the same time, it does seem unwise for any student who has had a few years' experience in a dramatic department, or in a little theatre, to consider that he is ready to step on to Broadway. Such experience is no certificate that one is prepared to impose oneself on the legitimate stage. If the student could serve an apprenticeship with a chosen man of reputation, or with a professional theatre group, upon completing his early stage training, the situation would be more satisfactory. However, no dependable means has been established whereby this is possible.[3]

In any event, it is well for the youth of our theatre to spend time moulding his artistic being into something worthy of the goal he wishes to attain. He must gain more experience; and if he is honest with himself, and fair to the theatre, he will fight for a place to obtain it.

In the course of his study the student should remember that dramatic art will never be greater than those who promote it are great. It will never attain its highest possibilities until it demands the best of those in its field. If the theatre can lay any claim to art, then it cannot stand in the way of progress which must come through the freedom of the individual.

Let those who aspire to do worthy things in our theatre bear in mind that play production cannot attain its ultimate artistic realm until it is concerned with a great play, æsthetically staged in its proper environment, played by actors of deep insight and high sincerity, and directed by a man of compre-

---

[3] Eva LeGallienne began a free school in connection with her professional repertory theatre in the fall of 1928. However, as she has had her company out on long road tours for the past two years, the school has been temporarily discontinued. Miss LeGallienne hopes to reëstablish her school in the future. I sincerely hope she may, for it is badly needed.

hension, of vision, and of a profound understanding of human nature. Then, our theatre will be raised to a level that will command the respect it deserves. It is an art worthy of that place.

PART ONE

HISTORY

THE THEATRE'S FIRST THREE THOUSAND YEARS

by

ALFRED HARDING

Alfred Harding has been in charge of the editorial work of the Actors' Equity Association since 1923. He served as reporter and dramatic editor, and as critic for the Washington *Daily News* in 1921, and as reporter for the New York *Morning Telegraph* in 1922. During 1930 and 1931 he was correspondent for the Montreal Daily Star. His book —*The Revolt of the Actors*, published in 1929, is probably his best known piece of work on the theatre.

THE THEATRE'S FIRST THREE THOUSAND YEARS

by

ALFRED HARDING

CHAPTER I

GREECE AND ROME

The Great Greeks

THE art of the theatre is the oldest of the arts known to man. Before ever there were written records, or pictures, or even the beginnings of speech, individual prehistoric men demonstrated to their fellows how they had stalked or been stalked by their natural enemies and how, in the encounters which followed, they had emerged victorious. They were, invariably, success stories; the conquered never returned to tell what fate had befallen them.

Yet, with all this ancient background, the history of the theatre as a medium for the portrayal of a story by actors on a stage before an audience is a matter of less than three thousand years. And that is no more than yesterday and the day before as history is reckoned.

The first recognizable ancestor of the theatre we know is discernible through the mists of history in Greece in 535 B. C. That was about the beginning of one of those rare great periods of history.

It must have been fun to be alive in Greece at that time. For here was something quite new to that ancient world—

5

a radical experiment in social pioneering—and it was working. Hitherto every one of the great civilizations the world
had known had flourished or fallen with the fortunes of its
ruling caste, a relatively small group holding in subjection
a great mass of miserable, oppressed, and hopeless people
through the agencies of a dominant priesthood and a ruthless army.

But as Greek civilization emerged from its cocoon of
barbarism it developed a federation of city states, cemented
lightly by ties of a common ancestry, religion, and language
and united briefly in moments of extreme peril. Within each
of those sovereign city states the citizens had rights and
privileges as well as obligations; they exulted in their city's
triumphs, shared in its prestige, and sorrowed in its humiliations. Their priestly class confined itself to its temples and
their rites and made no attempt to control the thinking of the
people. It was, in short, an eager, inquiring, independent
civilization whose horizons, physical, intellectual, and cultural,
were expanding before men's eyes. Not even the swelling
shadow of the Persian Empire, already darkening the eastern
skies above the colonies in Asia Minor, could damp the ardor
of the Greek spirit. Life was a pageant, fine and stirring and
well worth the living. At such a time and to such a people
the theatre first made itself manifest.

It was no new invention, even so, but rather a development
of events which had been long in the shaping. The Greeks
worshipped many gods—they loved Dionysos, conqueror of
death and lord of the vine. His festivals, and particularly
the Dionysos Eleuthereus in the spring, were occasions for
widespread rejoicing. Business was abandoned, the law courts
were closed, the whole city and all who were in it held high
holiday. Masked, or with faces daubed with the lees of wine,
processions streamed to the places of worship, roaring choruses

of praise to Dionysos, improvising dance steps—caught up for the time being from the ordinary routine of living, transformed into the intimates, the equals almost, of the god they served.

Some of the songs were familiar to all; others were composed on the spur of the moment; there would be snatches of dialogue between the leader and inspired members of the group. Here was a fit background and stage for the next short, but immensely important step—from the narration of a story to its enactment.

In 535 B. C. the festival of Dionysos Eleuthereus, known also as the City Dionysia because its celebration was within the walls of Athens in distinction to others held in the groves and fields, was organized, and Thespis of Icaria won the first prize offered for tragic poetry. It is this same Thespis (because of whom actors are still known as Thespians) who is credited with the introduction of an actor in addition to the leader of the chorus. He was probably that first actor himself, as well as being the dramatist and director of the production. The chorus was still the heart of Thespis' drama, and the acted part of the play was little more than a series of interludes to bind together and to explain its songs and dances —but the first step had been taken. Action was now an integral part of the drama.

Ten years after this world première Aeschylus, first of the trio of Greek tragic poets whose efforts raised the drama to heights rarely achieved since, was born in Eleusis. While he was establishing his literary reputation, the long lowering Persian storm burst, and every Greek hand was drafted to meet its menace. Responding brilliantly to the crisis, these citizen soldiers met and turned back the superior forces of Darius and Xerxes in the land engagements of Marathon (490) and Plataea (479), and in the naval battle of Salamis

(480). Aeschylus served with the Athenian contingent at Marathon and Salamis and acquitted himself creditably on both occasions.

Athens had furnished the leadership in this repulse of the Persians, and during the next few decades the city rode high. It was the actual capital of Greece. Treasure poured into its coffers from its tributaries and from commerce with its neighbors. Literature, drama, and the arts sprang into full bloom. Whatever the Athenians touched at this period turned to gold under their hands. Their writers opened vistas of thought which even today have not been completely explored. In the realms of thought and beauty the few years which followed Marathon are still the high water mark of human achievement.

It was in the midst of this glorious age that Aeschylus came to full flower. Writing for the festivals of Dionysos he used themes naturally limited to the gods and the legendary heroes and the conflicts in which they became involved. Over and over again in his stories of conflicts between gods and heroes, or between the greater and the lesser gods, he preached of the disastrous impact of sin, not only upon the sinner but upon his descendants for long generations until by hard won atonement the sin was expiated.

He was not a smooth writer, or an easy one. There were still tricks of speech and drama to be learned by his successors, but for lyric grandeur and nobility of thought and expression, Aeschylus of the *Oresteia* stands on a lonely peak.

Between 490 and 458 Aeschylus is supposed to have written ninety plays of which the complete texts of seven remain. One of them, *The Suppliants*, is the oldest of extant dramas. He won the tragic prize twelve times, and after his death the rule requiring new plays for each festival was relaxed to permit subsequent production of his works.

Two special contributions beyond his plays Aeschylus is also credited with having bequeathed to the theatre. He introduced a second actor to the scene where only the chorus leader and one actor had stood before—and new possibilities of drama came with him. And he set the fashion of writing trilogies—that is, three plays about a single central theme. The plays were short, not much more than a thousand to eleven hundred lines apiece. The three together took not much longer to present than a modern drama. That form, however, permitted progress in time, change of locale, and reason for a difference in costume, which served the same purposes as our division into acts. The acts of the Greek drama were simply interludes where the chorus came in. They did not divide the play into its natural parts as acts now do.

During the last ten years of his work Aeschylus overlapped the creative lifetime of Sophocles (495–406). In Sophocles many students of the theatre feel that tragic writing reached its finest flower. If he had lost something of the magnificence of Aeschylus, he had gained something of the humanity which was lacking in the older writer. Certainly he was the better technician of the two—one of the greatest the world has known. The gods loomed somewhat less impressively in his writings than the noble men who were their adversaries.

Of approximately one hundred plays Sophocles is supposed to have written, only seven have come down to us in complete form. *Oedipus the King* is generally held to be his masterpiece, though votes are also in for *Electra, Antigone, Oedipus at Colonus,* and *Ajax.*

Sophocles introduced the third actor. With his appearance the Greek dramatic cast reached proportions to which it ever after rigidly adhered. That is not to say that dramatists were committed to casts with only three characters, but it did impose a limit upon the number of characters with lines to speak who might appear on the stage together. By the use of various masks and costumes these three actors could and did portray scores of characters in one play. But when dramatic action required the presence of more than three of them on the stage together, the number in excess of three were required to remain silent during that scene. Sometimes that convention rather strained credulity, for it was necessary to have a character hear speeches to which he would ordinarily reply, and forego that reply or hear it made by another character. But it was not without certain advantages. It concentrated the attention of the audience, made the identification of the speakers easier (for there were no play bills or programs), and it resulted in less congestion on what was still a pretty small stage.

TWO ON THE AISLE IN ATHENS

Greek tragic writing was at its height during this period, and production was typical of what we call the classic drama. If through the magic of some time-machine, we could be transported two thousand years to Athens in the middle of the fifth century B. C., this is the sort of production and these the conditions we should find:

While the fingers of dawn still probe futilely at the black bowl of the horizon, all Athens is astir. The dark streets are full of hurrying forms all converging on the theatre of Dionysos, nestled in the slope of the Acropolis. Clutched in each hand, or tied securely in the fold of a robe, is a small stamped metal disc, or two obols in cash (about six cents). Admission used to be free, but since the riots a few years ago, and the complaints that foreigners were getting all the best seats, this charge is now made. Small as it is there is already grumbling that it is making the theatre too expensive for

many of the citizens, and a law is pending which will require
the admission price to be provided by the state to any citizen
who may demand it.

The gray light that precedes the dawn is scarcely more
than a suggestion, but already the rows of benches are rapidly
filling. Are our seats up there? Half way to heaven! We
aren't likely to miss anything in the audience—if they'd only
move the performance out there.

Far, far below us, for we are near the top of the theatre,
is the circle of the orchestra, beaten hard by the feet of
generations of dancers, a small altar to Dionysos in its center.
Across the floor of the orchestra, opposite us, is the low stage
on which the action will take place, backed by the "skene,"
or stage building. Three doors pierce its wall through which
the occupants of the palace or temple it may represent will
make their entrances and exits. But since only those who
dwell there, or are legitimately there, can use those doors,
the entrances from the wings are reserved for those who come
from a distance. The entrance to the right of the audience
is nearer the city, and persons coming thence, or from that
neighborhood, would naturally enter from it; the entrance
to our left gives onto the road to Piraeus, Athens' seaport,
and so it is through that entrance that persons from a distance
would appear. It helps to place people, and so it is a useful
convention.

Around the rim of the orchestra runs a row of thrones.
The larger one in the center is naturally for the Priest of
Dionysos. Each of the sixty-seven bears a tablet indicating the
office or the position of its occupant.

From the orchestra fourteen aisles radiate like the spokes
of a wheel. They go up and up, seventy-eight rows. The top,
near which we are sitting, is a hundred yards from and a
hundred feet above the orchestra floor.

Back of the thrones are the reserved seats, more than twenty rows of them. They are conferred by the state on certain officials and classes or for particular services. So there are places for the priests of various religions, for members of the Council of 500, for the orphans of soldiers fallen in battle, for the judges of the various contests, for foreign ambassadors and for certain public benefactors. Those who have reserved seats can take their time about arriving, and the more important will be met and conducted to their places by state officials. If they are popular, they are greeted with applause, if unpopular, with caustic remarks and hisses or the ancient Grecian equivalent of the Bronx Cheer.

And then come all the rest of us two obol people, eighteen to twenty thousand of us. We come with rugs and cushions, for the wooden benches are backless and low for the average man, and we carry supplies of food and drink. Though we may have eaten before leaving home, we are going to be here a long time. We present a gay, colorful appearance—white, red, brown, and yellow robes, vestments, and uniforms—even women up in the top rows—this is one of the few chances they have of getting out in public. No wonder our allies and visitors are impressed.

By now the dawn is fully here. The Priest of Dionysos stirs on his throne. A procession marches in from the wings— the chorus—and the play is on. It may be that we are witnessing the world première of *Electra* or *Oedipus the King*.

It is a marvelously responsive audience. Not only does it know all the stories on which these plays are based, but the average level of intelligence is high. Woe to the playwright who offends with a false quantity, or the actor who stumbles in his lines. Groans, hisses, and a concerted kicking of sandaled heels against the backs of their benches may force the player or the play to be taken off. But wise and noble sayings or great performances are welcomed with enormous pleasure, with shouts and the clapping of hands, and the play may be halted for an encore. Nor was it always unpremeditated—claques were then, as now, a factor in the theatre.

It would still be possible to over estimate the intellectual calibre of these audiences. They were from all classes and all ranks in the nation, and there were all kinds of people in them. There were those who slept through the entire performance and others who, no doubt, talked in the finest passages, or who ate and drank noisily. There were fools, and show-offs, and good hearted but dumb people, too. But, on the whole, the Athenians of that time were grand audiences and worthy of the plays they were summoned to see.

Contemporary with Sophocles in time, but a whole world away in thought, was Euripides (480–406), third of the glorious trio. Sophocles was conservative, polished, witty, urbane—a man of the world. Euripides was a scholar, aloof, withdrawn, and definitely on the radical side.

Athens was changing, too. The old exaltation and nobility, which had been characteristic of living in the days of Marathon and Salamis, had faded. Sparta had challenged Athenian leadership in Greece, and all the Grecian world had been embroiled on one side or the other. Half a century of merciless warfare had spilled the best blood in the land and impoverished all the contestants. Now, as the fifth century was ticking its way off the calendar, Athens was being crowded to the wall. Defeated by land and sea, deserted by her allies, she lay at Sparta's mercy, forced to make the best of her conqueror's hard terms. The long walls which linked the city to her sea-port were to be destroyed, and all her galleys, save twelve, were to be handed over to the victors, and Athens was to bind herself to do the bidding of Sparta in all things. All Greece rejoiced as the walls fell and the galleys went up in smoke, for Athens had never been an easy mistress, but with the fall of Athens, less than two years after the death of Sophocles and Euripides, the great days of Greece were gone—never to return.

The shadow of these coming events was dark over Euripides, and they colored his writing. If, because the theatre was still bound to a religious festival, his themes had to be the old familiar stories of the gods and heroes—well, he could write them, but he would show them as they were— and the record indicated that the gods were capable of some pretty dirty tricks. Of men, too, he would write as he knew them, and there were elements of divinity in the human characters he depicted. So, less noble than Aeschylus, not such a technician as Sophocles, he was more human and sympathetic than either.

It was his bad luck to be forced to compete with Sophocles at the height of his career, and of his ninety-two plays only five gained the prize. It was not only that, though. He had the misfortune to be ahead of his time. Brilliant and tolerant as the Athenians were in many respects, they were still not ready for a playwright who opposed war, or who questioned the realities of religion too closely. On one occasion his audience, believing he had revealed too much of the Eleusinian Mysteries, turned on him, and he saved his life only by taking refuge at the altar of Dionysos in the center of the orchestra. Brought to trial, he was subsequently acquitted, more, however, on his martial record than because he had demonstrated his innocence of the charges brought against him. The taint of suspicion still clung to him and somewhat later the author of *Medea, The Trojan Women, The Bacchae,* and other plays was sent into the outer darkness of exile, to die at the court of Philip of Macedon.

Whether they liked, or respected, or feared, or hated Euripides, the fifth century Athenians were sufficiently good judges of literature to seize upon his plays with avidity. New productions from his pen were awaited with an excitement hard to realize in these days of many and easy diversions. With his passing, the sun of Greek tragedy had set.

The tragic contests continued for some time still. New plays were being produced as late as the reign of the Roman Emperor Hadrian, in the second century A. D., but after the fifth century B. C. revivals of the earlier masterpieces became more common and from the third century B. C. they were customary. The last recorded production in Athens occurred in the fifth century A. D.

Altogether the contests of the City Dionysia had a run of close to a thousand years. Yet in the first hundred years of their existence they reached and passed their peak. The remainder of the course was a long slope—down hill all the way.

If tragedy could not survive the impact with disastrous facts, comedy rose to new heights during the period of Athens' greatest stress. It, too, was a product of the festival of Dionysos, but where tragedy evolved from a contemplation of the noble aspects of the god, comedy stemmed from the orgies which were no less an integral part of his divinity.

During the earlier days of the contests, each poet was required to take on the entertainment for a whole day, and the bill consisted of three tragedies and a comedy. Very often the poets made use of the characters and themes of the tragedies for comic relief in the afterpiece. But gradually the Lenaea became the comic contest, and the City Dionysia turned definitely to tragedy.

The Lenaea was largely a domestic festival. It fell toward the end of January, when winter held the Mediterranean in its grip, and travel was both difficult and dangerous. It was easier and on the whole safer to permit the poets freedom to speak their minds at such a time than when the whole of Greece was looking on.

Freedom of speech was no academic abstraction to the comic poets of Greece. Never in the world has a group of playwrights been so personal, bitter, and rough as the writers of the old comedy in Athens. There were literally no lengths to which they might not—and did not—go. When they laid about them at the social evils of the time, their weapons were more likely to be bludgeons than scalpels. Theoretically it was all good, clean fun and no harm meant. But the citizens who doubled up on the hillside while Aristophanes went after Socrates in *The Clouds* could later have sat in the dicastery, or grand jury, which condemned that great thinker to the fatal cup of hemlock.

No doubt about it, this Aristophanes (448–385), was one of the great comic writers of all time. A good deal of his stuff, by modern standards, is pretty low and rough, but it is still enormously funny. Just a few years ago a spirited revival of *Lysistrata* became a Broadway sellout. And then it came into conflict with the moralists of the law in Los Angeles, of all places, and it was rumored that a process server was scouring the city for several days in a futile search for a "Mr. A. Aristophanes," reported to be the author of the raided play.

Like many satirists, Aristophanes was little pleased with the life he saw about him. He turned longing eyes to a time only just passed, the golden era of Athens. Lamenting its passing, he damned those cults and isms whose presence betrayed the change. Yet he was not always a Jeremiah. Along with denunciations and burlesques he could still write delightful topical verse—the sort of stuff W. S. Gilbert did in the *Bab Ballads* and the Savoy Operas.

Eleven of the fifty plays with whose authorship he is

credited still survive. They are the only complete Greek comedies left to us of the thousands which must have been written. Reading Aristophanes provides a distorted but basically correct picture of the social structure and thought of his times. Perhaps it might not be unlike the picture of our own civilization which scholars of 4500 A. D. might try to piece together by studying comic strips from our daily newspapers or scattered reels of the annual Ten Best Motion Pictures.

Menander (342–291) was the last great Greek playwright. He came at a time when the final flicker of national greatness was lighting the Grecian world. Sparta had been toppled from the top of the heap by Thebes, which in turn had been displaced by Macedon under Philip. The latter's son, Alexander the Great, in his brief but meteoric career, welded the Greek world into an empire once more with the torch of the Macedonian phalanx and carried Greek thought and culture to every corner of his vast empire. But Alexander was the empire, and upon his death Greece disintegrated again into a loose sprawl of city states. It was no longer the virile, independent, eager race which had emerged from the Persian wars. Two centuries of almost constant strife had exhausted Greece; two centuries of contact with the Orient had softened her.

Comedy was softer, too, less personal, less extravagant, less topical. Instead of making game of actual persons or movements, it held up to ridicule certain universal types— the boastful soldier, the sly slave, the overbearing father. Not so devastating as the satires of Aristophanes, perhaps, but rather better plays and considerably more human. And if they, themselves, did not survive the tooth of time, they exerted indirectly an influence which has not ceased to this day. Those same stock figures, or their offspring, are still the basic characters of the productions of the Minsky Brothers, and Hurtig and Seamon, and the other burlesque wheel showmen.

BORROWED PLUMAGE: THE ROMAN THEATRE

Geographically Greece faces the East, for there are few good harbors on her western coasts. On the other side, however, the island-strewn Aegean Sea offers a series of stepping stones to the Asiatic littoral. And so the fortunes of Greece have always been largely bound up with the Orient.

With Italy this situation is reversed. Her finest harbors look toward the West, while her eastern shores are precipitous and uninviting to mariners. Italy, then, faces the West, and her eyes are fixed on Europe. For centuries these two great Mediterranean peninsulas turned their backs to each other, had little contact with each other, and each knew only vaguely what was going on in the other and cared less.

When Alexander the Great died in Babylon, in 323 B. C., sighing at the age of thirty-two that there were no more worlds to conquer, his enormous prestige in the East was scarcely known at Rome, though his next move would probably have been directed against her. Yet within fifty years of his death, and not twenty years after the death of Menander, Rome had established contact with the outposts of Alexander's empire and was preparing to stuff it, with all its civilization, its culture, and its vices, into her capacious and insatiable maw.

Rome, at this stage, was about five hundred years old. It had just completed the conquest of the Italian peninsula south of the Arno, and was about to embark upon the succession of foreign campaigns which were to subjugate a large part of the then known world.

The Romans of the Republic were, above all, a practical people. Five centuries of struggle for existence had taught them the value of order, discipline, and application, and they submitted to their requirements willingly and without apparent regret. The concepts of justice and the law which were then being formulated are still the fundamental law of a great part of the world. The military roads and aqueducts which were then being laid down excite the admiration of engineers to this day, and still serve the purpose for which they were constructed. In many respects, and in none less than their innocent admiration for sheer size, the Romans of that day possessed many of the qualities of the American people during the formative years of the United States.

Beauty, independent of utility, was something the Romans could take or leave. Solidity, massiveness, dignity, they could appreciate, and frequently achieved. But certainly there was no such hunger for beauty as the Greeks knew from the beginning.

In all matters esthetic the Romans were ever great borrowers and adapters. From neighbors and subject peoples they borrowed their religion, literature, art, and drama. During all this first five hundred years, they had developed no literature of their own. The first authentic piece of Latin literature is a translation of the *Odyssey* of Homer. Even that was not written until the end of the first Punic War, still a quarter of a century in the future at this time. From the Etruscans, a people of greater antiquity and more advanced civilization, they had borrowed a form of dramatic verse known as the Fescennine Verses which were performed at harvest and vintage festivals and which might in time have developed into drama as the Greek festival of Dionysos had done. But the development was long overdue. The first Etruscan troupe had made its début in Rome in 364 B. C. by performances there to propitiate the gods who were, at the moment, inflicting a pestilence upon the Roman people. It was to house this company that the Circus Maximus was built. Yet though these borrowed skits, songs, and dances had been known for close upon a century, they had never taken sufficient hold on the Roman imagination to produce a single Roman writer.

And then, in rounding out the occupation of the peninsula, Rome discovered the civilization of Greece. All the southern shore had been settled by Greeks and was so completely Hellenic that it was known as Magna Graecia. Tarentum, most important of these Greek cities, incurred the easily inflammable wrath of Rome. The city was invested and taken in 272, and Rome found itself face to face with a civilization vastly superior to anything it had ever known hitherto. It was leisurely, cultured, extravagant—in a word, everything that Rome was not. But it was a softer, sweeter, more gracious life and, apparently, lots more fun to live.

Because it was first revealed in a Greek city this mode of life was termed "Greek" by the Romans, although in its essentials it was probably oriental. Whatever it was, the Romans liked it, and they began to adopt its ways, as they had adopted the ways of their Etruscan and Samnite neighbors somewhat earlier. A valiant effort was made to keep Roman living and thinking on the same high bare plane it had previously inhabited. But legislation, precept, and example were powerless to stem the rising tide of alien culture and luxury.

It would be idle to speculate as to what might have happened if there had been a fully developed Roman dramatic literature. But after one look at the Greek drama available for the taking, Rome gave over forever the attempt to create a dramatic literature of its own. Henceforth its dramatists contented themselves with copying and adapting Greek plays for Roman audiences.

The first Roman to try his hand at that game with any degree of success was Titus Maccius Plautus (Flatfoot), 254–184 B. C., who wrote possibly one hundred and thirty plays, for every one of which he went back to Greek sources. And yet in the twenty plays by which we know him, Plautus stands revealed as something more than a mere coypist. Despite their alien source and the restrictions under which he labored, he managed to impart the Roman stamp to his work. His technical difficulties were not lessened by the fact that it was still a serious offense to make a butt of any citizen, or of Rome. The Twelve Tables of the Law prescribed whipping for such defamers. But Plautus, through calling his characters by Greek names, and setting the scene of his plays in Athens, was able to poke a vast amount of fun at the old Roman virtues and authority. As a matter of fact he was handicapped by the limitations of his audience even more than by the law. It was a sentimental audience, and easily moved. It did not particularly care to exercise its intellect. It wanted a good time, a chance to laugh at somebody or something. Make it laugh, and it would eat out of your hand. It was, all in all, an audience similar to that which supports revues and musical comedies today, and it got just about the same kind of fare handed to it.

The only other significant comedy writer was Publius Terentius Afer (? –159 B. C.). Although his early record is obscure, Terence was born in Carthage and was at one time a slave. It was to Menander that he went for his material, and he brought it back almost straight. Not the showman that Plautus was, Terence was essentially a scholar and stylist. He was intent on rendering the Greek originals in the finest and most elegant Latin at his command. How many more plays he wrote than the six we have is not known. They were lost in Arcadia whence he repaired because of charges of plagiarism, and where, brokenhearted by their loss, he died shortly afterward.

While Plautus and Terence were doing their best to create Latin literature, they exercised very little influence on contemporary Latin thought. The class for which they wrote was never large or much interested in the theatre as such. The very great majority of Romans went ahead getting their fun from the Fescennine and Atellan Verses and the performances of mimes and pantomimes. The importance of these two writers is derived from the fact that they preserved and kept available a great deal of Greek literature that must otherwise have perished; and also from the influence they exerted upon the classical scholars of the Renaissance when they were exhumed after many centuries of darkness.

Tremendous changes occurred in the political and social structure of Rome during the two centuries that stretched between the time of Terence and that of Seneca, who lived during the reigns of Caligula, Claudius, and Nero, in the first century A. D. It was a period of desperate and almost continual warfare—wars with Carthage, hostilities between Rome and her Latin allies, civil wars and class wars in Rome. In those wracking years the fate of the nation hung often in the balance, and the flower of its manhood was almost exterminated. Many of the great families which had provided Rome with a soul had simply ceased to exist.

The ruling class which now occupied their seats and sent its proconsuls in the wake of the conquering legions was no longer the hard, practical, self-denying citizenry that had set Rome on her path to glory. The staves of the legions might still bear the proud device SPQR (Senatus Populusque Romanus), but they represented a different breed of people. Once hereditary and autocratic, the Senate now took its orders from an Emperor who made and unmade Senators at his whim and might elevate to its formerly exclusive ranks even freedmen, recently slaves. Nor was the change in the Roman people less striking. A race of frugal, hard working, patriotic citizens had vanished in the mists. The Roman citizens of the Empire disdained to work or fight. Work was for slaves and new conquests glutted the markets no matter how badly the slaves were treated. Fighting was the job of professional soldiers. And so they lived without end or aim on the bounty of the government, which supplied food and amusement as the price of power.

And yet, because Rome in all her long existence never got around to the secret of representative government, this violent, capricious, and vicious mob was the nominal and, at times, the actual authority in the greatest empire the western world had yet seen. They, and other citizens of the Empire who were actually in Rome, were alone entitled to the vote that stood for the voice of the Roman people.

The sudden acquisition of great wealth is a stern test for any man, or organization, or people. By this time Rome was rich, immensely rich with the booty of all the civilized world. As the tide of gold rose about her, the old Roman virtues of justice, order, and discipline were washed away. A man's origin, his mode of life, his character, were of no significance. If he had amassed sufficient wealth, all honors, position, exemptions were his for the asking.

The theatre but mirrors the life of a community. It does not control that life. While there has never been a theatre less national than that of Rome, it would have been less than human if, in the first century A. D., it had not become a place for the exhibition of a drama spectacular, but somewhat empty; filled with violent, if sometimes meaningless action; and written in verse shaped for florid declamation, bombastic and mannered in the extreme. For that was the life of Rome by that time—the brilliant surface of a shell enclosing a great deal of nothing.

The one important Roman writer was Seneca (about 1–65 A. D.). He rewrote the old Greek stories of Agamemnon, Medea, and Oedipus, without the inner feeling which had produced the original versions. For Seneca was a politician, a Senator, a Consul, the lover of empresses, a philosopher, and a prolific worker in many literary fields. He was no believer in the ancient gods whose stories he told, nor was his audience. And so his plays were literary, and, dramatically speaking, lifeless. Seneca's importance is due to the fact that when the scholars of the Renaissance discovered classical drama, it was the work of Seneca with which they first became acquainted and not the original plays of Aeschylus, Sophocles, and Euripides upon which Seneca had drawn.

They found in his work, too, references to the Greek unities of time, place, and action, about which a great deal is said, even today, without any very clear idea as to what they are and why they were formulated. They were based upon an observation in Aristotle's *Poetics* in which he wrote: "The action of a play should be represented as occurring in one place, within one day, and with nothing irrelevant to the plot." They were common practices in a theatre which possessed no actual changes in scenery, or methods of indicating different times of day. The unity of action, or of theme, or mood, was the only one of any actual importance. Even that unity was violated by the best Greek writers on occasion. But what Aristotle merely recommended as a good idea, as developed by Seneca, became the rule to which the French and Italian classicists of the Renaissance gave slavish acceptance. For quite a while they succeeded in persuading writers that this drama of Seneca's was *the* drama, and that anybody who intended to write tragedy had to copy it.

From its very beginnings the Roman theatre was essentially a place to see something performed. And so the stage which, in Greece, had been at first nonexistent and then only an adjunct to the performance of the chorus, became of prime importance. It was made much longer and wider, and the wall of the "skene" was raised to imposing proportions, clear to the top of the colonnade surrounding the auditorium. It was broken into stories by rows of heavy columns set atop each other, and the space between was filled with niches containing statues, busts, and ornamental objects. In at least one theatre of which there is record the first story was of marble, the second of glass, and the third of gilded wood. It required active, not to say violent, plays to compete with a background like that. And here is a description of a play and of its reception by the audience reported by Horace, in one of his *Epistles*. The time is somewhat before the period during which Seneca was active, but the conditions were approximately the same. Said Horace:

"The audience, even while the actors are speaking their lines, calls for a bear baiting or a wrestling match. Pleasure has moved from the ear to the restless eye and to entertainment with no meaning. For four hours, or more, the curtain is down while troops of cavalry fly past and hordes of men on foot. Captive Kings are dragged in with hands bound behind their backs. War chariots lumber by and are followed by carts, carriages, ships, bearing ivory and all the spoils of Corinth. That hybrid creature, the giraffe, then catches the attention of the crowd, or it may be a white elephant. And what actors' voices are strong enough to be heard above that din? The spectators ask each other: 'Has the actor said anything, yet?' 'I don't think so.' 'Then with what are you so pleased?' 'Oh, that beautiful purple tunic he is wearing.' "

Under such conditions the lot of the actor was wretched in the extreme. Where in Greece he had been a minister of Dionysos, occupying an honored position in society, exempt from military service and, in his journeyings, granted a diplomatic immunity even in wartime; he was the scum of the earth in Rome. There was no religious significance to the presentation of plays here, and the theatre, for the first time in its career, became purely a question of entertainment. It was merely a matter of slaves and freedmen earning their living by means of a despised trade. No citizen could become an actor without forfeiting all his civic privileges. A soldier appearing on the stage might be punished by instant death. The actor was infamous, excluded from public functions, honors, and military service. If he, or his son, married the daughter, granddaughter, or great granddaughter of a Senator, the marriage might be annulled. He was under the absolute control of his manager, who might be a slave himself, but who had the power of life and death over his troupe, and might order the most merciless flogging for any faults in a performance. In short the actor was generally held to be, as he was classed by a praetorian Edict, one with deserters, panders, thieves, and robbers. And, apparently, he deserved that classification often enough.

Yet from that debased and disgraceful status there arose the world's first great actor. Roscius (Quintus Roscius Gallus) promoted himself from the ranks during the last days of the Republic, about the time of which Horace was writing. He was a comedian of singular power and restraint, and he deserved and enjoyed a popularity never previously bestowed upon any actor in Rome. He became a friend and protégé of the orator Cicero, who defended him in court on one occasion; and of the Consul Sulla, by whom he was raised to

Senatorial rank. He died in 62 B. C., rich and respected, proto-
type of the successful actor.

Clearly enough, the Roman public never gave its real interest or support to the literary dramas of Plautus and Terence and Seneca, no matter how ably they might be interpreted by Roscius, or Aesopus, his tragic counterpart, or any
of their less able fellows. The Romans found other forms of
entertainment more to their understanding and liking. They
never lost their fondness for the vaudeville of the mimes.
They developed a real passion for pantomimes (in which a
whole performance is acted by a single player successively
presenting the various characters in a play to the accompaniment of a chorus and an orchestra). But the darling of the
Roman heart was the gladiatorial combat—fights to the death
between assorted beasts; between beasts and men; between
individual men with similar arms, or individuals equipped with
different types of weapons; between whole troops of men. In
these bloody combats the real spirit of Rome under the Emperors is revealed. Before these more vital forms of entertainment the legitimate theatre was overshadowed, and for some
time before receiving its *coup de grâce*, it languished in the
shadows.

Meanwhile there were rising two forces which eventually
were to end the theatre in Europe for centuries: Christianity
and Barbarism.

Christianity hated the theatre on several counts. It was, in
the first place, a survival of paganism and celebrated the
deeds of various pagan gods and heroes, against whom the
church had declared war to the death. And the church was
the religion of the poor and oppressed, despising and decry-
ing the rich and highly placed and all their manifestations,
of which the theatre was one of the most obvious. Finally in

the theatre the church could descry only too many evidences of "the world, the flesh, and the devil," which it was willing to forswear for salvation. So the church proscribed the theatre and preached against it, though it was never able to prevent entirely its people from attending the theatre as long as the theatre remained.

Beyond the ramparts of the empire established by Trajan at the close of the first century A. D., the barbarians were piling up. Behind the spears of the legions, henceforth on the defensive, an oppressed and miserable people did not care who governed them and rather expected that under a different rule some of the more terrible inequities of life might be corrected.

And so, from the fourth century A. D. (and from now on all dates will be of that vintage), succeeding waves of Goths, Vandals, Franks, Huns, and their kindred tribes washed against the ramparts finding holes here and there; filtering through, taking over whole provinces with little or no resistance; and gradually absorbing the once omnipotent realm of Rome. The whole eastern end of the Empire, roughly corresponding to the domain of Alexander the Great, split off from Rome and went its own way for a thousand years becoming increasingly more Greek than Roman. The west splintered under each impact of the barbarian waves. At any time after the sack of Rome by Alaric the Goth, in 410, the Empire might be deemed to have perished, though the date 476, when the line of Emperors came to an end with Romulus Augustus, is usually assigned as the formal end of the Roman Empire.

The barbarians had no more use for the Roman theatre than did the church fathers. There was nothing like it in their past, and they found themselves little enough in sympathy

with its ways. It was, on the whole, they thought, rather
Roman and hence weakening and degrading.

And so the theatre after a thousand years of varying fortunes, found itself at last at the end of its string. Forgotten
by the people; despised by the new lords of the land; hated,
feared, and proscribed by the now dominant Christian religion, the theatre fled into exile. Its buildings were allowed
to decay and fall into ruin, were converted to other purposes, or were torn down for building material. Its scripts were
written over, destroyed, or retained as grammar texts in mon-
asteries. Its people became vagabonds, outlaws, wanderers over
the face of the land.

CHAPTER II

THE CONTINENTAL THEATRE

In Cassock and Cotta

THE theatre went into exile; its people remained. There were
no longer theatres in which to perform; the plays were patch-
work quilts of remembered scraps, handed on by word of
mouth. They had no standing at all and no real right to
life. But still they persisted in living and in playing. In
little, unrelated groups they drifted about from town to town,
putting on their tattered remnants of productions in castles,
at fairs, at crossroads, on street corners—wherever they could
get together an audience. They got by any way they could,
doubling in brass between drama and singing, dancing,
juggling, throwing knives, walking tight ropes, competing
with and even turning their hand to wrestling, animal training, and all the repertoire of small time vaudeville.

The last contemporary reference to a dramatic production
in Rome appears in a letter dated 533 A. D. There followed

four hundred years of privation, neglect, and hostility for the theatre; of unremitting pressure, social, religious, and economic. Yet at its end, as at its beginning, there were still actors plying their uncertain and ill-rewarded profession. And people question whether the theatrical profession can weather a depression which has to this point run barely six years!

The church of Christ was principally responsible for the exile of the theatre. For centuries that church was its unrelenting foe. Even today there are sections of it which do their best to keep the theatre's grave ploughed under and planted over. Yet it was, in the end, that same church which restored the theatre to society once more. No change of heart was involved, or any liberalization of the clerical viewpoint. But existing conditions led the church to believe that under proper supervision, and with its thoughts directed to higher things, the theatre might yet prove a mighty instrument of salvation.

The centuries which followed the fall of the Empire were years of wretchedness and distress in Europe. In the midst of the ruins of a once great and luxurious civilization life became rude and mean and barbarous to a degree difficult to realize. The peace and order and comparative security of the Pax Romana were utterly destroyed. If there was no longer legal slavery, serfdom bound the people to the soil and to its owner just as effectively. And if a liege lord became embroiled with another of his kind, everybody in their trains became involved, too. It was a bloody and brutal and seemingly futile time, with present peoples only island mountain tops just beginning to emerge from a swirling ocean of racial chaos.

Only in one quarter was there any peace, or serenity, or order; only there any love of wisdom, or of the arts, or even such rudimentary science as had survived. But for the flicker from the chancel of the church, the light of learning would have vanished from the western world. The church, too, was the one democratic institution of the time. There, alone, could low-born worth hope to attain the heights. And so the ablest as well as the noblest men and women of the day embraced its life.

Toward the close of the tenth century the Dukes of Saxony succeeded to the throne of the Holy Roman Empire established by Charlemagne. Saxony lay on the eastern march of Europe, and had contacts with the empire in the East. When Otto II, of Saxony, married the daughter of the Eastern Emperor, a stream of Hellenic thought and culture was drawn in her wake to the northern wilderness to which she departed.

One of the fiefs of Saxony was the abbey of Gandersheim, and in the abbey at that time there lived a nun possessed of an eager, restless, and creative mind. Whether it was in the abbey's library, or in contacts with the ladies of Theophano's train that Hrotsvitha, the Benedictine nun, discovered the plays of Terence, is a matter of minor import. The wonder of it is that in that secluded convent, in a milieu as alien to the theatre in thought and spirit as could well be imagined, she was inspired to write six plays at a time when nobody in the world, as far as she knew, was doing anything of the kind. They related the stories of saints and martyrs, and their telling was stamped and colored and conditioned by her profession. But working alone, buried alive in Gandersheim Abbey, Hrotsvitha created a dramatic literature which is not wholly forgotten today. For two of her stories, *The Fall and Conversion of Theophilus* and *Paphnutius,* tell respectively the originals of the stories we know as *Faust* and *Thais.*

There seems to have been no connection between the isolated labors of Hrotsvitha and the introduction of drama in the liturgy of the church, perhaps a hundred and fifty to two hundred years later. It is quite likely that this latter was the spontaneous blossoming that occurred in several widely separated places at about the same time. It was becoming increasingly difficult to teach the complicated theology and ritual, which by this time the church had accumulated, to a practically illiterate people. But they could be made to assume meaning if they were enacted before the congregation. Certain parts of the mass and some of the notable feasts, especially the nativity and the resurrection, particularly lent themselves to such interpretations and were most often and most lovingly presented.

In the beginning these were isolated incidents, performed by the priests, and in Latin. But they grew into series of incidents and some of the rôles were handed over to the lower orders of the ministry; and a mixture of Latin and vernacular was developed which eventually shifted entirely to the vernacular. With these changes the plays, known either as "Mysteries" if they were founded on stories from the Bible or "Miracles" if based on the lives of the saints, were moved out of the chancel to the vestry, or porch of the church, and then right out of the church into the public square.

By this time the plays, religious though they still were, had passed into the hands of the laymen. Organizations to stage them were developed, like those groups which still present Passion Plays periodically; or certain guilds were handed sections of the production, for the presentation of which they were responsible.

For the first time, the locale where the action of these plays took place began to matter tremendously. Heaven and Hell were very real places. They had to be depicted in the most impressive manner possible. And so either a series of set stages was grouped about a central acting space, with the action alternating between it and these stages in turn; or these set stages were built on cars, and as the action required it, each was wheeled in. A variation on this arrangement was a progressive circuit of places in a town at which audiences assembled, and to which, in regular order, a section of the play was brought on its wheeled stage. As the stage got farther and farther from the chancel, it got further and further from the control of the church. The Devil and his attendant demons assumed a prominence which the teachings of the church did not warrant, and Hell became easily the most spectacular and probably the most interesting of all the stages in the production. The Devil, as a matter of fact, became the chief comedian of the pieces (perhaps because he was the only character with whom the playwrights and directors felt they could take liberties), and though always defeated in the end, he was by no means lacking in popular appeal.

The church did not always like these changes; it could not always approve of the new notes which these productions struck, or of the people who struck them. The church, as a matter of fact, came to hold much of its former opinion as to the general undesirability of show business and its people. But it was too late to dismiss the theatre again. By the time the church had reached this conclusion, the theatre was out of its hands and safely established in the hands and hearts of the people. And never since that time has it or any other person or institution got quite the strangle-hold on the theatre which it held for so long.

The church had not been so much concerned with the theatre as drama, as it had been with the theatre as propaganda. It is not surprising that no great playwright or play was produced during this period. And yet it was during this transition period that definite stage sets were developed and a new method of presentation evolved, a couple of contributions quite worth making.

ITALY: FROM THE CLASSICS TO GRAND OPERA

Europe was ripe for a general upheaval. The feudal order which had evolved from the wreck of the Roman Empire may still have been a fine and imposing structure to the eye, but its foundations were rotten and its roof was sagging. And there were forces abroad which would have put a severe strain on the old frame even when it was strong.

The period of stir and change and reorganization which began in the twelfth century has been called the Renaissance, or rebirth of civilization. To most people the Renaissance is something that occurred in time long past—not quite so far off or so dead as that other period known as ancient history, perhaps, but pretty dead and gone just the same. And yet many of the forces which were liberated at that time have not been finally resolved, as yet. Historically speaking, we belong to one of the later stages of that Renaissance rather than to any period which succeeded it.

People were no longer satisfied to stay put. They were leaving the land to which they had been attached through several static centuries and were moving about from place to place. Often enough these moves finally stranded them in some town working in some new job and exposed to a lot of new impressions and experiences. The old order of living, the old explanations as to who they were and what they must do and think were no longer acceptable. The new and growing classes of artisans, merchants, and professional men were active, turbulent, and insatiable in the exploration of the physical, intellectual, and moral aspects of the world in which they found themselves. They developed inventions, discovered trade routes long forgotten, or never known. They encountered new peoples, new modes of living, and new habits of thinking, with zest and a keen desire to experiment with them all. Their political power grew with their wealth and knowledge and experience.

When the Roman Empire had gone down before the barbarian invasions, Italy had disintegrated into a number of independent, competitive, and generally irreconcilable petty states. It was nominally a part of the Holy Roman Empire, but the periodical attempts of the Emperors to translate those claims into fact drew retorts and reprisals from France, Spain, and the Papacy, each of whom had equally valid (and untenable) claims to various portions of Italy. Despite the persistence and the occasional fervor with which these claims were preferred, the development of a distinctive Italian culture was not thwarted or even, in all probability, materially delayed. For it was here, rather than anywhere else, that the travail which marked the Renaissance was first manifest.

After centuries of universal ignorance and indifference a few people were at last aware of the fact that they were heirs of a once great and complex civilization, fragments of which were available all about them. And so these people turned the country upside down for manuscripts, records, anything which might give them clues to the reconstruction of life and thought in that civilization.

The spoils of these researches were divided up among a number of Academies, each of which devoted itself to some particular aspect of that ancient culture. One of the earliest of these specialized groups was the Roman Academy. Its members had barely got beneath the surface in their research, when their dazzled and delighted gaze lit upon the remnants of the Roman theatre, and they knew that they had discovered what it was they wanted to study. Now they found not only manuscripts of the plays, but a good deal else which helped them to an understanding of what that theatre was, and what it had meant to its early practitioners. They found the *Poetics* of Aristotle, both in the original Greek and in translation, and thus they learned some of the theories behind the plays, including the classical unities; and from *De Architectura*, of Vitruvius, they learned a great deal about the theatres themselves, their proportions, and the construction and management of various theatrical effects. These were deciphered and followed with scrupulous devotion to detail, and from somewhere in the early fifteenth century the members of the Academy put on productions of Plautus and Terence for and with each other, in some of the more suitable rooms of their various palaces.

But they did not do so merely as literary exercises. This was lively and living theatre, for which the best artists were drafted to execute scenery in accordance with the laws of the newly rediscovered art of perspective. And before very long their ingenious artists had worked out three more or less standard sets, one for each of the then accepted types of plays. Tragedy, for instance, was played before the background of a public square, or stately houses, or public buildings, or monuments. The scenery for comedy, on the other hand, might indicate less pretentious dwellings, or an inn, a church, or a brothel. For the satyr plays, a rural landscape was required— trees, herbs, flowers, or country houses. With those sets a group felt prepared to mount any play. And the same general sets are the nucleus of the scene loft of every vaudeville, stock, and burlesque theatre today—to say nothing of supposedly metropolitan legitimate theatres.

This admiration for the classics was not approved in every quarter. By some, such devotion to pagan gods and heroes, and the amoral creatures of classical comedy was considered unseemly, to say the least. For that reason the Roman Academy and all its works were suppressed by Pope Paul II, in 1468. But this was a purely personal view of the situation and it was not the policy of the church. Under Paul's successor, Sixtus IV, in just a few years, the Academy was not only revived, but was actually encouraged. And by 1500, there were copies of the Roman model in Venice, Mantua, Milan, Naples, Florence, and Vicenza.

All these early productions were, of course, in either Greek or Latin. To such an extent were they still considered the only languages fit for cultured people, that Petrarch and Dante suffered considerably because they had elected to cast their work in the mould of the "vulgar" tongue. It was not until the sixteenth century that plays were written in Italian.

But when Italian plays finally appeared, they brought with them a situation quite new to the theatre. Up to this time it has been possible to speak of "The Theatre" wherever it has been found, for generally speaking, it has been the same institution everywhere. But now the theatre, like everything else, will be aware of the division of people along lines of national languages, national cultures, and the consciousness of nationality. It is as though the theatre were a great arm, in the tracing of which we have finally arrived at the fingers.

The first to try tragic writing in the new Italian tongue was Gian Giorgio Trissino, whose importance begins and ends with that distinction. His plays (*Italia Liberata* was the first, though *Sophonisba* was the better known) were printed several times between 1515 and 1562, when *Sophonisba* was produced. They are correct enough imitations of the form, but the drama is just not there.

Early Italian comedy is another story. Ludovico Ariosto, Niccolo Machiavelli, and Pietro Aretino threw Plautus and Terence and the other classics out of the window, and sat down to write about the people and the life that was going on about them. It was the life of the brilliant and dissolute courts of Rome, Florence, and Ferrara, where people lived fast, died hard, and were avid for new ideas and new sensations. Several of Ariosto's plays, including *Orlando Furioso*, still survive and are esteemed in Italy. They reflect the boldness, the coarseness, the liveliness of the time and the society for which they were written.

None of these dramatic activities could be called popular drama. Every one of them was an attempt on the part of learned and cultured men to interest, instruct, and entertain other learned or cultured people. They were written for no bigger audiences than could be gathered together in the ball rooms of the palaces. And the physical theatre, which had been shaped originally by the hills of Greece and Rome, and then by the stages of the miracle and mystery plays, was now reformed to meet the limitations of a ball room.

This does not mean, however, that there was no popular drama. It means simply that these formal plays were too remote from the people and too highbrow for them to care for, or even to know about. But there was a form of entertainment available which they could understand and did approve of—that form of entertainment which we know as the commedia dell' arte.

Now just where the characters of the commedia dell' arte came from, and how they all got together is something on which scholars are not in agreement. The ancestry of some of them can be traced back to nearly forgotten characters in the later Greek and Roman comedies; characteristics of some of them were holdovers from the puppet theatre which had continued to lead a separate life of its own through all these dark centuries; others, no doubt, represented bursts of genuine inspiration on the part of individual actors. Wherever they came from, and however they got there, the commedia dell' arte people eventually became a sort of permanent stock company. The appearance and general traits of each of these characters were generally known, as was his relationship to the other characters in the company.

But if the audience knew the characters in the play and how they were likely to react to general situations, there was no telling what was going to happen in any particular performance or how the characters were going to behave in response to any concrete stimulus. For here was no orderly progress of a play from curtain to curtain. There was, instead, only a skeleton plot, a scenario of the high spots of the play. All the rest, words, actions, gestures, were filled in by the players as they went along. So each had only a vague idea of what he would do in response to a cue, and not the faintest idea of what any other player on the stage would say or do at any moment.

There lay both the strength and the weakness of the commedia dell' arte. At its best, in the hands of creative artists trained by years of association to a high pitch of ensemble playing, it was a glorious art and must have been enormously stirring to watch. But like extemporaneous prayer it must be *good* or it is no good. And unfortunately the number of people who can extemporize well at anything is pretty limited. The lower grade of commedia dell' arte companies, which tried to make up for the lack of inspiration by speed and noise and dirt, degenerated into approximations of modern burlesque companies.

Nevertheless the commedia dell' arte enjoyed a tremendous vogue for well over a century and a half. Its exponents overflowed into practically every European country. Wherever they went they served as an advance guard for the professional theatre—and as an inspiration, as teachers, and as models for its budding playwrights and actors.

The most famous of these commedia dell' arte companies was an Italian troupe headed by Francesco Andreini and Isabella, his wife. They went by the name of I Gelosi (The Zealous Players), and they seem to have rated that distinction. Every one of the twelve or fifteen men and women on the roster (for there was no prejudice against women in these companies) was a real star in some particular line of business. They journeyed far and wide, and on one of their tours to France, in 1577, they were kidnapped and held for ransom by the Huguenots. Henry III, then occupying the French throne, was forced to pay through the nose in order to redeem I Gelosi for a scheduled performance in the State Hall, at Blois.

The commedia dell' arte companies enjoyed a very general success and esteem. Nowhere was that so universal or so long lived as in Italy. The highbrow productions of the Academies could not even be classed as opposition to these sturdy competitors in the vulgar tongue. And no native drama developed for a long time, partly because of the very popularity of the commedia dell' arte; partly because of the continued disrupted state of the country; and partly because of the extent of the divergence among the various dialects.

Then, just about this time, grand opera put in an appearance on the Italian scene, and something in that flamboyant and mellifluous hybrid struck an answering note in the Italian soul. This, said the Italians in effect, is what we've been waiting for all this time. And as far as the majority of Italians is concerned, grand opera remains still baseball, bull fighting, and a couple of other national pastimes all rolled into one.

At any rate, from the early part of the sixteenth century until well on to the middle of the eighteenth—for nearly two hundred and fifty years—there were no Italian playwrights, and no Italian theatre save for the commedia dell' arte and opera. Italy, which had given the initial impulse to the drama of the Renaissance, now lagged behind all those other nations which had once, as pupils, sat at her feet.

The only real threat to the continued routine of opera and commedia dell' arte, developed from the spirited protest of Carlo Goldoni, a playwright whose name still means something in the world theatre. Goldoni did not like the manners, morals, or methods of the current commedia dell' arte troupes, nor was he much more favorably impressed with the earlier comedy writers, running back to Aretino and Macchiavelli. So he turned for his inspiration to France, where Molière was then in full flower, and began to write comedies of common life. His characters were still of the same general family as the commedia dell' arte, and yet they were recognizable human beings. Their speech was that of the Venetian bourgeois from whom Goldoni had sprung.

Dramatic invention and acting were at a low ebb at that time, and Goldoni's fresh slant caught on quickly. In a brief time he was Italy's leading playwright, working under contract for various managers, and turning out as many as sixteen plays a year. It seemed for a while as though his one man revolt might change the whole character of the theatre in Italy. And yet the suddenness of his downfall indicates that, successful as he may have been, his viewpoint was essentially not that of his countrymen.

One day in a bookstore Goldoni encountered Carlos Gozzi, a critic, and the ensuing argument terminated in a quarrel. Caustically Goldoni informed his opponent that it was easier to criticize a good play than to write one. Stung by the implications of the remark, Gozzi retorted that he could do that too. His play, *The Three Oranges,* was a satire on the Goldoni method, mixed with not a little personal ridicule of his rival. It took Venice by storm, and so discomfited Goldoni that he beat a dignified retreat to the Italian company resident in Paris. And there Goldoni spent the rest of his life, learning French when past fifty with such a good effect that two plays in his adopted tongue were performed at the Théâtre Français. He was eighty-six when he died in exile, in 1793, bequeathing to posterity a legacy of upward of two hundred and fifty compositions for the stage.

Once his hand let go its grip on the Italian theatre, it fell away toward the rut from which he had tried to hoist it. Not all the way back to the pure commedia dell' arte, perhaps, for Goldoni had made some of its conventions and characteristics too ridiculous to be taken seriously any longer, but back to the heroic loves and loyalties of standard tragedy, the comic-strip roughhouse of stock comedies. And there, to all practical intents and purposes, it has rested since.

Thenceforth Italy's chief contribution to the theatre has been a succession of great players, of whom Tommaso Salvini (1829–1913), Adelaide Ristori (1822–1906), and especially Eleanora Duse (1859–1924), rank with the best the world has produced.

SPAIN: THE DRAMA OF CLOAK AND SWORD

When the Moorish tide that had swept up out of Africa in the seventh century began to recede, it crawled south past the rocks of a handful of petty Christian states which had never been completely inundated. For eight centuries they harried and were harried by the Moor, relentlessly, and on the whole successfully pushing him back out of Europe. In those eight centuries Spain gradually became aware of its nationality. It became, also, fanatically Christian, proud of its place as an outpost of Christendom; with a tradition of martial valor and high personal loyalty to both church and king.

And then, suddenly, about the time the Moorish job was

finished, Spain mushroomed. A few lucky breaks in exploration, a couple of royal marriages of convenience, and the handful of petty states had become one of the great countries of the world, and its Emperor, Charles V (1516–1556), the chief actor on any stage on which he might step.

The elements responsible for Spain's greatness were too unstable for permanence, the disruptive forces too strong. Under Charles' son and grandson the sun of her greatness was already declining. When the commedia dell' arte players brought the professional theatre there from Italy, Spain was already past the zenith of her power.

Yet the tradition of greatness was still strong in Spanish literature, the manners and customs, the feelings of those great days, still in the minds and hearts of her people, as it persisted for generations after that glory had faded from the European sky.

Although he was not the father of the Spanish theatre, Lope de Vega (1562–1635) was incontestably its great figure. If ever there was a one man show in dramatic literature, he was that show. During his long and fantastically varied life, he turned his hand to every one of the then known forms of playwriting, and when they failed to provide him with requisite models, he invented others as he needed them. Fifteen hundred of his works may be classified as plays, another three hundred divided between dramatic sketches, religious processionals, and works of a miscellaneous nature—eighteen hundred in all.

In the end, none of them has won a permanent place in the world theatre, but at this distance it is difficult to say how much he may have to answer for and how much his time. For this was Spain of the Inquisition, and original thinking and questioning of the established order were simply not permitted. As a craftsman he was far ahead of anything the theatre had yet seen, and his plays were immensely effective in action. He was the theatre of his time and place more completely than any other dramatist ever has been.

Only one other Spanish writer stands comparison with Lope de Vega. (Cervantes, though he wrote plays, was a failure as a dramatist). Pedro Calderon de la Barca was not a literary tornado like his predecessor, but wrote himself out in barely a hundred plays. He was still the soldier, courtier, and churchman, with the limitations such loyalties impose upon the creative artist, but he is reckoned to be somewhat more creative, more genuinely poetic, penetrating deeper beneath the surface of life. There are no better Spanish tragedies than *The Physician of His Own Honor*, *The Constant Prince*, or *The Mayor of Zalamea*.

And with Calderon's death in 1681, Spain had reached the end of her brief period of theatrical greatness. Of competent journeyman playwrights there has been a sufficiency; of really significant figures, not one.

As in Italy, the rise of another and more satisfying form of entertainment accounted in no small measure for this neglect of the theatre. In Italy it was grand opera; in Spain that formal, stylized combat, the bull fight. Now this sport is curiously akin to the commedia dell' arte at its best. The plot of the piece, the chief characters and their relation to each other are all known to the spectators from the beginning. But while these broad outlines are generally followed, it is quite possible for almost any of the actors to introduce some innovation without notice. And in the bull ring a muffed cue can be, and often is, fatal. It is that element of dramatic suspense which holds the devotees of the sport right up to the final stroke. The best dramatic and critical genius has been drawn to its service. Lacking this, the Spanish legitimate theatre has languished.

FRANCE: DRAFTING THE "CLASSIC" FORMULA

France was a perfect hotbed of dramatic activity during the Middle Ages. Religious festivals, miracle and mystery plays were all widely performed during the thirteenth, fourteenth, and fifteenth centuries. Religious brotherhoods for the presentation of sacred plays, though not necessarily in churches, were in full bloom during the fifteenth century. In the same century student organizations in the universities began to produce plays. Some of them were translations of the classics, but there was sufficient ability available to turn out original plays of a high order of vitality, such, for instance, as *Maistre Pierre Pathelin,* still an eminently playable work.

It was for one of these companies, and somewhere after 1550, that Stephen Jodelle wrote *Cléopatre Captive.* It was not much of a play, staggering beneath a load of Senecan "classical" mechanics, but it employed for the first time the Alexandrine verse scheme for dramatic composition.

Unintentionally, perhaps unknowingly, Jodelle had constructed the mould into which French tragic writing was poured by his more competent successors. For when Alexandre Hardy showed up from his literary apprenticeship in Spain, about the turn of the century, it was to this verse scheme with its rhymed couplets and six beat line that he went for his model, and before this indefatigable inventor of tragi-comedy retired in 1623, with six hundred dramatic compositions behind him, Pierre Corneille, first authentic genius of the French theatre, was about ready to make his début on the scene.

By this time France had found herself as a nation. A lull had developed in the long series of wracking wars with the English, the Spanish, and the Holy Roman Empire. The struggle between the crown and the nobility had ended in a decisive victory for the former, and the Bourbon line was set firmly on the throne. France, in short, was at the beginning of the great creative surge which was to carry it straight to the top of the continental heap.

As Paris became more and more the center of the French world, its gay and sophisticated court took the theatre to its slightly hardboiled heart. And it was primarily for the court, its hangers on, and a thin but spreading fringe of intellectuals and wealthy bourgeois, that the great French plays were written.

The first professional company hung out its banner about the year 1600 in a little room sixty by eighteen feet in the Hôtel de Burgogne, so called because it stood on land owned by the Dukes of Burgundy. The acting arrangements were simplicity itself. A bare platform without settings or properties was the stage. Chairs were provided for a few of the audience. The remainder stood. This "theatre" was still under lease to the Confrérie de la Passion, and the brothers collected rent for it, though for more than fifty years their own performances had been forbidden by law.

The Théâtre du Marais was the second theatre in Paris. And this was the company for which Hardy wrote. As its house dramatist he became the direct literary ancestor of Pierre Corneille. For on one of its tours of the provinces under the management of its star, Mondori, it played in Rouen, and there it came under the eyes of Corneille, then a fledgling lawyer. The young attorney threw over whatever practice he had built up and went to Paris with Mondori.

Corneille's work for the Théâtre du Marais attracted the attention of Cardinal Richelieu who, along with his other great gifts, also had an ambition to write and a considerable affection for the theatre. But he disliked the mechanical drudgery of writing, and so he used to outline the characters and plot of the play, and establish its general tone, and then turn its actual writing over to one or more collaborators. Corneille was one of a set of five chosen on one occasion, and he had the temerity to change the plot of the act which had been assigned to him. Richelieu, furious, threw him out, and he retired to Rouen for further study and writing, but with never a backward glance at his withered law practice.

In the course of his study he encountered a play by Guillen de Castro based on the life and exploits of the Cid, a Spanish legendary hero. Corneille took over the idea for his own, and some time afterward was back in Paris with *Le Cid*, the hit of the Paris dramatic season of 1636. It was, of course, performed without benefit of clergy, and Richelieu, still burning over the implied slight to his dramatic craftsmanship, commanded the Academy to condemn it. Now that institution was pretty well under his thumb, but it was a tough assignment he had handed it, and the Academy hedged. Its condemnation was no more than half hearted, and had no effect on the play's popularity. *Le Cid* was translated into all the principal European languages, an almost unprecedented honor at the time, and was widely copied.

"Within a dim, candle-lit auditorium," writes a later commentator describing that historic première, "is an audience of a most mixed sort. Courtiers and dandies fill the boxes and, on this special occasion, the best benches on the main floor. And close by them are litterateurs, officers, travelers, tradesmen, even down to the court pages, idlers, and adventurers, an element so unruly the actors will be lucky to get through without a disturbance, or battle. This audience is admitted by a brawny and heavily armed door man whose duty is to exclude by violence all who refuse to buy tickets. All except nobles, against whom a mere proprietor or ticket taker may not stand out. The stage is curtainless, on it are spread several 'mansions' or 'stations,' indicating the locale and the place

where the actors will stand. There are practically no properties. When the auditorium candles have been snuffed two actresses appear. . . ." and the play is on.

By the time Corneille laid down his pen, the rules for classical French tragedy had become pretty well set. They demanded a strict adherence to the unities of time, place, and
action; the division of every play into five acts; the removal
of violent action from the sight of the audience, to be recounted
rather than witnessed; that plays be confined to lofty themes
and noble characters; and that all comic relief and sub-plots
be eliminated. In short, even by this time there was general
agreement on the formula which Voltaire, some hundred
years later, codified as follows:

"To compact an illustrious or interesting event into a space
of two or three hours; to make the characters appear only when
they ought to come forth; never to leave the stage empty; to
put together a plot as probable as it is attractive; to say nothing
unnecessary; to instruct the mind and move the heart; to be
always eloquent in verse and with the eloquence proper to each
character represented; to speak one's tongue with the same purity
as in the most chastened prose, without allowing the effort of
rhyming to seem to hamper the thought; to permit no single line
to be hard, or obscure, or declamatory—these are the conditions
which nowadays one insists upon in tragedy."

These are hard rules even for a master dramatist, but
faithfully observed and in the hands of genius, they make for
great art within certain limits. But such writing demanded not
only great writing, but an audience able and prepared to appreciate, even relish, a dry art, an intellectual art divorced
from sentiment and personal feeling. This appreciation, the
brilliant and dissolute courts of the great period of the French
monarchy were prepared to furnish.

But even while these rules were being formulated, there

was rising the greatest comic genius of the French theatre. And he would have none of these rules, or of the conventions they are set to guard. As it suited his purpose, he ignored or flouted them. For his radical views on art and life, the Academy refused him the membership he deserved, until he had been in his grave for a century.

Jean Baptiste Poquelin (Molière), was born in 1622, before Hardy had retired or Corneille was discovered. He was one of those souls destined for the theatre, whose existence apart from it seems almost inconceivable. The senior Poquelin, upholsterer to the King, had small regard for the theatre, and did everything he could to discourage Jean Baptiste's evident preference for it. His opposition was not sufficient to deter his son, but it did lead him to adopt another name when he fled school for the theatre. And today the chief distinction of the name Poquelin, is that Molière deserted it.

When Molière took a little inheritance from his mother and gathered a small troupe about him, they all modestly voted to take the name of the Illustre Théâtre, and set up shop in a covered tennis court in the Fossé de Nesle. For two years they put up a gallant fight for recognition, and for two years all Paris appeared to be in a conspiracy to stay away from their theatre. Finally, their money gone, and their credit after it, they gave up the unequal fight and took to the road.

And there the Illustre Théâtre remained for all of fifteen years, growing in ability, in wealth, and in experience, adding to its repertoire the comedies Molière was beginning to turn out. But it was still a road company, with its eyes turned ever on Paris, and its plans under way for another invasion of the capital.

The big chance for which the Molière troupe had worked and waited so long came its way on October 24, 1658. A command performance before the new King, Louis XIV, himself, and under the patronage of the King's only brother. The assurance that in addition to the royal family every courtier who could manage to get himself invited would be in the audience.

Molière picked a tragedy by Corneille, *Nicomède*, and for good measure *Le Docteur Amoreux*, a farce of his own. It was just as well that he did so, for in spite of their own opinion of their ability and the years they had put in at it, neither Molière nor his actors were really at home in the heroic alexandrines of Corneille. But the audience was delighted by the farce, and the King said, yes, let them stay on and share the theatre of the Petit Bourbon with the Italian actors, and keep on calling themselves the Troupe of Monsieur, only Brother of the King.

During the next year Molière brought forward *Les Précieuses Ridicules*, a satire on the affectations of posing womankind, and that play raised him to the forefront of French dramatists. In the next few years there flowed from his pen a succession of marvelous comedies in which he painted a gallery of social characters whose names and faces are bywords to this day. Of all dramatists, only Shakespeare excelled him in the number of characters who are universally recognized as touchstones: *L'École des Maris*, *Le Bourgeois Gentilhomme*, *Les Femmes Savantes*, *Le Médicin Malgré Lui*, *Le Misanthrope*, *L'Avare*, *La Malade Imaginaire*, and best of all perhaps, *Tartuffe*.

It was not all easy sailing. *Tartuffe's* attack on hypocrisy was construed as an assault on morality and the church, and its production was fought bitterly, delayed three years, and made possible only by a change in title to *L'Imposteur*. Molière married Armande Béjart, his leading lady, who was twenty-five years his junior, and found that he could live neither with her nor without her. He died in harness, February 17, 1673, collapsing on the stage during a performance of *La Malade Imaginaire,* and succumbing shortly after he was carried to his house.

The resentment of the church was not appeased by death. Standing on the technical ground that he was an actor, the Archbishop of Paris refused to grant him Christian burial. At the intercession of the King, the most that was granted was burial without a service in an obscure grave of a disreputable churchyard at night.

What Molière had done was to bring to its peak a very special kind of comedy. It consists, in brief, of selecting certain universal weaknesses, or social follies, stripping them of pretense and sophistry and holding them up to the X-ray of reason and truth. It must be done coolly, impartially, without tenderness or sympathy for the characters. To do it successfully necessitates walking an intellectual tight rope. Evoking sympathy for the characters sends one off into sentimental comedy; provoking laughter by the introduction of sudden improbabilities, by the use of the long arm of coincidence, or by the use of the custard pie school of acting, drops one into farce or burlesque. The French have always felt that these were not true comedy, and further, that they are the guardians of the true comic spirit. For this detached, impersonal, and slightly hardboiled attitude toward human foibles, the French are supreme, and Molière is their head man.

At the height of Molière's career he received a manuscript from an unknown dramatist who had, however, something of a reputation as a poet. Molière turned down the play, but he saw in it such evidences of ability that he encouraged its author to continue writing. And so he did, and came back at Molière with another, *Le Thebaïde,* which Molière produced at the Palais Royal in 1664. That was the introduction to the theatre of Jean Racine (1639–1699), in whom classical tragedy reached its full flowering.

In the sixteen years during which he continued to contribute steadily to the French theatre, Racine turned out a group of superb vehicles for actors. There is probably not a finer part in the French language than his Phèdre. Mostly he built on Greek and Roman classical myths, as attested by *Le Thebaïde*, *Andromaque*, and *Iphigénie*, though he went back to the Bible for *Esther* and *Athalie*, and came to practically contemporary history for *Bajazet*. But he always adhered to the formula of great themes and noble characters.

Racine was a master craftsman. He further simplified and concentrated the play form, tightened up dialogue and action, and refined the literary content of his plays. But his somewhat cold, architecturally perfect and extraordinarily articulated plays build to perfectly tremendous climaxes.

In 1680 he married a very devout woman. He had always been a religious man, his early preparation had been for the church, and his marriage tipped the scales against the theatre, which was still officially under proscription by the church. So now Racine made his peace with the church, and retired to spend the remaining twenty-nine years of his life as an elegant gentleman and scholar.

In the same year in which Racine retired, the King reorganized the existing theatrical charters, and concentrated them into the Théâtre Français, which was given a monopoly of the acting privilege. Louis personally selected the twenty-seven members of the original acting company, and drew up a salary schedule calling for a division of the profits on a sharing basis.

And when its first theatre, in the Rue Mazarin, suffered because of the traffic jams of coaches and chairs before its doors,

Louis ordered his own architect to draw plans for a new and modern theatre about an old tennis court in the Rue des Fossés St. Germain des Pres. There, on April 18, 1689, the customary three knocks on the stage floor signaled for the ascent of the curtain on the initial production of Le Théâtre de la Comédie Française, the official title under which the French National Theatre continues to produce to this day.

Under Louis XIV France had climbed to the apex of the monarchy's power. During the century which followed the founding of the national theatre, the great machine of state slid straight down hill to the revolution with increasing velocity. In that period there was only one writer for the theatre who in any way challenges comparison with Corneille, Racine, and Molière. And even he loomed somewhat bigger as a playwright to his contemporaries than he seems now, down the vista of the years.

Jean François Marie Arouet, better known by his pseudonym, Voltaire (1694–1778), included a great deal of material for the stage in his voluminous writings. But his principal contribution to humanity was a passionate crusade for liberty of thought, which played no small part in the ultimate downfall of the monarchy and the rash of democratic experiments which spangled the maps of the world about the beginning of the nineteenth century.

One real contribution he did make to the theatre, for which practical theatre men should ever be grateful to him. The tremendous popularity of Le Cid had caused managers to admit the audience to the stage for the first time in French theatrical history. And there they had clung persistently since, encroaching farther and farther on the domain of the actor until, toward the end of this régime, the action of the play had to be performed in a narrow strip between parallel rows of benches. The prestige Voltaire enjoyed enabled him to clear the stage of these intruders, and to return it to the actors and their allied craftsmen.

These latter were increasingly important. The *manner* of a play's presentation became of more importance than the play, itself. Writing, acting, costume, and make-up were as standardized as so many Ford cars. The French theatre was a bed of Procrustes, in which feet were lopped off, necks stretched, and paunches ironed out to fit the mould of the classical unities.

About this time (1767) *Hamlet* was being adapted for the Théâtre Français by Jean François Ducis, one of its members, presumably well acquainted with its requirements. Among the surgical feats he deemed requisite before the play could be presented by his company were these: The number of principal parts was reduced to four. Of the twenty-three characters in the play, Hamlet himself, the Ghost of his father, Ophelia, the Grave Diggers, Horatio, and Laertes were all dispensed with, or relegated to the side lines. Only the King, the Queen, Polonius (now become the King's confidant), and a character written in to serve as confidante of the Queen, now remained. They held the stage and reported the violent and bloody deeds of a singularly violent play. They told the tragic story of Ophelia's love which this production emphasized, and to which further poetic passages had been added— all in rhymed alexandrines, of course.

THE THEATRE MEETS THE REVOLUTION

The sands of the *ancien régime* had almost run out. The revolution had not yet broken, but it was in the air. Even in the cloistered precincts of the Théâtre Français a keen observer might have noted its signs. For here was the company of the King's Comedians producing *Le Barbier de Séville,* and *Le Mariage de Figaro*, satires on the existing social order, so mordant and radical that the latter play had to win a production over the personal veto of Louis XVI, himself. That it could get a production, nevertheless, and that its presentation on April 27, 1784, was greeted with a riot, were surely indicative that times were changing. The author of these plays, Beaumarchais (Pierre Augustin Caron, 1732–1799), was himself a thoroughgoing rebel and two fisted battler for his own rights. He campaigned against court censorship and control of productions, insisted on an author's right to cast his own plays, wrote detailed stage directions (and made them stick), refused to be cheated of his royalties by the sociétaires or anybody else, and by his stand on these matters blazed the trail for authors' guilds in the future.

Something of that spirit of independence was implicit in the acting of Michel Baron, first of the natural school of players who, in defiance of tradition, broke the line of verse to fit the thought it expressed, modulated his voice and varied his gestures and stage business to his conception of the character he was playing. But no shrinking violet, old Baron. "The world," he once declared, "has known only two great actors, Roscius and myself. Every century has its Caesar. Two thousand years are necessary to produce a Baron."

And now not even the blindest and most self-centered of the sociétaires could fail to perceive that the revolution was here. The Bastille had fallen before the Paris mob on July 14, 1789, and members of that same mob were soon roaring down the aisles of the Théâtre Français, and disrupting its production schedule with their demands.

One of the items of that season was *Charles IX*, a historical drama of the massacre of the Huguenots on the Eve of St. Bartholomew, some two centuries before. This play, by Marie-Joseph Chénier, was not much of a drama, perhaps, but the spectacle it provided of a King of France ordering the butchery of his own subjects was meat that made the wolves in the audience howl.

The company was still generally royalist at heart, and had been none too keen about making the production in the first place. And the furious reception it was accorded disturbed and distressed its members beyond measure. They took counsel together, and determined to take the play off the instant a drop in attendance gave the slightest excuse for such a move. But in so doing they reckoned without several potent factors. For, on the first night of the new production a patron rose in the orchestra and demanded the return of *Charles IX* the next evening. The company tried to proceed with the lines, but the audience drowned them out. The management was ready for that one, however, and as soon as a lull occurred, trotted out one of its members to inform the malcontents that the company would have been most willing to continue *Charles IX*, but, owing to the illness of two of the important members of the cast, it was, as the audience could see, quite out of the question.

The demonstrators were prepared for anything but an appeal to reason, and were taken aback at this answer. It was one of those psychological moments when anything might have happened. What did occur was the appearance of the player of the leading rôle in the discarded production, who informed the audience that one of the actors in question was not so ill, and the other had a pretty good substitute available. The fat was in the fire, again.

Now François Joseph Talma was playing the leading rôle in *Charles IX*, but he was one of the younger members of the company, playing that rôle, as a matter of fact, only because the actor entitled to it by seniority had walked out on it because of his royalist sympathies. For him to appear at this time and in this manner was distinctly talking out of turn. But he had picked his spot, for there was no question as to where the sympathy of the audience lay. The company surrendered. *Charles IX* went on the next night—to the accompaniment of another riot, but it went on.

The conservative members of the Comédie were scandalized at Talma. The actor whose announcement he had spoiled challenged him to a duel. When that failed to dispose of the radical, he was read out of the organization. His friends made up a theatre party and the next performance was lost in a hideous din. The management protested that if they would only wait until the next evening, they should have a decision about M. Talma. His friends fell for the soft answer, and returned the next evening—to find themselves confronted by an almost equal number of royalist sympathizers. That night the performance was all in the front of the house. The actors did not even make a pretense of going through their parts.

The company was still nominally under the supervision of the Four First Gentlemen of the Bedchamber, and to this authority the conservatives made an appeal for support on their stand. Pending that decision the company would continue —without Talma. But Talma had friends in the company, too. Dugazon, leading comedian and one of the best loved of the group, walked out for Talma. And *his* friends in the audience took their turn at smashing benches and railings.

When the decision came down it proceeded, significantly enough, not from the Gentlemen of the Bedchamber, but from the city authorities. It was brief and to the point: "Take Talma and Dugazon back." Hoping against hope for support from the court, which surely would not abandon them in this crisis, the conservatives did nothing about the order. On the evening of September 26, 1790, a mob forced its way into the theatre and put a stop to the proceedings. Next day the authorities cracked down on the company and closed the theatre.

The inference was plain. Until Talma and Dugazon came back, the company need not expect to be allowed to play. The stubborn management held out for two months before running up the white flag and inviting the strikers to return. But things had gone so far that even that return provoked further trouble. Several of the actresses of the company resigned, alleging that the presence of these radicals rendered the maintenance of the company's tone impossible. All this to the accompaniment of passionate demonstrations of loyalty and a good deal of rough stuff on both sides of the footlights.

The situation was fundamentally impossible, and nothing could have saved the whole company from dissolution if the National Assembly had not cancelled the monopoly which, to this point, the Comédie had enjoyed. Talma led his group out of the Comédie and organized a rival company.

The Talma company was frankly a radical outfit. Somewhat less frankly the old Comédie Française became a royalist propaganda bureau. It tried to assume a hearty republican air along with the new name of the Theatre of the Nation under which it reopened after the bloody Short Terror, which attended the execution of the King and Queen; but its heart was never really in any such masquerade, and, as it could, it tried to put the brakes on popular opinion and turn it to the right. In such an attempt a play was produced lampooning the radical leaders of the Commune. If they thought they had seen riots before, they learned the real meaning of that word, now. On one occasion cannon were trained on the doors of the playhouse. A last, spasmodic rally of the conservatives wrung a victory from the sympathizers with the Commune, and after a few days of forced closing, the Theatre of the Nation was reopened.

But the tide was running fast, and the former Comedians of the King could not swim with it. In September, 1793, the whole company was arrested and thrown into prison. The situation of the actors was really desperate, for the Long Terror was then at its height. Anyone with known royalist leanings or connections was likely to fare badly. And the bias of the Comédie Française was only too well known.

From documents later available, it seems probable that indictments against the actors, tantamount to a death sentence under prevailing conditions, were actually drawn. It is supposed that, ironically enough, they were drawn by a former actor who had never succeeded in making the grade in the Théâtre Français, or, indeed, in any reputable company. But it happened that another actor, one Labussière, was clerk of the powerful Committee of Public Safety. This man is credited with having saved the lives of more than eleven hundred condemned men and women, through the simple expedient of destroying documents in their dossiers to which he had access. His sympathies were enlisted on behalf of the wretched members of the former Comédie Française, and, by one expedient or another, he succeeded in having action on their cases delayed until the worst of the Terror was past.

But the company was done for as an organization. As its members straggled out of prison, they joined forces with the Talma troupe which had managed to ride out of the revolutionary gale by trimming their sails to its shifting blasts. They were now ensconced in their own Théâtre de la Rue de Richelieu, a site still occupied by the Comédie Française.

Their position was enhanced rather than diminished by the rise of Napoleon Bonaparte. Along the way Napoleon had become friendly with Talma, and interested in the reborn Comédie Française. When he became Emperor, his subsidies to the company exceeded the largest grants ever made by the

King. Nor, with the enormous expansion of his realm and the activities it entailed, did his interest wane. In the midst of his disastrous Russian campaign he could still find time to dictate the Decree of Moscow, by which the Comédie is yet governed.

Napoleon blazed across the European sky like a rocket and was extinguished, and fell upon the rocky isle of St. Helena. Louis XVIII returned from exile to occupy the throne of his ancestors. Metternich persuaded the Congress of Vienna to try to freeze the map of Europe and to hold in perpetual arrest the hands of the world clock. Reaction—political, social, religious, and literary—was in the saddle, and France, as all Europe, was at its feet.

THROUGH ROMANCE AND REALISM TO THE PRESENT

To many people, no doubt, the return to order and stability and established authority was grateful enough after the years of revolution and war which had preceded it. But the seeds of revolution were never all uprooted and cast in the fire. There were always some spirits in revolt against order and constituted authority. And, as usual, their rebellion was first manifest among the arts.

When we think of "Romance" and "Romanticism," it is apt to be with rather a different connotation from that of those French dramatists and novelists of the nineteenth century who adopted the term as a label for their movement. What they meant to imply by its use was an independence from the restraints imposed by the canons of classical writing. All those limitations incidental to the observance of the unities of time and place and action, the choice of themes and characters, the treatment demanded, they felt were too narrow, hampered too much the free flow of genius.

The Romanticists felt that they simply had to get away from all such restrictions at any cost—that they required absolute freedom to write about any sort of person, and in any medium that seemed to be indicated, to run the entire gamut of settings at will, to juggle with time, and in general, to follow only the dictates of their own artistic consciences.

Just such deviations from the commonly accepted standards had marked those early, far flown tales of love and adventure in the vernacular, which were the first tentative steps from the leading strings of churchly Latin essayed by the romance peoples. Bristling with technical faults, these stories had displayed a zest for life and a vitality which had more than made up for their formal weaknesses. It was this zest and vitality the Romanticists now hoped to recapture by jettisoning their own classical restraints.

But it often happens that when revolt is staged against existing conditions, the achievement of freedom is symbolized and emphasized by a general reversal of previous values and virtues. As it worked out this time, the Romantic writers, after having been confined so long to noble characters and deeds, now flung themselves with ardor into tales of criminals and outcasts (though still more sinned against than sinning). And, released from the bonds of a rigid and inelastic play form, their dramas often enough simply didn't jell. Freed from classic discipline of thought and word, they went rioting off into all manner of extravagance of speech and action.

Unfortunately it is these extravagances, rather than the estimable intentions of which they are the unkempt flowerings, which are recalled by use of the term "Romantic." And yet such a connotation is not due to gross stupidity, or pure perversity, for those extravagances were characteristic of the movement from its inception, and became increasingly dominant with its development.

So much for the theory of Romanticism and for certain of its subsequent practices. Historically it was one phase of the general surge of liberalism which ran like wildfire through Europe in 1830 and which, in France, culminated in the downfall of Charles X on July 29, 1830, after three days of bloody street fighting and his replacement by the definitely more liberal Louis Phillipe.

The conservative element, though beaten, was not overwhelmed. It gave ground on all fronts but sullenly, resentfully, and with sudden flare-ups of inexplicable animosity. Just how much of that general resentment was implicit in the reception of *Hernani* can only be guessed. But Victor Hugo's wild and melodramatic drama of love among the bandits was so far outside the pale of contemporary good taste and good writing that the conservatives would probably have felt bound to oppose it anyway.

In the curious way in which such things happen the play at the Théâtre Français became the symbol of the conflict between the radicals and conservatives of the moment, the standard by which loyalty to certain contemporary social and political tenets could be measured. And so again, as in those fierce days of the Terror, the actors of the Théâtre Français enjoyed the somewhat equivocal honor of playing practically for each other while all Paris demonstrated for or against their drama.

In those demonstrations the extravagances of the romanticists were early apparent. Shrieking their affiliation with the play and the movement by their costumes no less than their behavior, they turned out for a fight or a frolic in violet and scarlet waistcoats, pale green breeches, yellow shoes, and flowing curls beneath Rembrandt hats. Romanticists both ways from the skin!

There were riots in the theatre and on the street before it.

Books and pamphlets screamed at each other from neighboring bookstalls. There was even a quota of duels, in some of which people were killed or injured. But the revolt was not to be halted by such measures. *Hernani* was a success, and so was the movement for which it stood.

Despite the apparent evidence to the contrary in their almost schoolgirl crushes on the Napoleons, the French are not an essentially romantic people. Basically they are a sober, frugal, and realistic race. And so all this rank verdure of the Romantic movement was just so much surface growth, lacking those roots of popular taste which alone could have assured it ultimate survival.

The temperament of the French people has much closer kinship to the Realistic school of thought, which holds that the function of the artist is to photograph people at work, or at play, or in love, to remove the fourth wall of their houses and allow the audience to eavesdrop on their activities.

For such writing keen observation and logical, orderly thinking are the prime requisites. That is a long cry from the magic poetry of the early Greeks. But if the dramatist is less a poet than a reporter, that reportorial quality, when combined with technical proficiency in the handling of dialogue and situation, may make for extraordinarily exciting entertainment. They were the qualities, above all others, which Eugène Scribe, and later Victorien Sardou, brought to their dramatic writing. Their plays were beautiful examples of dramatic construction, adhering to proved formula with all the faithfulness of a modern detective story and with, it must be admitted, about the same general significance.

It was odd to see the French theatre, once (and only comparatively recently, still) the battle ground for political, social, religious, and economic ideas, remain absorbed in the problem of who slept with whom, or with the disposition of the state papers, while France became successively a republic, a kingdom again, an empire, and, for the third time, a republic.

But these plays were swell jobs, mechanically speaking, and their characters were so universal in their appeal that they stood translation marvelously. They were as popular in Germany, England, and the United States as at home. And so once more the wheel had turned. After an interval of more than three hundred years, the barriers of language, of national prejudices and aspirations no longer isolated the theatres of Europe. Plays could again be written for production in a world theatre.

The French were the leaders in this revived world theatre. But its writers, gifted and conscientious as some of them were, and increasingly aware of the responsibility of conveying a social message through their plays, were not to be compared in stature with the earlier giants of their theatre.

As had been the case in Italy, the declining years of the nineteenth and the early years of the twentieth century produced a line of great players of whom two, at least, deserve to be ranked with the small company of world geniuses. In the exacting rôles of French classic drama Rachel (Elisabeth Rachel Félix, 1821–1858) and Sarah Bernhardt (1844–1923) disclosed an aura of authentic genius (as well as a common tempestuousness of temperament), which entitles them unquestionably to membership in any reckoning of the world's elect.

Yet the assent to this state of things was never unanimous. There were always rebels among the intellectuals and the younger actors who were ready to rally around any standard that might be raised against the administration of the Théâtre Français. And in its devotion to the wheel horses of classical drama and its readiness to yield to the importunities of the actor-managers for the fleshpots of parts and acting, there was plenty to incite rebellion.

The Moses who came forth from the local bullrushes at this juncture was a young clerk in the Paris Gas Company named André Antoine. At the moment he was only a clerk, but prior to that job he had been first a member of the official claque at the Théâtre Français, then its leader and, growing more and more enamored of the theatre, a student of acting and direction.

Early in the eighties Antoine joined the Cercle Gaulois, an amateur dramatic society in the Montmartre section of Paris. He soon found himself in open disagreement with the club authorities over the selection of its monthly plays, which were of the same general pattern as the Théâtre Français. Antoine was all for putting on programs of one act plays by the more radical and realistic playwrights, and the committee promptly turned him down.

When he persisted in his plan he was forbidden the use of the club's name and prestige and, which hurt still worse, the use of its hall for his presentations. He was told, in effect, if he wanted to try out his ridiculous theories to go and hire a hall. And the owner of the tiny hall, seating only three hundred and forty-three people, in which the Cercle Gaulois lived and moved and had its being, added that if he wanted *his* hall it would cost Antoine one hundred francs in advance.

This was a formidable sum for anyone living on the meagre salary of a clerk in the gas company, but slowly and painfully Antoine set about accumulating it. At the same time, he began to gather about him a group of fellow spirits, and to drill them in the plays they would present *when* they had a hundred francs and a hall.

It was not until March 30, 1887, that it was possible to

present the first bill of the Théâtre-Libre. This name was chosen because the group intended to free itself from the hampering restrictions and the timid and timeserving policies of the commercial theatre. It was the parent and the model for the countless little theatres which have followed the trail it then began to blaze.

Its disregard of the financial probabilities kept the group in hot water from the beginning. Antoine, a magnificent director and prophet of the theatre, never knew how to control the purse strings of any of the organizations with which he was associated. But the plays and the playwrights that were presented to France by the Théâtre-Libre! Tolstoy and Turgenev; the French première of Ibsen's *The Wild Duck;* work from the pens of Björnson, Strindberg, and Hauptmann; the early work of Brieux. In 1906, Antoine was appointed director of the Odéon, and without his guiding hand the Théâtre-Libre was unable to survive its mounting difficulties. But, before its extinction, it had lit a fire which has burned, and which still burns brightly on many alien hearths.

About the same time the Théâtre-Libre was getting under way in France, a similar movement was being initiated in Germany. There the Deutsches Theater of Adolf L'Arronge, the Lessing Theater of Oscar Blumenthal, and the Freie Bühne of Otto Brahm undertook to do very much the same sort of thing the Théâtre-Libre was doing in Paris. It is a melancholy commentary on modern trends that most of the leaders of this valuable movement would have encountered considerable difficulty and would probably have been barred entirely from that work because of their race, if the present régime had been in control of Germany at that time.

Then came the organization of the Independent Theatre, by J. T. Grein in England, and the Little Theatre Movement was off on its world career—a career of splendid service and of incalculable value to the theatre.

GERMANY: FROM HANS WURST TO HITLER

The territory which is known as Germany was familiar to cartographers by that name long before it became a member of the family of nations. Nominally a part of the Holy Roman Empire, it was actually an agglomeration of some three hundred principalities, duchies, free cities, and fiefs of the church, some of which were no more than a few square miles in extent. But diverse as they were in other things, all were united in their hatred of effective federal control and were equally eager in the maintenance of their independence of the Emperor. And, aided by the form of government which had been devised for that purpose and by the number and variety of the Emperor's problems, they succeeded in their ambition tolerably well.

The imperial government consisted of the Emperor and the Diet. This body consisted of representatives of the more important landholders (the seven members of the Empire's electoral college), the lesser landholders, and the free cities. The consent of the Diet was required for all the important acts of the Emperor, and its members saw to it that the Emperor was never provided with an army, an administration, or sufficient funds to set up either one.

Prior to the Reformation the religious theatre of Germany was second to none in the vigor and variety of its productions. In the work of Hans Sachs (an actual poet-shoemaker of Nuremberg [1494–1576] and not merely a bass in the troupe of Meistersingers in Richard Wagner's opera of that name), there was a rudimentary German folk drama which, if it did not rise very high, was a genuine beginning.

But any significance it might have had was wiped out with the promulgation of the Edict of Worms, in 1521, by which the Emperor, Charles V, proscribed Martin Luther as a heretic, and ordered his arrest at sight. That edict precipitated a series of blighting religious, social, and economic wars, which transformed Germany into a cockpit churned by the bloody spurs of contending Protestant, Catholic, German, Austrian, French, Danish, and Swedish armies for more than two hundred years. In all that furious and frantic time there was no leisure, or security, or order for creative writing, or any disposition on the part of the rulers of the time to encourage it.

A few unhappy theatrical companies occasionally wandered in from foreign territory and, dodging armies and plagues, made the most of the patronage of those courts which opened their doors to them. Sometimes they moved on again; sometimes they remained and their members and their material became Germanized. In the end there was no knowing what of the residue was native and what was borrowed.

Italian commedia dell' arte troupes, French farceurs, English tragedians—the result was a sort of vaudeville routine of sketches, dancing, juggling, acrobatic turns, and songs, from which gradually emerged the swelling figure of Hans Wurst, a colossus who so dominated the stages of Germany that for many decades he was practically the German theatre.

This Hans Wurst was an amalgamation of the Italian Harlequin and any Burlesque Wheel tramp comedian, retaining the worst features of each. He was a sort of "Peck's Bad Boy," physically mature but mentally and morally arrested. Yet he was so perfectly what the audiences wanted that he was dragged into even the presumably serious plays. There was "The World's Great Monster, or The Life and Death of the Late Imperial General Wallenstein, Duke of Friedland, with Hans Wurst," an announcement analogous, perhaps, to

"The tragedy of Hamlet, with Popeye the Sailor Man." At any rate, good or bad, explicable or not, Hans Wurst *was* the German theatre for a matter of a couple of hundred years.

And then, quite suddenly, about the beginning of the eighteenth century, there was an improvement in conditions throughout Germany. The loose sprawl of states and cities began to coagulate about Austria in the south and Prussia in the north. The duel between them may have seemed endless to most of those involved in it, but there were intervals, and in those lulls the arts and sciences took root and sent out sprouts wherever the soil was favorable.

The town of Leipzig, in Saxony near the border of Brandenburg, was such a place, to some extent because it was the seat of a great university. To Leipzig, in 1724, came Johann Christoph Gottsched (1700–1766), and within a few years he had made himself dictator of the literary circle of Leipzig. He was a man of definite limitations, both a pedant and a prig, but he had a consuming hatred for Hans Wurst in all his manifestations and a burning desire to establish a great national literature. Since there was not at that time any great German literature or even any pretty good German literature, Gottsched decided to give Germany the best of the foreign material then available. By nature Gottsched had more affinity for the French classicists than for any other group, and he set out to transplant their works and their manner of writing to Germany.

Casting about for some medium to transmit his ambitions to the theatre he encountered the "Royal Polish and Electoral Saxon Court Comedians" headed by Johann Neuber and Frederika Carolina, his wife, or, perhaps, *vice versa*. Now Carolina Neuber was no great shakes as an actress, but she was a splendid organizer and executive, and she was animated by as great a distaste for Hans Wurst and his works as Gottsched himself. It was no job at all to strike up an alliance between Gottsched and the Neubers, by which they agreed to provide the players, and Gottsched the plays and invitations to the various courts to present them.

But Gottsched and the Neubers were too far apart in taste and in outlook ever to make a go of such an alliance. They were, as a matter of fact, too far ahead of their time to receive the popular support which alone would have brought success to their venture. And any chance they might have had went by the board when they quarreled over one of their productions. Gottsched's wife had prepared the translation of Voltaire's *Alzire*, and naturally he expected it to be used. But the Neubers had another translation which they found preferable. The fury of their assault on Hans Wurst was now directed against each other and to the destruction of the common cause to which they had given so much time and effort. United they had never had more than an outside chance. Clawing at each other's throats, they went down to inevitable defeat and death in poverty and obscurity.

Their effort had ended in apparent failure and humiliation, but the German theatre owes them a debt of eternal gratitude. Before they went their separate ways, the throne of Hans Wurst had been yanked from under him, and the theatre had been hauled from the rut in which it had been so long stalled.

During the life of the partnership the Neuber troupe gave occasional employment to a brilliant young student in the Theological School of the University. And in the quarter century which followed the dissolution of that partnership, while the star of Gottsched and the Neubers was setting, and while the grenadiers of Frederick the Great were knocking off one military nation after another, the fortunes of Gotthold Ephraim Lessing (1729–1781) were in the ascendant. By the time the citizens of Hamburg got around to the formation of a committee to organize a national theatre, some time in 1765 or 1766, Lessing was Germany's leading dramatist. And, indeed, *Minna von Barnhelm,* and *Miss Sara Sampson* still hold a place in classical German repertoire.

So it is no wonder that the committee asked Lessing to become house dramatist for the national theatre, responsible for providing a continuous flow of acceptable plays. But Lessing had no desire for the job of a hack writer, no matter how disguised. What he proposed, instead, was handling publicity for the theatre and writing its advertising, in the form of critical reviews of its productions. That was the inspiration behind the *Hamburgische Dramaturgie* which began its career coincidentally with the National Theatre, in 1767, and was published regularly twice a week until the failure of its parent enterprise snuffed it out, also. It presented the first real dramatic criticism, certainly the first exposition of the principles of dramatic art, ever to come out of Germany. It was enormously popular, widely read and almost as widely pirated, and it exercised a deep and lasting influence on the German theatre.

Lessing had almost as little regard for French classicism as Gottsched and the Neubers for Hans Wurst. His dramatic crush was William Shakespeare, then scarcely known beyond the borders of his native England. The build up and ballyhoo he lavished on the Englishman made his work an integral part of the repertoire of every Central European state. Today he is more frequently played and more really a factor in the theatre of Germany than in England or America.

Mismanagement and lack of real interest by the Hamburgers laid the National Theatre low in 1769. But in that short time the nucleus of a fine company had been assembled. Even though that company was scattered by the failure of its theatre, and while Prussia itself was tumbled from its proud position by Napoleon's military juggernaut, the actors kept the German theatre alive and vigorous. When Germany's greatest dramatists stepped out on to the scene, there was a theatre waiting for them and players capable of presenting their plays.

It was for no less a person than Johann Wolfgang von Goethe (1749–1832) that the stage had been set. Goethe is one of the great IFS of the theatre. *If* he had only been single-minded about his dramatic writing, as was practically every other one of the theatre's geniuses, there is no telling to what dramatic heights he might have risen. But he was at least equally interested in poetry, philosophy, and science; and, in consequence, his dramatic writings, great literature though they are, are not as good plays as the work of writers many notches below him as a thinker or a poet.

It was not for lack of opportunity to know the theatre, or because he had no chance to put his theories to the test, that Goethe's plays lacked stage-worthiness. For twenty-six years, with some intervals, he was director of the court theatre of Karl August, Duke of Weimar. In that capacity he wrote, staged, and acted in every variety of dramatic entertainment. He even developed into something of a martinet toward his actors, drawing up rules for every situation and every shading of emotion, to which his actors were held as closely as recruits to the manual of arms. But he just didn't have the flair for drama, the feeling for perfect dramatic rightness which so many of his literary inferiors possessed in abundance. A dramatic scene might be halted for a philosophic dissertation, or for a poetic passage—great stuff in itself, but not great drama.

And yet, imperfect in this respect, he is still the greatest dramatist Germany has yet produced. The creator of *Faust*, of *Egmont*, of *Clavigo*, of *Götz von Berlichingen*, of *Iphigenia*, of *Tasso*, and the rest, is an authentic genius who belongs to the line of Aeschylus, Sophocles, Euripides, and Shakespeare.

Goethe's work at Weimar, and the generally favorable attitude of its Duke, drew other literary men to it, and in time it became the literary capital of Germany. Among those who drifted there was a poet and dramatist who had already made something of a name for himself with a passionate and melodramatic play, *The Robbers*. But Goethe and Johann Christoph Friedrich von Schiller (1759–1805) did not take kindly to each other at first, to some extent, perhaps, because the younger man was so presumptuous as to criticize unfavorably his distinguished colleague's play, *Egmont*.

Eventually, however (but a good six or seven years later), that breach was healed and they entered into an enormously stimulating and fruitful friendship which was terminated only by Schiller's death. They each had something of value to contribute to the friendship. Schiller was not the literary titan that Goethe was, but he had a much better grasp of dramatic technique. In that last spurt of seven years, with death closing in on him, he produced *Conspiracy and Love, Mary Stuart, The Maid of Orleans*, the *Wallenstein* trilogy, *The Bride of Messina* and *William Tell*. They are not only rousing historical dramas, still capable of stirring audiences' pulses; they have also a fine lyric note of nationalism very welcome to German ears at that time, for German prestige, won so recently and with such difficulty by Frederick the Great, was being trampled into the dust of Austerlitz and Auerstadt by the boots of Napoleon's hard marching, hard fighting veterans. Leipzig and Waterloo were a long way in the future, too far to be easily foreseen, and to the ardent patriots of Weimar and throughout Germany, these stories of tyrants and conquerors who got their proper comeuppances were highly grateful.

After Schiller's death, in 1805, Goethe carried on at Weimar

under increasingly difficult circumstances. The Duke fell more
and more under the spell of his mistress, a silly and incon-
sequential former opera singer, who bothered the life out of
Goethe with her suggestions for the management of the court
theatre. Goethe was something of a tyrant in the theatre himself, and these suggestions did not set very well with him.
But he held on until 1817, when she insisted on the presentation of a drama designed to star a trained poodle. This was
too much for the creator of *Faust,* and he resigned from his
post and turned gladly to his beloved poetry, science, philosophy, and memoirs for the remaining years of his life.

Goethe and Schiller had been enormously aided in their
theatrical activities by a succession of fine actors. Three of
them from that brief period are still counted as the best Germany has produced: Konrad Ekhof, Friederich Ludwig
Schröder (still called "The Great Schröder" by theatrical
historians), and August Wilhelm Iffland.

The fires of patriotism which Schiller had labored so hard
to kindle continued to burn through all the period of reaction
and conservatism which set in with the downfall of Napoleon.
And when at last a Germany united by victories over Austria
(1866) and France (1871), stepped out to play its rôle on
the world stage, it was with a people tremendously aware of
its possibilities and enormously proud of its race.

In the next generation the theatre in Germany became the
most active and vital of any in the world. In matters of direction, settings, lighting, and ensemble playing it was both excited and exciting. If there were no more gigantic playwrights,
such writers as Gerhardt Hauptmann, Hermann Sudermann,
and Frank Wedekind displayed a growing sense of social
responsibility as well as considerable technical proficiency, and
made the German theatre not the least valuable of its country's
exports.

And then came the World War, in 1914, and the German theatre, like that of all combatant countries became subordinated to the national effort. Even the war's end brought little respite to the country's theatre, for the people were too disturbed, too poor, and too miserable for really good work to be possible.

About the time the theatre was beginning to emerge from the nightmare of inflation, the revolution hoisted Adolf Hitler and his National Socialist Party into the saddle. From that moment the theatre, with the press, the schools, and religion became simply one more agency for the diffusion of the Nazi creed.

Whatever the value of that formula, it places very definite limitations upon the development of the art of the theatre. Wherever that concept of the state, and of the relations of its citizens to the state, exists, little original or significant drama can be expected. At the moment (1935), the German theatre continues in a state of suspended animation.

CHAPTER III

ENGLAND

In Good Queen Bess's Glorious Days

WHEN Elizabeth came to the throne of England, in 1558, London was still a walled town in which there was not a single professional theatre. What theatrical activity there was, and it was considerable, was mostly manifest in the schools and in the community presentations of the miracle and morality plays.

But England stood on the threshold of one of those marvelous periods that come all too rarely to men and nations. Within the fifty-five years that marked her reign, the map of the world was redrafted, and English admirals were responsible for many of its new contours. Claim to the ownership of those new worlds was also contested, it is true, by Spain, but that claim was met and sunk with the Spanish Armada in the English Channel in the summer of 1588. Now England's wealth was increased enormously and was matched by the growing sense of her national sufficiency and of her destiny as a nation. It was a time when it seemed that not only anything could happen, but that it was happening right before one's eyes. In short, it was a period when just to be alive and a part of all that was going on must have been enormously exciting and stimulating.

And, as had happened at similar moments in Greece, in Spain, and in France, this aura of national prosperity and prestige was reflected in a burst of literary activity that is still the glory and the wonder of the English language. Poets and playwrights tumbled over themselves and each other proclaiming the richness and complexity of life and the pleasures and penalties of living.

The first playhouse was erected in London in 1576, and it was a structure sufficiently unique to be called simply The Theatre. But long before there was any formal home for their work, scattered bands of players were carrying the drama the length and breadth of the country.

The ordinary run of these players had no standing in the eyes of the law. They were outcasts classed with rogues and vagabonds, and their approach to a village justified, no doubt, the ancient cry:

"Mother, mother, take in the wash! The actors are coming!"

The better or more fortunate companies were able to persuade one of the nobility to extend to them the protection of his name. Proclaiming that they were of his household, and wearing his livery, they enjoyed a reasonable immunity from petty persecution and often enjoyed considerable prosperity.

Touring the country without any fixed place for performance, these companies had to play wherever they could, or wherever they could best get an audience together. More often than elsewhere this proved to be the courtyard of an inn with the stage set up at one end. The better elements of the audience watched the play from their windows, or from the balconies that ran around the courtyard—the common herd stood in the yard in front of the stage. And thus it was that when The Theatre and its fellow playhouses were built, they followed the plan already familiar to players and audiences alike; they were circular or oval structures enclosing an open courtyard or pit, at one end of which a bare platform for acting was erected.

There was not, nor could there be, any attempt at the painted sets and perspectives already common on Italian stages. But never having known such refinements, the audience never missed them. A placard might announce whether the stage was for the moment a palace, a hut, or a seashore; or a comment by one of the characters would serve to define the scene of action. And immediately the audience filled in the background in its mind's eye, or forgot about it in its absorption over the action—and that, forthwith, there had to be, and plenty of it. Not again, until the motion picture Cyclops cast its roving eye about the world, could a playwright sweep his play and its characters so fluently and freely about the map as the Elizabethan dramatist.

The first English play of which there is any record is *Ralph Roister Doister* by Nicholas Udall, headmaster at Eton, probably written by him for the school's Christmas entertainment some time between 1534 and 1541. Written by a schoolmaster for schoolboys, it runs along the easy lines of Plautus. The first genuinely English comedy is *Gammer Gurton's Needle*, by John Still, Bishop of Bath and Wells, which was first performed at Cambridge in 1566.

About the same time the first English tragedy was performed. *Gorboduc*, the story of a mythical British king, by Thomas Sackville and Thomas Norton, was first performed about 1561, though it did not appear in print until four years later. This play, on a Senecan model, is, however, chiefly interesting because there was then employed for the first time in dramatic construction the unrhymed iambic pentameter which we also call blank verse, and which has served as such a glorious instrument in the hands of the greater dramatists then waiting in the wings.

In the approved style of the day the entrance of the great man was preceded by a crowd of lesser performers: John Lyly, romantic, elegant, artificial; Thomas Kyd, whose play, *The Spanish Tragedy*, was a dime novel best seller about 1590; George Peele, Robert Greene, Thomas Lodge, Thomas Nashe—courtiers, soldiers, tavern brawlers, involved in vigorous controversies which often ended in imprisonment, exile, or death—they wrote swift-moving, stirring and effective plays which made the theatre a vital and popular part of the life of the times.

But Christopher Marlowe (1564–1593) was more than a supernumerary. He would have been a great writer in any language and at any time. Only the overwhelming greatness of Shakespeare has dwarfed his gifts. If there had been no Shakespeare, the four plays Marlowe wrote before he was killed in a drunken row, at the age of twenty-nine, would still have made the theatre of his time a notable era. *Tamurlaine the Great, The Tragical History of Dr. Faustus, The Jew of Malta*, and *Edward II* proved his right to consideration as a dramatist, a poet, and a craftsman of the first rank. If he had lived—but he lived prodigally and died miserably and was overtaken and surpassed by the greatest and most versatile dramatist the theatre of any land has ever known.

About 1585 or 1586 there came up to London from the quiet little Warwickshire town of Stratford-on-Avon, a young man named William Shakespeare. There was nothing in his background or history to that point to indicate that here was the supreme dramatic genius not only of his own land and time, but of all times and all places. He came of good, though not exceptional family, his schooling had been average, or less, and nothing he had done there appears to have left any particular mark on the community. About all he had to show for himself to the point of his departure for London, at twenty-one or two, had been a restless inability to fit into the peaceful Stratford pattern, which had manifested itself in a hasty and apparently none too happy marriage to a girl eight years older than himself, and in local scrapes which probably hastened his going.

There is a tradition that he made his start in London by holding horses for theatre patrons, and there is little doubt that, at the beginning, he was probably reduced to turning his hand to anything that came along. Whatever the truth of that particular story, he was soon graduated into the theatre, at first as an actor in the company of James Burbage, at The Theatre, and then as a play doctor, adapter, and author attached to the company.

It was the custom of the time for the managers to buy plays outright from their authors and to revamp them as their desires or the requirements of their companies dictated. Sometimes, as in the motion pictures today, a whole battery of playwrights worked on one manuscript. Since the majority of plays produced were not ascribed to any author, and only one out of every three or four was preserved in any form, it is not possible to say with any degree of definiteness just how many plays Shakespeare worked over, or with whom he collaborated, or just what was done by each.

But by the time Marlowe came to his end, Shakespeare was definitely established as one of the outstanding men of the English theatre, and within three years of that time was listed as one of the owners of The Globe, to which the Burbage company had moved themselves and their productions recently.

And before his retirement, in 1611, to spend the last five years of his life as a rich and respected gentleman in his native Stratford, Shakespeare produced thirty-seven comedies, dramas, and histories, which can be definitely ascribed to him in addition to those others on which he probably lent a hand.

His versatility is only one of his claims to theatrical greatness, but it is true that where every other one of the world's greatest dramatists turned instinctively either to drama or to comedy, Shakespeare was supreme at everything to which he turned his hand, and his plays include every known form of dramatic writing. Certain of his characters, Hamlet, Iago, Richard III, Falstaff, Lady Macbeth, are still the yardsticks by which players who aspire to prove their dramatic stature measure themselves. Probably no other author has created so many characters who are familiar to everyone, and if there is another source of quotations more prolific, it can only be the Bible.

Nor was it that he worked in an age where his contemporaries were little men. Ben Jonson, John Fletcher, and John Webster would have been giants in any age. And, in addition to them George Chapman, Francis Beaumont, Thomas Dekker, Thomas Middleton, John Ford, James Shirley, Philip Massinger, Thomas Heywood, and Samuel Rowley were all on the job during his lifetime. Never have there been so many first rate dramatists at work at any one time in the history of the theatre. There have not been so many notable names in all the rest of the English theatre since then. And yet William Shakespeare dwarfed that impressive field and was tops in every line of dramatic endeavor.

It was a tough audience to which Shakespeare addressed himself. The sight of the flag flying over the wooden O of The Globe, indicating that a play was on, brought a curious, mixed audience on the run to view it.

There, standing on the ground before the stage, we would find a crowd of apprentices playing hooky from their jobs; a sprinkling of local gangsters; soldiers and sailors on leave; tourists up from the country; and a few street walkers with an eye to any business that could be picked up.

In the gallery where, of course, we are, there are a knot of students who have probably cut their classes to be there; business men giving their customers a treat on the house; over on the other side, certainly some of the gentlemen of the court, and with them, masked as they would have to be at a place like this, some of the ladies.

You might suppose the group up there on the stage a part of the acting company if you didn't happen to know the play hadn't begun yet. Some of them are smoking long pipes (a habit picked up from the red Indians by Sir Walter Raleigh's men, and becoming vastly popular); others are talking and showing off their fine figures and the costumes which enhance them. These are some of the really important people at court, friends of the sponsor of the company, men about town who are quite as interested in being seen as in seeing Mr. Shakespeare's new play about some Danish prince, Hamlet, is it?

A boisterous, vigorous, volatile audience this, which has come to the theatre to be thrilled and amused and has to be caught in the first few minutes of the production if it is to be caught at all. Action first and fine sentiment afterwards, and woe to the play or the player too slow or too tame for its hot fancy. It would be luck, indeed, if the audience merely dismissed the tedious proceedings on the stage in favor of cards and dice.

Of those who were contemporary with Shakespeare and whose work continued after his retirement and death, the most important, without question, was Ben Jonson (1573–1637). Highly considered as a writer of tragedies at the time, his most important contribution to the theatre was the theory that every person has some distinguishing characteristic, or humor, and that true comedy comes from the elaboration of that underlying humor in each character. This is the theory on which the whole art of cartooning is predicated, and Jonson's satiric comedies of humor were really tremendously clever and well drawn dramatic cartoons. In *Everyman in His Humor, The Poetaster, The Alchemist, Bartholomew Fair,* and, above all in *Volpone,* he did this exceedingly well, almost as well as Shakespeare. It is true that he lacked the tragic genius of his fellow craftsman. But to be almost as good as Shakespeare at anything is a distinction that can be accorded to comparatively few.

REFORMATION AND RESTORATION

There seems to be a rather widespread belief that the Puritan movement came from nowhere to take over the government of England—as though, almost, England went to bed one night without any Puritans in sight and woke up the next morning to find them on the throne, and in every municipal building, running the nation. But far back in Tudor times, when the Church of England was being cut loose from the Papacy, there were people who believed that its reforms had not gone far enough, that too much ritual and too many trappings still remained. Because they wished to reform or purify the church still further, they were known as Puritans.

Now to many of these people the theatre was anathema, a veritable anteroom to hell. They held it responsible for at least encouraging all the religious, social, political, and economic ills of the times, from emptying the churches and perpetuating pagan customs, to causing God to visit the plague on London in 1603.

The theatre, on its part, struck back at the Puritans with every weapon of ridicule and abuse in its armory. The Puritan leaders and customs were pilloried in pamphlets and plays, and, just to show its unconcern for their disapproval, the theatre plunged into new excesses of word and action which justified most of the harsher things the Puritans said of it.

But the quarrel between the theatre and the Puritans was not entirely on moral grounds. The Reformation in England had liberated two great forces, the power of the throne, and the power of the people, which, sooner or later, were bound to come into conflict. Quite generally the theatre and its people were on the side of government, of constituted authority, and that trait, if nothing else, would have damned the theatre to the Puritans.

The struggle was already so far developed that in 1602, with Elizabeth still on the throne, and Shakespeare in the bloom of his finest creative years, the town council of his native Stratford enacted an ordinance prohibiting the performance of any plays "in the Chamber, the Guildhall, nor in any parte of the howse, or courte, from hensforward."

And it grew with the development of the theory of the Divine Right of Kings proclaimed by her successor, James I, first of the Stuart line until, in 1625, the same year in which James' son, Charles I, came to the throne, a Puritan, William Prynne, began the monumental labor of cataloguing every crime ever recorded as having occurred in or about the theatre, or by anyone connected with the theatre. The result of this research, published seven years later under the title *Histrio-Mastix*, was an eleven hundred page indictment of the theatre and everything and everybody who had anything to do with it.

Prynne had the misfortune to issue this volume at the precise moment that Queen Henrietta Maria was rehearsing in a new court pastoral, and when the attention of the King was drawn to the fact that Prynne, in commenting on the riots that had somewhat earlier greeted a French company with actresses (a thing unknown to the English stage of that time), had remarked that women players were "notorious whores," the swift vengeance of outraged divinity fell upon the hapless blasphemer. Prynne was stood in the pillory, his ears were cut off, he was branded "S L" (Seditious Libeler) on both cheeks, he was fined and to top it off he was given a sentence of life imprisonment.

Then, eight years later, came the complete rupture between the King and Parliament, and with the first defeats inflicted upon the Cavaliers by the Roundheads under Oliver Cromwell, all the theatres were closed by act of Parliament, in 1642.

So, once more, the theatre went underground, its plays and its players proscribed. But this exile was neither so long nor so rigorous as some of the others which have been visited upon it. For at all times in England in the eighteen years this act stood officially, there were those sympathetic toward the theatre and its people, and there were, undoubtedly, theatrical performances given in Royalist castles and private homes.

Oliver Cromwell still sat on the throne of England when, in 1656, Sir William D'Avenant returned from France, where he had been in attendance on "Bonnie Prince Charlie," and obtained permission to stage an "opera, made a representation by the Art of Perspective in Scenes," at his town house in London. And there on a stage eleven feet high and fifteen deep appeared the first professional actress ever to grace the English stage.

The closing of the theatres fourteen years earlier had made such an event almost inevitable. In the interval all the carefully trained boys who had played the women's parts in Elizabethan productions had grown to manhood, and none had been prepared to take their places.

And, in their pilgrimages to the Stuart courts on the Continent, English travelers had in the meantime become accustomed to the sight of women playing their own sex and doing it better than their boyish competitors.

The actress who made this historic appearance was Mrs. Edward Coleman, wife of the composer of the opera, and though she was so inept an actress that she never got her head out of the book during the entire performance and, apparently, retired from acting immediately afterward, she deserves, nevertheless, a place among the innovators of the theatre.

Two years later the Lord Protector died, and after tentative experiments with his son Richard, and with government by Parliament under the control of the army, the country turned once more to the Stuarts. Charles II, son of the executed monarch, was invited to resume the throne that had been pulled from under his father. And with his return, in 1660, there began one of the most amazing epochs of the English stage.

The new king was more than friendly to the theatre and its people. Before his coronation, even, he had granted patents to Thomas Killigrew and Sir William D'Avenant to produce plays. They were the only licensed companies in the entire kingdom, for outside London the Puritans were still in the saddle. These companies first played in tennis courts, similar to the establishments of their French contemporaries, and then Killigrew, at the head of His Majesties' Servants, set up shop in the Theatre Royal, Drury Lane; while D'Avenant's troupe, under the patronage of the King's brother, the Duke of York, established the Opera (in distinction to Killigrew's Theatre), at the Dorset Garden.

These two theatres were run almost entirely by and for the court and reflected its tastes, its tone, and its standards. Since this court was preëminently brilliant, sophisticated, and mercenary, these terms became outstanding in characterizing what is known as the Restoration drama.

It had no connection with the English theatre which had preceded the revolution. That was old stuff, and rather apologized for. The new drama looked rather to the Continent, which was natural enough, since the King himself, and many of the court had lived there for years. That was the period when Corneille was setting the pace in the French theatre, and so the Restoration drama burgeoned with plots in which the characters were all noble and the themes lofty, from which all comic relief and sub-plots were eliminated, and in which the story was told in rhymed couplets. The two outstanding practitioners of the heroic drama of the Restoration were John Dryden (1631–1700), best remembered for *The Conquest of Granada* and *All for Love,* a retelling of the story of Antony and Cleopatra, and Thomas Otway (1652–1685), who before he succumbed to illness and malnutrition at the early age of thirty-three, contributed *The Orphan* and, best of the dramas of that type, *Venice Preserved.*

But if the Restoration theatre depended for remembrance on its drama, it would occupy a much smaller and less conspicuous niche than it does. For its genius was essentially comic.

Up to the last fifteen years, say to the end of the World War, the Restoration comedy was thought too coarse and unmoral for general consumption. Advanced students might be led gingerly about its borders, rather than through it, holding metaphorical handkerchiefs to their noses and learning that since it was classical, it wasn't nearly as dirty as it seemed. Brilliant, yes,—but what a pity such great gifts were put to such mean uses! In fact, the general judgment of that time, which is still chronologically a part of the present generation, was pretty well summed up when Brander Matthews writing of Restoration comedy, about the turn of the twentieth century, said:

"Congreve and Wycherley, Farquahar and Vanbrugh helped themselves to Molière's framework only to hang it about with dirty linen."

There was enough surface truth in that observation to hurt. The writers of the Restoration owed plenty to Molière, no doubt. Their hard glitter of wit was characteristic of him; so, too, was their detached and aloof attitude toward their characters. The characters, who were, after all, dramatizations of certain basic human characteristics? That had been done by Ben Jonson long before Molière. Dirt? Lots of it—to many people much more than is necessary. And there you come to the matter of taste, for scarcely two people will agree on just how much dirt is necessary. But they lived and wrote for an age which was much more frank and free in expression than the period just before the World War.

And so William Wycherley (1640–1716), best remembered for *The Country Wife*, and *The Plain Dealer;* Sir John Vanbrugh (1664–1726), *The Provok'd Wife;* George Farquahar (1678–1707), *The Recruiting Officer* and *The Beaux' Stratagem;* and William Congreve (1670–1729), *Love for Love* and *The Way of the World*, seemed to be well on their way to become museum pieces, periodically read and discussed, but not a part of the living theatre.

Whether or not the World War was wholly responsible for our altered attitude toward the moral standards of our elder brothers, it is true that the prolonged and world wide period of economic pressure and the extensive remodeling of our social structure which it ushered in, have evolved audiences quite able and prepared to appreciate the gay and licentious plays of the Restoration writers. Some of their words may be a little strange, for styles in words change with fashions in clothes; but there is hardly a character or a situation of theirs which might not be (and probably has been) appropriated by modern playwrights—and enjoyed by contemporary audiences.

These brilliant plays were given good productions. Inigo Jones had brought back from the Continent the continental playhouse, and England had turned its back forever on the inn courtyard and "wooden O" theatres; and the two companies available in London were filled with able players.

In one bound, actresses had taken over the stage so long denied to them. Paradoxically enough that move was facilitated by the work of one of the last and probably one of the greatest of the boy actors of feminine rôles. Edward Kynaston was so completely devastating in the parts he played that he became the idol of the ladies of the court. They descended on the theatre in which he was appearing and bore him off to ride through the park, perhaps in his stage costumes. The consequent scandal was such that the very persons who had most inveighed against the immorality of women in the theatre now cried to heaven against the practice of men playing in women's clothing. But Kynaston only somewhat hastened a process which was inevitable. The general attitude toward the theatre was changing, anyway, and regardless of whether or not he had appeared, women would not have been denied much longer the privilege of portraying their own sex on the stage.

At any rate in the company of William Betterton, who had succeeded to the management of the Opera on the death of D'Avenant and who was, himself, a splendid actor, were Mary Saunderson (Mrs. Betterton), the first Juliet, Ophelia, and Lady Macbeth of her sex in the English theatre; Nell Gwyn, whose spectacular career as uncrowned Queen of England overshadowed her really brilliant gifts as a madcap comedian; Anne Bracegirdle and Aphra Behn, first of the professional playwrights of her sex to achieve the honor of burial in Westminster Abbey. But in spite of this profusion of talent in writing, producing, and acting, there were simply not enough patrons to make two theatres go. When they were merged in 1682, the resultant company, known as the King's, took over Drury Lane, which was, for a long time, the only company in all the land possessed of a royal patent, or license.

In other ways it was evident that the theatre was sliding from the peak to which it had climbed in those first years after the Restoration. There were no more playwrights of the calibre of Wycherley, Vanbrugh, Farquahar, and Congreve. The little men who trailed in their wake tried hard enough to follow their patterns, but, as little men do, copied only their more sensational and less estimable characteristics. The tone of the theatre, questionable enough before, fell to a very low point.

Public taste was going through one of its cycles of change, no doubt of it. It did not require the general agreement with Jeremy Collier's *A Short View of the Immorality and Profaneness of the English Stage,* published in 1698, to demonstrate it. Quite as definite was the public favor accorded the rather milk and water comedies of Sir Richard Steele (1672–1729),

and the academic tragedy (with political overtones), typified
by *The Tragedy of Cato* of Joseph Addison (1672–1719).
These men deservedly, however, are better remembered for
their collaboration on the Spectator Papers. Yes, England was
sobering up after the spree of the Restoration. Charles'
brother, James II, forfeited the confidence of his people and
thereafter his throne. Indicative of the temper of the time
was his replacement by his daughter Mary, and her husband,
William of Orange. Another era of the English stage was at
hand.

A THEATRE OF ACTOR-MANAGERS

This time it was the turn of the actors, exploring and
elaborating upon the characters bequeathed by vanished playwrights. To this period belong such players as Colley Cibber,
Anne Oldfield, Peg Woffington, Charles Macklin, and the
darling and the hero of actors from that time, "Little Davey,"
David Garrick.

There may have been greater actors in the English theatre
than David Garrick (1717–1779), but none more completely
captured the imagination and affection of his fellow workers
than this little, none too impressively built descendant of
Huguenot refugees, who, in his dash to the stage, fled from
under the wing of the great Dr. Johnson and from his family
wine business.

The actors who had immediately preceded him had made
acting pretty much a matter of routine. Whatever splendor it
had had in the hands of its originators, this stylized acting
had now brought that art down to the level of declamations
inserted in a series of tableaux. From the beginning Garrick
would have none of this. There was a great shaking of heads
at his comparatively natural style. "If this young fellow is

right, we are all wrong," said James Quin. And the weight
of the evidence is to the effect that they were.

Within half a dozen years of his début, in 1741, Garrick
had made such strides in popular favor that he was able to
purchase a two-thirds interest in the building and business of
Drury Lane. And from that time, until his retirement, thirty
years later, he was the unquestioned ruler of the English
theatre.

The enthusiasm of his fellow actors is understandable in
the light of what Garrick did to and with his company. He
worked them tremendously hard, and was a good deal of a
martinet with them, but he built the finest acting company
the English theatre had yet seen, with much more scope to
character acting and ensemble work than had been given by
any of his predecessors. He overhauled the scene lofts and
costume closets and reorganized them at considerable expense. And finally he gave his company Shakespeare and the
other Elizabethans in a form which, if it was not as they had
been written, was much closer to it than the "improvements"
added by the Restoration and post-Restoration adapters. The
sobriety of his own life and the discipline on which he insisted in his company gave actors a standing and general acceptance in society they had never known in England. And
when, on top of all this, he was the first actor of his day,
particularly in the rôles of Hamlet, Lear, and Macbeth; was
as amiable and charming off the stage as on; and was so able
a business manager that he retired with a fortune of well over
a million dollars, it is not much wonder that the actors feel
as they do about him.

Garrick may have been the greatest manager of the period,
but he let slip through his fingers the only two playwrights
who had anything worth saying. Both *She Stoops to Conquer*,
by Oliver Goldsmith (1728–1774), and *The Rivals* and *The*

School for Scandal by Richard Brinsley Sheridan (1751–1816), were produced at the rival Covent Garden. Maybe Garrick was tired, or had lost his keenness—anyway he missed out on them.

It looked as though a new and even more brilliant era of playwriting was at hand. At twenty-five Sheridan was the author of two eminently successful plays, had bought Garrick's interest in Drury Lane, and had thereby acquired the finest acting company in England. When he reopened that playhouse with his own great comedy *The School for Scandal*, it would have been silly to bet against him. And yet, after that start, he wrote only one more play, *The Critic*, and then laid down his pen. It may have been that in four plays he had written himself out. More likely it was because after his election to Parliament, in 1780, politics became the greater interest. At any rate there were no more comedies from his gifted hand, and his control of Drury Lane was only nominal.

It may be of interest to note that as a member of Parliament, he was so vigorously opposed to the war with the American Colonies that the Continental Congress tried to make him a gift of a hundred thousand dollars; and that he opened the government's case against Warren Hastings for corrupt administration as Governor General of India; but as far as the theatre was concerned, his career might as well have closed with the final curtain on *The Critic*. It would have been better, perhaps, if it had, for under his absentee managership the splendid company at Drury Lane was allowed to disintegrate. Finally, in 1809, the theatre, now the second largest in Europe, caught fire, and Sheridan, engrossed in a Parliamentary debate, refused even to go to see what could be done.

It is curious that he and Goldsmith should have bobbed up when they did. Not so brilliant technically as the Restoration writers, they were considerably more human in their characterizations. And for some reason or other, there they were, a little island of brilliance in a sea of general dullness that stretched for a hundred years in either direction.

With Sheridan devoting more and more time to his political career, the actual management of Drury Lane was entrusted to the stage manager, John Philip Kemble, brother of Sarah Siddons, the company's star, and member of a dominant stage family whose descendants are still active in the theatres of two continents. Sarah Siddons (1755–1831) was probably the finest tragic actress the English stage has produced. Lady Macbeth was her great part, and she played it on and off. Sir Walter Scott has recorded his amusement at the stately blank verse in which she rebuked one of his servants at Abbotsford: "I asked for water, boy! you've brought me beer." But she was a great actress, with taste, feeling, and genuine nobility. For nearly forty years she queened it over the London stage and well deserved the tribute paid by Sir Joshua Reynolds in his selection of her as model for his painting *The Tragic Muse*.

While the Kembles were in control of Covent Garden, the theatre was burned, and John Philip Kemble in an attempt to recoup some of his losses raised his ticket prices, adding sixpence to the admission to the pit, or orchestra, and a shilling to the stalls. This change precipitated a series of demonstrations which has never been approached, let alone matched, in English theatre history.

For when the curtain went up on the performance of *Macbeth* on that eighteenth of September, 1809, the audience began to shout "Old Prices—Old Prices" and to stamp and catcall, to pound on the seats, and in general to broadcast its dissatisfaction with the management. The company, under orders from Kemble, proceeded with the performance—in pantomime.

For sixty-one consecutive performances from that night,

this was the routine at Covent Garden: the curtain would rise, a character would appear and open his mouth to speak his first line, and as he did so the audience would go into action with a steady, sustained chant in unison "O-P! O-P!" In the course of the weeks this strike lasted, the Covent Garden audiences developed a variety and vigor in the technique of mass protest that would have won the admiration of a Union Square radical, and which is certainly unique in English theatrical annals. In support of the strike, people gave O-P parties, an O-P dance was created, there were parades with O-P banners. Once they were in the theatre, and it was sold out for every one of these so-called performances, vocal protests were supplemented by every imaginable noise-making device. The hapless actors, drowned out from the first instant of the play, yet held to their task by a relentless management, dodged through their performances, with one eye always cocked in the direction of the auditorium for whatever might be coming their way. Often enough there was something. For three months a stubborn management tried to break up these demonstrations by resorting to arrests and hired rough necks; or to wear down the demonstrators by a dogged continuance of these performances. But this time the management had encountered a force even more fanatic and stubborn than itself. Finally Kemble sensed the uselessness of this conflict and surrendered at discretion. On December eighteenth the old prices were restored, and amity and accord once more reigned where discord and confusion had so long reared their ugly heads.

The period which ensued was quiet and, theatrically, rather dull. Yet beneath the placid surface, forces were gathering which were to sweep not only the theatre but all of life and living into new channels. There have been more changes, and more profound changes, in the approximately one hundred and fifty years since the beginning of the nineteenth century, than in all the forty or fifty centuries of recorded history prior to that date.

But, although the theatre was to be deeply affected by these changes and was, indeed, destined to suffer more from the machine age than any of its sister arts, their effect was not immediately perceptible. There was the orderly procession of plays and players in the patent houses, and the more or less bootlegged offerings of the other theatres, whose offerings were not legitimatized until the royal patents were revoked in 1843. There were scattered examples of fine acting, like raisins in half pay pudding: George Frederick Cooke, first of what might be called the Intuitive School of Acting, which depends on the inspiration of the moment and may be either marvelous or terrible; Edmund Kean (1787–1833), of whom Samuel Taylor Coleridge wrote "To see Kean play is like reading Shakespeare by flashes of lightning," and who earned a million dollars in his first thirteen years as a star, and who spent it all, and more, before his early death; Eliza Vestris (1797–1867), first of woman producers on the English stage; and William Charles Macready (1793–1873), whose quarrel with the American star, Edwin Forrest, precipitated the fatal Astor Place riot in New York, in 1849.

The changes of living and the new stresses and strains they imposed were beginning to force themselves upon the attention of playwrights, and to pull them away from the translations and imitations of the parlor and bedroom drama from across the Channel. Since these new dramas were largely concerned with what were at the time referred to as "social problems," they were called Problem Plays (with voices and eyebrows raised for the word "Problem"). But in *The Liars* and *Mrs. Dane's Defence*, Henry Arthur Jones and still more so Arthur Wing Pinero in *The Second Mrs. Tanqueray* and *Iris*, wrote plays of real emotional depth and characterization. If they, and that was particularly applicable to Pinero, fell short of the sublimity of Greek tragic writing, it was by the gap between the plane of Greek life in the fifth century B. C. and Victorian London. It would be difficult, because of the evolution in psychology in the last forty years, for a casual reader of today to guess the terrific impact of these plays upon the emotions of their audiences.

A somewhat gentler voice raised on behalf of womankind was that of Sir James Matthew Barrie, who wrote one of the great fairy tales of all time in *Peter Pan;* charming social sketches in *The Little Minister* and *What Every Woman Knows,* as well as the perennial one-acter, *The Twelve Pound Look.*

Where Jones, Pinero, and Barrie were primarily concerned with the position of woman in the newly unstable and shifting economic and social world, John Galsworthy went in for more inclusive and still less flattering pictures of modern society. What makes the work of the creator of *Justice, Strife, The Silver Box, Loyalties,* and *Escape* so terrible is the way in which he has depicted an impersonal society, motivated by no particular ill will, and often operating through essentially good and kindly men, wasting human resources, casually crushing unfortunate individuals who become enmeshed in its gears.

Those who are inclined to be alarmed at the possible subversive influence of this play or that, may well ponder the fact that these excellent dramas did not cause their audiences to go forth to destroy, or even to correct a criminally careless civilization.

It is rather harder to place correctly and estimate the work of George Bernard Shaw, for he is still very much alive and exceedingly vocal. And yet in more than time he belongs to the group of playwrights which thought and worked in pre-war days. When he first appeared on the theatrical horizon with his bundle of prejudices, his willingness to make a football of generally accepted standards of honor and of romantic love, and an apparently never-ceasing flow of brilliant conversation, he looked to be a very considerable fellow indeed. And in truth, anyone who could produce *Arms and the Man, Candida, Androcles and the Lion, Man and Superman, Getting Married, St. Joan,* and their companion plays is not a negligible person.

And yet, there was an early promise which he somehow never quite fulfilled, a hint of something important he had to say, to which he never got around. Perhaps he has lived too long for his own best interests, and has said too much. It may be that he is the victim of implications read into his work for which he is not responsible. But, on the guess of one prejudiced and highly fallible commentator, the plays of George Bernard Shaw are not likely to grow in stature down the perspective of the years.

With the plays of these men, and the acting of Henry Irving, Ellen Terry, Beerbohm Tree, and others, the English theatre was interesting and vital when the first World War broke out in 1914. Whatever pretense of "business as usual" may have been affected, the war paralyzed the theatre. There was too much tension, too much suffering, too much tragedy in every home for serious theatre. What was wanted, and all that was wanted, was something light. Revue, farce, or melodrama—anything to take the minds of soldiers and their families off the business of the morrow. The theatre took its place alongside the newspapers, periodicals and books to disseminate propaganda and to build up and sustain the proper morale.

England came out of the war with a staggering loss in manpower, with an enormous debt, and with the most acute unemployment problem the country has ever known. These are not factors conducive to theatrical prosperity. And they have been further aggravated by the world wide economic stringency and depression, and by the new competition of motion pictures and radio broadcasting.

Under such unfavorable conditions, the theatre has been hard put to it to survive at all, and it has, as has the American theatre, been considerably restricted in territory and in influence. And yet this crippled theatre produced a really significant play, quite, it seems, by accident. That was the story of an infantry company headquarters in a dugout on the western front in March, 1918, which R. C. Sheriff wrote for a rowing club under the title, *Journey's End.*

Future generations seeing revivals of this clipped, repressed, and unpretentious play will appreciate more clearly than from reading the stacks of books on the subject, why the English army was not crushed by the German drive that spring.

Currently England appears to be working out from under the depression. The theatre, however, is still operating on a depression basis, and under a depression psychology. The next act in its long and splendid drama is still veiled, but there is no reason to suppose that there is not another act all set behind that curtain.

CHAPTER IV

AMERICA

A Theatre from Abroad

THE theatre that first came to the United States, or what was eventually to be the United States, was a foreign theatre, pure and simple. Not only the players, but the plays in which they appeared, the costumes, sets—everything but the theatres themselves—were imported direct from England.

Even before the professional theatre got around to visiting this wilderness fringe of empire, the colonists had sought to relieve the tedium of their simple lives with masques, charades, and skits. Authority did not always regard kindly these efforts, for even in the royal and more liberal settlements in Virginia, the citizens of Accomac who ventured to beguile themselves and each other by putting on a playlet entitled *Ye Bare and Ye Cubb*, on August 27, 1665, found themselves shortly afterwards explaining it to the judge—but getting away with it.

The early history of the American theatre is largely a matter of conjecture. Pretty generally the theatre was suspect and frowned upon by godly people, and the newspapers and journals of the period did not consider its people or their movements of sufficient importance to chronicle. In all probability the first theatre to be constructed for that purpose within what is now the United States, was built at Williamsburg, then the capital of Virginia, in 1716.

But to all practical intents and purposes the history of the American theatre begins with the arrival of the Hallam company in the early summer of 1752. It was the property of William Hallam, proprietor of one of the smaller, non-patent London theatres who had been crowded to the wall by competition. The provinces appeared unpromising, but across the seas was virgin territory growing in wealth, with a background of attachment to the theatre and—well, it was worth a gamble.

So Hallam got together a company of fifteen players, none of whom was a star, but all of whom were pretty good players, nevertheless; picked up what odds and ends of scenery, costumes, and properties were available; and shipped them off to America under the command of his brother Lewis.

The repertoire consisted largely of Shakespeare and Restoration dramas, a couple of dozen in all, perhaps. There was plenty of time to get them in shape on shipboard during the long voyage.

The Hallam company arrived in Yorktown in June, 1750, and proceeded immediately to Williamsburg where its first season was inaugurated the following September fifteenth, with *The Merchant of Venice* in a theatre built for an earlier company.

The importance of the Hallams is due to the fact that this was the first company to produce standard plays in a professional manner and with a reasonable degree of competence.

The company played here and there about the country for the better part of two years, and then Hallam took it to the West Indies, where he died and the company was disbanded.

There was in the islands at the time a young actor named David Douglass, who had left England to seek his fortunes in the colonies, or to escape from his misfortunes at home. Douglass married Lewis Hallam's widow, and at once set about reassembling the scattered members of the Hallam troupe. Whatever his limitations as an actor, Douglass was a first class manager, the best the American theatre of that time was to know. Under his able and energetic leadership the company, known at first as "The Company of Comedians from London," and later in deference to the rising tide of Americanism as "The American Company," proceeded to open up new theatre territory all up and down the coast.

It is true that in order to circumvent local prejudices Douglass had occasionally to disguise the exact nature of his enterprise. When he first played Newport, Rhode Island, in 1761 (and his was the first professional company to invade Puritan New England), *Othello* was advertised as *A Series of*

Moral Dialogues; and when he returned the following season he called his theatre a "Histrionic Academy" at which "dissertations" were delivered.

But Rhode Island's statesmen were not deceived by this terminology. And inasmuch as he had simply assumed the consent of the local legislators, he had not bothered to ask permission. The local authorities were burned up by his attitude and took it up with the General Assembly of the state. That body promptly responded with a statute forbidding theatrical productions which, in certain respects, was even more drastic than that which had been previously adopted by the neighboring Massachusetts Bay Colony. This law remained on the statute books of Rhode Island until 1798.

All these productions, and the actors who appeared in them, were British. It was not until 1767, when the American Company presented *The Prince of Parthia,* by Thomas Godfrey, Jr., at the Southwark Theatre, Philadelphia, that an American playwright received a professional presentation, and the first native born American actor of record, a man named Goodman, made his début in the same company in Philadelphia in the following year.

This distinctly British tinge made things go hard with the theatre when the War for Independence broke out. One of the first measures adopted by the Continental Congress which convened in Philadelphia in October, 1774, was a recommendation to discontinue "expensive diversions and entertainments." And in truth there was little professional activity to discourage. Most of the actors either were drawn into the service, or drifted back to the West Indies.

What theatre remained was almost wholly amateur and was largely due to the activities of British officers in garrison. Generals Burgoyne, Clinton, and Howe all included the management of such companies in the routine of their administrative duties, with General Clinton's troupe being given the edge on its rivals by contemporary critics.

Even before the formal cessation of hostilities, in 1787, theatrical production was once more under way. The prejudices of war time were still operative, however, and it was often necessary to assume protective camouflage. Philadelphia's Southwark Theatre had to be renamed "The Opera House, Southwark," forerunner of a long line of Opera Houses. There musical comedies could be presented as "operas" under the bland assumption that, of course, operas were all right. *Hamlet* was described as "a moral and instructive Tale as exemplified in the History of the Prince of Denmark"; and *The School for Scandal* coyly appeared as "A Comic Lecture in five parts, on the Pernicious Vice of Scandal."

The American Company was reorganized in 1785, under the joint management of John Henry and Lewis Hallam, Jr., and quickly asserted its supremacy. It was so far the best company in the American Theatre that none was able to compete with it successfully. Whenever the American Company came into a town, its rivals folded up and moved on. Not until internal dissension and financial quarrels disrupted this organization, did any other company stand a chance at playing day and date with it.

Up to this time all the companies, big and small, good and bad, had been coöperative repertory organizations. They were, or aimed to be, permanent companies presenting a repertory of plays, from the receipts of which the operating expenses were paid. In any surplus which remained at the end of the season, assuming that there was a surplus, the actors all shared *pro rata*. If the manager was also an actor, he might receive a share for each of his contributions. In Hallam's original company, for instance, eighteen shares were established. Each of the twelve adult actors, including Hallam, himself, received one share. Hallam, in addition, was voted two full shares more—one for his services in a managerial capacity and the other for those of his children. The remaining four shares were assigned to the property.

This system was possible only in a company which was making money. Bad business was certain to be followed by bad feeling. Under adverse conditions it was extremely difficult to maintain reasonable discipline; morale was simply shot to pieces.

And so, from about the time of the dissolution of the American Company, in 1792, managers began to engage their actors on a salary basis, taking any risks implicit in production—and the profits, too.

In addition to their salary there was one graft to which actors were entitled that helped to keep them in line. Each of the principal members of the company was entitled to one or more benefits during the season. Pretty generally he was allowed to select the play—one, of course, in which he appeared to advantage—and, in the beginning, he was entitled to the gross receipts of the performance. But it was not long before the managers were holding out the actual operating expenses.

Whatever the arrangement, it was up to the actor to get as many people as possible into the house for his benefit, and he could usually be depended on to drum up all the trade he could. People took their theatre pretty seriously in those days, and so a benefit performance might be made the occasion for a demonstration in favor of one actor or against another, which stopped little short of actual rioting. It might be flowers and a mob waiting to pull the actor's carriage to his hotel; or it might be boos, rotten eggs, and the police to see that he got home all in one piece.

THE STARS IN THEIR COURSES DISCOVER THE ROAD

Until well past the Revolutionary War, the theatre had stuck pretty closely to the fringe of settlements along the Atlantic Coast. But as the swelling tide of the new country pressed against the barrier of the Appalachians and began to trickle down the western slopes, the theatre rode upon it. None of the first class companies was involved in these first migrations; but little groups of the lesser players, unable to compete with the better companies, or possessed of the restless, pioneering spirit of the time, went along with the westward tide.

They went as everybody else did—by wagon and boat if they could afford it, on horseback and afoot if they could not. Their fare and accommodations were those of any other emigrants on the trail, and so were the conditions under which they practiced their art in the rude frontier outposts of Pittsburgh, Cincinnati, Chicago, St. Louis, Nashville, and the considerably more civilized New Orleans. No difficulties of terrain were too great to be overcome, no conditions of playing too primitive. If people who might serve as audiences had gone there first, the theatre went after them. It followed the Mormons out into the Great American Desert; and when the discovery of gold drew thousands to the Pacific Coast, about the middle of the nineteenth century, the theatre was waiting for the miners when they came up from their shafts or back from panning the streams.

As transportation facilities were developed, the better class of players followed in their wake. George Frederick Cooke,

Edmund Kean, and Charles Kemble never left the Atlantic Coastal Plain; but by 1828 Junius Brutus Booth was playing in New Orleans; in 1843 William Charles Macready got as far west as St. Louis.

These were all foreign stars who made American tours almost as they would embark on tours of the English provinces. The first native born American star was Edwin Forrest (1806–1872) and the first actress to deserve that appellation was Charlotte Cushman (1816–1876).

The rise of Forrest and the incipient pride in his nationality precipitated the first demonstration of feeling against alien actors. On one of Forrest's visits to England he was hissed during a performance in London, and his admirers believed that it was at the instigation of Macready. They resolved to even the score at the first opportunity.

That was vouchsafed them in May, 1849, when Macready came to America for what he had expected to be his farewell tour, after which he planned to retire from the theatre and settle near Cambridge, Massachusetts. He was announced to open in *Macbeth* at the Astor Place Opera House, New York, on the evening of May 10, 1849.

It was not a particularly fortunate time or place for the appearance of an English star. The relations between Great Britain and the United States were strained at the time over boundary disputes and economic questions; the Know Nothing Party, grounded in opposition to all foreigners, was at the height of its power in New York, and to many New Yorkers anything British was anathema. It was not hard to stir the mob spirit into active life.

As the performance got under way, the mob bore down on the Astor Place Opera House to break up the show. Those who managed to force their way into the Opera House were thrown out by the police, but the mob rapidly swelled to such proportions that it was evident the police would not be able to control the situation. Fearful of just such an occurrence, the Seventh Regiment of the New York National Guard had been held under arms and was ordered to the scene. But the presence of soldiers merely inflamed the mob. After the guardsmen had endured for some time a barrage of paving stones, brickbats, and anything that could be hurled, the order was finally given to fire. Before the encounter ended, thirty-four rioters had received wounds from which they subsequently died, and many more had been wounded less seriously. Nor had the militia escaped unscathed. One hundred and forty-one of their number had been injured more or less seriously, and the theatre had received considerable damage.

The performance had been abruptly terminated by the rioting, and Macready was smuggled out of the theatre to the seclusion of a private home. Two days later he proceeded secretly to Boston whence he sailed immediately for England. Cambridge saw him no more, nor did any other place in America.

The peregrinations of these and other stars profoundly affected the existing structure of the theatre. Where the early stars had brought their own companies in a repertory of the classics, from 1820 it was increasingly customary for the star to travel by himself, visiting in turn the resident stock companies for brief engagements in the parts for which he was famous.

As long as the number of stars was comparatively small and was confined to actors of extraordinary merit, the plan was not without its benefits to all concerned. The stars found themselves relieved of managerial routine and many managerial expenses, and could concentrate on their performances. They were generally much more highly paid than the members of the resident companies. But the managements could afford this, for stars drew better houses. The actors in the supporting casts had the opportunity of learning from the best in their business. And the audiences saw the finest actors of the day in all the great rôles of the theatre.

If there had only been a balance wheel to regulate the number of stars and pass on the qualifications of applicants, the system might have enjoyed a much longer run. But the fact that stardom was so pleasant and lucrative was its undoing. Stars multiplied out of all proportion and indeed out of all reason.

But once accustomed to stars, the public had no use for companies which did not furnish them. The managers, now feeling that stars were their only salvation, began to scramble for them and to bid up their services to a point where even crowded houses might leave the management in the red because of the percentage accorded the star.

There was only one place where the manager could cut down, and that was on the salaries of the members of the resident company. Able actors were replaced by those whose primary recommendation was that they could be obtained cheaply. Inevitably the standards of production and performance were lowered, and the public which at first would not support good stock companies without stars, now turned its back entirely on poor companies. Without stars and more stars the managers were sunk. Even with them, the stock system suffered a decline which practically pointed to eventual extinction.

Everybody in the theatre, except the stars, found the going harder as the resident stock system hit the skids. Members of the supporting casts below the rank of stars found fewer good companies offering engagements. Salaries were bad and getting worse, and the standard of acting was dropping in an alarming manner. That was due not only to the unfortunate financial situation, but to the attitude of the stars themselves. Desiring to shine as brightly as possible, they did not encourage competition from their support. The best that a stock actor could do was to make himself and his part as inconspicuous as possible while a star was on the horizon.

Eventually the stock companies in the smaller towns became so bad that they could not furnish even adequate support to the best players. But the stars, concerned only with their own personal interests, and lacking an intelligent selfishness in the welfare of their local representatives, did nothing to help the resident companies. It was not, as a matter of fact, anything that one or even a few of them could have done. Nothing short of a Stars' Protective Association and a theatrical code of fair practices would have sufficed, and to the individualists of the day nothing would have seemed less feasible or desirable.

Something had to be done about the support, in certain of the more important rôles, however; the resident companies were getting too terrible to be depended on. And so the stars began to take one or two players with them for the more important rôles, leaving only the minor parts to the local players. This practice may have helped solve the immediate problem of the stars, but it was only another headache for the resident stock companies. Except for a few companies in the larger cities, resident stock companies practically passed out of the picture.

But that does not mean that the theatre had been killed, only that a new form of theatre had superseded that which had prevailed. From the practice of carrying a couple of important players along, it was a simple and easy step to organizing a whole company for a tour. With his own company, a star could have the precise support he might desire, much better costumes, scenery, and properties than he might expect to find in impoverished local companies and, by adding his own stage hands and, probably, the nucleus of an orchestra, he was completely independent of the local situation. Of course the star, once more an actor-manager, had the old problem of finances back in his lap again, but the very fact that he accepted it so willingly is proof that to his mind the advantages outweighed the penalties.

Since the stars had been accustomed to playing several rôles, these first combination companies were repertory organizations. Gradually it became customary for a star to concentrate on one play for which the company was organized specifically, and which would be played for the entire season or, if there were sufficient bookings, for several seasons.

In the first years of this system the local managers retained their houses, and some of them continued desultory activities in the intervals between the stands of the visiting companies. But public support was less and less given to such efforts, and one after another they gave up the attempt and pretty generally confined themselves to the management of their theatres, becoming not theatrical operators so much as theatrical landlords.

These economic shifts were gradual and did not proceed on any orderly plan. At any given moment it would not have been possible to say that one system had been replaced by another. But, in general, the resident stock system was in force prior to 1820; the stock star system was at its height between 1820 and 1860, and from that time declined before the impetus of the traveling combination company, until by 1890 the star on a solo tour was a thing of the past, largely because there were no more companies for him to visit.

Who was personally responsible for the innovation is a matter of some dispute. Both Dion Boucicault and Joseph Jefferson laid claim to any honor that might be involved, and both were pioneers in it, unquestionably. The economics of the situation was probably more the determining factor than any person, and these two, and any other managers who may have attempted the same solution at this time, were simply quicker to sense the change than their fellows.

The development of transportation facilities had played an important part in the transition. As long as travel was slow and difficult, permanent organizations maintaining independent existence in their own bailiwicks were quite in order. The railroads were the solvent which liquidated this isolation. In 1849 there were still less than six thousand miles of railroad in the United States. By the end of 1860 they had grown to nearly thirty-one thousand. As late as 1850 there was no direct rail connection between New York and either Boston or Albany. Ten years later the railroads stretched from New York to the Mississippi and were reaching out across the plains.

The emphasis in these periods and well into the reign of the traveling combination company was all on the player. It was an era of virtuoso acting which was probably better in retrospect than at the moment. There were giants such as Edwin Booth—and those still alive who saw him are convinced that no greater actor ever trod the boards of any theatre—and there were Edwin Forrest, John McCullough, Joseph Jefferson, and Charlotte Cushman. But aside from the top ranking players and a few of the metropolitan stock companies, the general level of acting was no better than it is today, and in all probability was not so good.

Native playwrights hardly entered the picture at all. They had no protection from copyright laws and, aside from occasional competitions announced by stars in need of plays, received little encouragement from the managers. John Howard Payne, best remembered for *Home, Sweet Home* and other songs, one of the best and most prolific of American dramatists in the early part of the nineteenth century, made what little money he got from his plays from occasional benefits. It was vaguely supposed to be customary for the author to be given a benefit on the third night of his play's presentation, but there was no organization to enforce the observance of this rule, which was disregarded at least as often as it was observed. And any time the manager felt it was too burdensome, he could avoid it by the simple expedient of not giving a third performance of the play. But as long as any play was available for the mere cost of a printed copy, royalties were not an item to bother a manager. Even as late as 1886, A. M. Palmer, an important New York manager, was boasting:

"It has never been my habit to use any author's work without compensating him, and if I had the money I had paid in my time to authors and their representatives, it would amount to a very tidy sum—all I would want to live on for the rest of my days."

But then Mr. Palmer may have been a man of singularly simple and easily satisfied wants, for his offer to W. S. Gilbert for the rights to a run of *Engaged* was twenty dollars a performance.

So American authorship languished and the repertory of practically every company was composed of the classics supplemented by a few standard contemporary foreign plays.

THE EMPIRE OF THE SYNDICATE

Quite unsuspected, even by those who were in the thick of things, a new factor was forming which was to change the whole aspect of the American theatre. On one hand were a number of theatres that had been divorced from their resident companies, and on the other were a lot of homeless traveling combination companies. Now a theatre without actors is nothing at all. It is less than that, because it cannot, as a rule, be used for anything else. And despite eulogists to the contrary, a company without a theatre in which to play is not much better off. Something simply had to be done to bring them together and to assure at least a semblance of order and public decency.

At first this was accomplished in an unbelievably casual and haphazard fashion. New York City had by that time overcome the cities which had been its rivals for the theatre, and was then, as it is now, the theatrical capital of the country, and Union Square was the theatre's Rialto. During the brief weeks between the middle of June and the first of September, its sidewalks, park benches, and the hotel lobbies, bedrooms and bars which were adjacent to them swarmed with actors, authors, agents, producers, and theatre managers, all intent on making the vital arrangements which were to care for their needs during the next thirty or forty weeks.

Everybody rushed around seeking the most desirable contacts and avoiding all others until forced to their consideration. In an atmosphere of bustle and bluff, on scraps of paper or mere handshakes, between drinks and mental reservations, the business of the theatre got itself attended to with a minimum of ceremony and efficiency.

The wonder is that this crude system, or lack of system, by means of which plays, players, and audiences were brought together, worked at all. In the majority of cases it did work, else the theatre would have broken down altogether. The important producers and theatres got along well enough. But the one night stands had a pretty tough time. They were always the last booked, and those bookings were accepted with the definite reservation that they would be observed only in case nothing better turned up. Aware of that probability, the one night stand manager contracted for more productions than he could possibly have played. But he felt tolerably sure that many of the attractions booked would probably fail to turn up. If it seemed likely that two would arrive simultaneously, some sort of arrangement could probably be made to delay one or speed up the other. If the worst came to the worst, and both landed in town together and neither of them would give way, a sort of theatrical double header might be managed.

Even with the best intentions and the most scrupulous care there were bound to be conflicting engagements, open dates, long jumps, and worthless stands for the companies, and dark periods for the houses, simply because the job of routing two hundred and fifty companies into five thousand theatres in thirty-five hundred cities, which was the extent of the theatre by 1880, was an impossibility without adequate machinery.

In self-protection these theatres began to form mutual alliances for defense and offense. Little groups of theatres in contiguous territory got together and agreed on the terms they would offer touring attractions; on their routing through the territory; on the principle that if one of them was mistreated, all would refuse to have anything further to do with the offender. They found that by so doing they could get better attractions, on better terms and with much less trouble and expense. And since managers of touring attractions could now book several weeks in two or three transactions instead of having to negotiate time and terms with a whole flock of individual theatre owners, they raised no serious objections to this system.

But as the theatres began to crystallize into circuits, and the producing interests to consolidate in New York and a few other centers, the gap between theatres desiring attractions, and attractions seeking opportunities to play yawned wider than ever. So, all during this period, there were also evolving a number of booking offices. In its essentials a booking office is nothing more than an employment agency. The client is the theatre, and the labor which is recruited is a theatrical company rather than an individual actor. Originally the business was done on a lump sum basis. For a fixed fee, ranging between twenty-five dollars and two hundred and fifty dollars a year, the booking office undertook to supply the theatre with suitable attractions during its season. But this was a clumsy arrangement, at best, and before long it was shelved in favor of a percentage of the theatre's receipts.

Throughout the entire country the era of pioneering was drawing to a close. The frontiers had been reached, and behind them the country was filling up. The multitude of small, independent, competing business men was beginning to be liquidated and replaced by combinations of big businesses. The trusts were not creatures of the theatre, but they were happening all around it; they were in the air, and the theatre could no more have hoped to escape their infection than a class in a school invaded by an epidemic of measles.

The theatre trust which emerged from the confusion of productions, circuits, and booking offices was known as the Theatrical Syndicate, and in its day was one of the tightest knit and highest geared of all of them. It was organized on August 31, 1896, by a combination of three existing partnerships.

Briefly, the aim of the Syndicate was the control of the legitimate theatre of the entire country through the control of its bookings. To get any Syndicate bookings, a theatre had to hand over the control of its policies to the Syndicate's booking office; to obtain a route through Syndicate territory, a production had to deliver itself into the hands of that same booking office.

But the Syndicate was in a position to deliver the goods to

those who were thus required to meet its terms. No other combination in the theatre could match the resources of its three partnerships. Klaw and Erlanger held the keys to any route through the South; Nixon and Zimmerman owned most of the important theatres in Philadelphia and had, to boot, a string of houses out through Pennsylvania and Ohio; Hayman and Frohman exercised an almost monopolistic control of the country west of the Mississippi. In addition, Charles Frohman was the most important producer in the country and, through his brother Daniel, afforded the Syndicate access to the productions of the Lyceum Stock Company, last and one of the greatest of the resident stock companies.

As the Syndicate lined up theatres and attractions, it grew like a snowball rolling downhill. When the first five year agreement drew to a close and a second was under negotiation, the number of theatres it controlled had risen from thirty-three to about sixty-five. At the height of its power the Syndicate controlled the bookings of more than seven hundred theatres. Now it is true that this is only a minor fraction of the total number of theatres available. What it represented, however, was practically every first class theatre in the country. It meant that any production which aspired to a tour of the leading theatres had to come to the Syndicate to get it. Conversely it implied that any theatre which wanted first class attractions could also be found on Klaw and Erlanger's doorstep.

The Syndicate was efficient. It eliminated a lot of wasteful competition. It straightened out a number of the worst booking tangles. It instituted a measure of order and discipline badly needed. In general the business side of the theatre was placed on a better basis.

But the Syndicate was not only a harsh and arbitrary master; it was also a capricious and selfish one. Ostensibly it was the agent of the theatre and charged the theatre a fixed sum or percentage. In actual practice the Syndicate sometimes charged both the theatre and production for this service; and the charge, instead of being standard, varied considerably, running sometimes as high as one-third to one-half of the net profits. Nor was this the worst feature of its practices. The firms which composed the Syndicate were also producers and theatre owners. As such they used the considerable power of their organization to further their own interests at the expense of their other clients. Productions and houses owned by Syndicate members, or in which they had an interest, got the best routes and bookings. The others got what was left over and paid handsomely, even exorbitantly, for it.

Owing to its peculiar construction the Syndicate could and often did say it never demanded or got a nickel for its services from the producer, author, or star. And neither it did. But the individuals and partnerships which composed it did receive such tribute. And the tribute was paid because the whole power of the Syndicate was brought to bear on anyone refusing such payment.

These harsh tactics soon provoked a revolt which, however, came not from the producing managers or the theatres, but from a group of actor-managers who rebelled at surrendering their bookings to Klaw and Erlanger, the Syndicate's bookers. The rebels included Joseph Jefferson, Richard Mansfield, Fanny Davenport, Nat Goodwin, James O'Neill, Minnie Maddern Fiske and her husband Harrison Grey Fiske, David Belasco, and Francis Wilson. Early in 1898 they got together and swore not to book through the Syndicate for the season of 1898–9. Each agreed to put up a forfeit of five thousand dollars to guarantee his observance of the agreement.

These stars did not have anything in common except their opposition to the Syndicate's demands. They did not even have a common name for their group. The Syndicate went to work on this common interest. To the most valuable, or those least grounded in opposition, it held out the bait of increased percentages and other concessions, and they capitulated. Having broken the backbone of the movement by this stroke, the Syndicate blacklisted the others and then proceeded to forget about them. After they had campaigned a while in the second and third rate opera houses and town halls, or even under canvas, they were willing to admit they had had enough.

They had not all had the fight knocked out of them, however. A second revolt, in 1902, was again headed by the Fiskes, who, this time, were joined by Maurice Campbell and his wife, Henrietta Crosman, by James K. Hackett, and by Weber and Fields, then just launching their producing career. But the factor which made their organization, the Independent Booking Office, really dangerous was the chain of popular priced theatres operated by Stair and Havlin.

Once more the Syndicate sensed the real heart of the opposition and aimed its attack at this vulnerable spot. Stair and Havlin were approached and offered control of the popular priced field in all the important cities of the country and the assurance of a flow of productions suitable for these theatres, if the firm would withdraw from the Independent Booking Office. This offer was accepted and since, at the same time, Weber and Fields surrendered their theatres to Stair and Havlin, this defection wrecked the rebels. By the time the season of 1904–5 rolled around, all except the irreconcilable Fiskes were back in the fold nursing their wounds.

AND THERE WERE SHUBERTS

But at the very moment when the Syndicate seemed to have crushed every vestige of opposition, it faced the challenge which ultimately broke its grip on the country's theatre.

Sam S. Shubert, eldest of the three Shubert brothers, of Syracuse, New York, got into the theatre early. At eight years of age he sold newspapers by day, and candy, programs, and souvenirs at the Syracuse Grand Opera House at night. Shortly he was an usher. But he was too good a man to be kept down, and he was promoted to be assistant treasurer as a grizzled theatre veteran of ten.

A year later, through the good offices of a friend, he became treasurer of the Wieting Opera House, Syracuse's first class theatre, still so small that he had to stand on a box when he handled the ticket window.

In 1894, at the age of sixteen he became a manager, taking over the road rights of Charles H. Hoyt's *A Texas Steer* and displaying considerable managerial skill in the conduct of its tour throughout the country. As his interests and holdings expanded, he took into partnership his two brothers, Lee and J. J., and the three set out to carve a kingdom of their own from the Syndicate Empire.

Their first attempts were confined to familiar territory. Beginning with the Opera House in Utica, they spread out into the surrounding cities. By 1900 they had established themselves sufficiently to justify the invasion of New York. There they made their début in the theatrical big league by taking over the Herald Square Theatre.

At first their relations with the Syndicate were entirely amicable. They played ball with it, booking their productions through Klaw and Erlanger and taking into their theatres what productions were assigned them by that office. But the rapidity with which they blossomed and embarked not only on producing activities, but also in the building of theatres during the next three or four years alarmed the Syndicate. And so it was decided to put the brakes on this ambitious and enterprising young firm.

As a preliminary measure the Syndicate served notice on the Shuberts that if they wished to remain clients, they must agree not to expand their producing activities or acquire any more theatres.

In the struggle that ensued, the Shuberts were technically the aggressors. Not only did they proceed with the construction of the Garrick Theatre in St. Louis, but they refused to book one of the Klaw and Erlanger productions in their theatres. But whatever the immediate cause, war was so inevitable that if it had not come then and in that way, it would surely have come eventually. The real reason was that there was no longer room in the theatre as then constituted for both the Syndicate and the Shuberts.

While affairs were still in the stage of ultimata and other diplomatic preliminaries, the brilliant career of Sam Shubert was brought to an end in a railway accident, in May, 1905. Since his journey had been undertaken on business connected with an alliance against the Syndicate, it has always been understood that his brothers held the Syndicate responsible for it, and no small part of the bitterness and relentlessness with which that warfare was waged was credited to that feeling.

Before his death Sam Shubert had approached David Belasco, then both a theatrical and legal opponent of the Syndicate. After his death his brothers pushed the alliance with Belasco to a consummation and also established an understanding with the Fiskes. Never a formal agreement, it was nevertheless definitely understood that all three were to play each other's theatres and attractions and also that the Shuberts would accept bookings from any other independent managers, whether or not they played Syndicate theatres at other times.

This policy of the "Open Door" adopted from the expressed policy of the United States in the Far East, which was then very much to the fore because of President Theodore Roosevelt's settlement of the war between Russia and Japan in the summer of that year, was radically different from the Syndicate's exclusive policy. It was the heart of the Shubert propaganda in the years that followed. And increasingly, as this struggle progressed, propaganda assumed an importance never before reached in any industrial warfare.

Once these heretical alliances were out in the open and war formally declared in July, 1905, the Syndicate set in motion the machine which had crushed all former revolts. Not a first class theatre in the country, aside from the few controlled by the rebels themselves, was available to their productions or to any managers who had the temerity to join them.

But the Shuberts had no mind to play the game with Syndicate rules. If there were no first class theatres for them, they would go out and build them. Of course they did not have sufficient money to embark upon such a campaign themselves, but by this time they had demonstrated sufficient ability to enlist the support of men who had. Their first string of theatres was built with money lent by a group of Cincinnati financiers including George B. Cox, Max Anderson, and Congressman Joseph L. Rhinock.

Once more their tactics were at variance with the Syndicate, which had never invested its own money in theatres to any appreciable extent. It had always preferred to let somebody else build the theatres and then acquire control of their policies. But the force of necessity provided the Shuberts with a string of theatres newer and better equipped than those controlled by their enemies.

With these and their own theatres, the Shuberts and their allies in the Open Door Campaign had about thirty theatres available for the season of 1905–1906. But they had managed to line up a group of stars which included Sarah Bernhardt,

Ada Rehan, David Warfield, Minnie Maddern Fiske, Mrs. Leslie Carter, Blanche Bates, Bertha Kalich, Jefferson De Angelis, De Wolf Hopper, Eddie Foy, Henry Miller, and Margaret Anglin.

At the end of their first season the Shuberts could claim not only that they had resisted all efforts of the Syndicate to put them out of business, but also that they had made considerable progress despite the effort. Their original thirty theatres had grown to about fifty, and they felt strong enough to carry the fight to the enemy.

For their next season's enterprises the Shuberts lured from the Syndicate such stars as Mrs. Pat Campbell, Cyril Maude, Arnold Daly, Louis Mann, Cyril Scott, Julia Sanderson, and Henry E. Dixey. And they went out for more theatres, building up their circuit to fifty-nine.

That circuit was still far short of the Syndicate, both in size and variety. It had nothing like the chain of one night stands which the Syndicate could offer, but its power was growing, and nothing the Syndicate could do, and it did everything it could, was able to stop the steady stream of defections both in theatres and players from its ranks to those of the Shuberts.

This furious struggle which, with intervals, lasted for nearly fifteen years, presented a golden opportunity to the actors of the country which, if they had only realized it or been prepared to take advantage of it, would have saved them much of the terrific effort which they were forced to make later. For the rule of the Syndicate had imposed real hardships on the players. Its control of theatres and productions enabled it to say what actors would appear in any given cast and on what terms. The functions of playing and management which, in earlier days, had been generally intertwined, now became separate, and a whole new generation of managers arose who were primarily business men, unacquainted with and without much sympathy for the traditions of the stage and the privileges enjoyed by the actor under them.

The business advances under the Syndicate rule were all in favor of the management. The actor, so long considered the backbone of the theatre, was now given the least consideration of all the factors concerned in the production of a play.

The theatre has always been something of a gamble, and those who work in it are prone to be gamblers. Probably there will always be an element of chance-taking in its operation. But from the time the Syndicate established its dominance, the actors in their relations to the managers had had to gamble with loaded dice—and the dice belonged to the managers.

Concessions made by actors when conditions were otherwise were now taken as a matter of course in all contracts, and there evolved a body of new theatrical customs, which was all in the management's favor.

About the same time the Syndicate was formed, the Actors' Society of America was organized to protect its members from unscrupulous managers. But the Syndicate grew so much more quickly and became so nearly omnipotent that the Actors' Society never had a chance to get started.

The challenge of the Shuberts was an opportunity which the Actors' Society might very well have capitalized. The Shuberts were so desperate for every possible foothold that they must have been willing to grant concessions to almost any extent that might have been demanded, in return for the assurance of the solid support of the Society's members. And the Syndicate was so sorely beset that it could not have refused similar terms.

But the Actors' Society did not lift a voice or a hand during this titanic struggle, and the work for the actors all had to be done later and at terrible cost.

There now ensued one of those curious and baffling truces with which the history of this conflict is dotted. Why, when locked in a death struggle for each other's throats, the Syndicate and the Shuberts should suddenly draw apart and join hands in the establishment of a vaudeville circuit is something they may be able to explain though they never have.

But at any rate in 1907 that is exactly what they did. In April of that year the United States Amusement Company was incorporated to present "Advanced Vaudeville." Its officers were A. L. Erlanger, President; Lee Shubert, Vice President; Marc Klaw, Treasurer; and J. P. McGovern, Secretary. Erlanger, Shubert, and Klaw constituted the Executive Committee and also served on the Board of Directors along with Al Hayman, J. J. Shubert, George B. Cox, Joseph L. Rhinock, Moses Reis, and Conover English. It was a pretty complete intermarriage of the two organizations. And Klaw and Erlanger were to do the booking! It must have been a terrific shock to the Fiskes, Belasco, and the others who had counted on the undying animosity between the Shuberts and the Syndicate to find them all contentedly feeding out of the same trough.

In staging an incursion into vaudeville, these managers were undertaking more than they had reckoned, however. For vaudeville, then a rich field, was as highly organized and as efficiently administered by as bold and ruthless a group as their own. B. F. Keith, E. F. Albee, F. F. Proctor, B. S. Moss, and Martin Beck were not the men to sit back and watch someone else step in and take advantage of conditions created by their efforts. In October, the United Booking Office, for the Keith-Orpheum interests, announced the organization of a circuit of thirty legitimate theatres.

The United Booking Office may have had this circuit up

its sleeve, or it may have been talking through its hat. It never was called on to back up its announcement. Though the United States Amusement Company had actually opened nineteen of its projected chain of theatres, and had signed up such stars as Harry Lauder and Vesta Victoria, it had been operating at a loss. The legitimate theatre managers were moving in a milieu which was foreign to them, the problems of which were strange, and they had found vaudeville only a headache. They were happy enough to receive an offer which would permit their graceful withdrawal from the field.

So it was not hard to arrive at terms. The United States Amusement Company agreed to dissolve its organization and its principals promised not to engage in any similar attempt for the space of fifteen years. In return for these promises the United Booking Office handed over two hundred and fifty thousand dollars, took over all current contracts of vaudeville artists from the legitimate group, and dropped all plans for a legitimate circuit of its own at whatever stage had been reached. "Advanced Vaudeville" was washed up in January, 1908, although the final formalities were not concluded for another year and a half.

With its end, the Shuberts recovered the theatres they had contributed to the pool and went on about their legitimate business, ostensibly on the best of terms with their late allies. But it cannot be supposed that the vaudeville failure had been without strain, nor could the Syndicate ever reconcile itself to the way in which the Shuberts continued to pick up theatres and expand their activities.

The quarrel flared up again shortly after the Shuberts' agreement with the United States Amusement Company, terminated on May 1, 1909. The fight which followed was the most bitter and desperate of all the series of wars. Managers, stars, and circuits were won and lost, rewon and again lost. Belasco and the Fiskes, after years of opposition to the Syndicate, found themselves forced to choose between two organizations almost similar in aims and methods, and went back to the Syndicate. For as they drew even with the Syndicate, it became more and more apparent that when the Shuberts had demanded an Open Door, they had meant an open door for themselves and their productions and that there were now, in effect, two Syndicates with one or the other of which everyone in the theatre must be affiliated.

Still handicapped by their lack of one night stands, the Shuberts shifted their emphasis from theatres to productions and at last acquired so many productions and stars that the Syndicate could not adequately supply the one night stands. When these latter learned that the Shuberts had the attractions, they were not long in renouncing their allegiance to the Syndicate. Early in 1910 the exodus began, and by the middle of that season a considerable number of them had slipped from the Syndicate's fingers.

The Syndicate was frantic. It pleaded and threatened, it offered better terms, it sent Marc Klaw on a good will tour of the country, but the one night stands, singly and in groups, slid from the Syndicate's ranks and disappeared over the horizon in the direction of the Open Door.

And with their going the Syndicate definitely lost its grip on the country's theatre. When peace was finally patched up, in 1913, it was between two equals content to hold for the time the balance of power.

By that time the Syndicate agreement was in its last period. When it expired, on August 31, 1916, after twenty years of existence, Nixon and Zimmerman had dissolved their partnership, and were out of the theatre; Frohman had gone down on the Lusitania, in May, 1915; Hayman had retired and was nearing the end of his span of life. The Syndicate had simmered down to Klaw and Erlanger.

THE ROAD THAT WENT DOWN HILL

Locked in this desperate struggle both the Syndicate and the Shuberts failed to recognize that the kingdom for which they were battling was beginning to disintegrate beneath their feet. That decline was first evident and has continued to be most severe in the cities outside the production centers which the theatre knows as the road. The curtailment had been so rapid and so severe that whereas there were three hundred and thirty-seven touring companies listed in the first week of December, 1908, when the Shuberts and the Syndicate were squaring off for the big fight, there were, in mid-December, 1934, just twenty-seven such companies in all the country.

The Syndicate-Shubert fight was not the whole reason for this decline, but it intensified the unfavorable conditions under which the decline started and created a condition favorable to the competing amusements which put in their appearance after the decline had set in.

There were too many theatres. There always had been, as a matter of fact, and the scramble for the road had resulted in the building of yet more theatres. And there were not nearly enough good plays and players to fill them. So all sorts of plays were sent out, manned by all sorts of players. They were still extravagantly billed in advance both by the producer and the local theatre manager. Now this trick might be put over occasionally, but it was not good for as many encores as were demanded of it. Theatregoers in the small towns could read; they knew who had played in those plays originally; many had seen those players before. When they had been fooled a few times, they quit going. There rose, unorganized but quite spontaneously, a buyers' strike against the theatre.

When the World War struck, in 1914, and still more so after the United States was drawn into it, the theatre found itself caught in a spiral of ascending prices. Not only did everything that went into a production become more expensive, but union labor, shabbily treated by managers in earlier times, grew strong enough to impose its own wage scales and working conditions on the theatre and took pleasure in making managers pay through the nose for former humiliations and inequities. Railroad travel grew more costly, and at the same time mileage books, party tickets, and free baggage cars were withdrawn.

If the theatre had been able to raise its prices, as other businesses did, it might have survived even these increased costs, but it was already at the limit of what it might charge. The one place where savings could be effected was in the cheapening of productions, either through cutting actors' salaries, or in the scenery and costumes, or in all of them. And such tactics merely increased the dissatisfaction of the road.

The good companies could still make money in New York and in the larger cities of the road in spite of increases. And so, with comparatively few regrets, the managers cheerfully abandoned the smaller towns and concentrated on the few spots where money was available.

It was all the easier and there was less complaint from the road itself because there appeared at this time other and cheaper forms of entertainment which either had not existed previously, or had not been anywhere near so attainable.

The automobile had been developing for some time, but up to this time its expense, comparative fragility, and the lack of good roads had combined to keep it a vehicle for wealthy city dwellers. Now the market was flooded with sturdy medium and low priced cars, and good roads began to push out into the country in all directions. The more general use of the automobile not only made it easier not to go to the theatre, but it encouraged those who went to venture further afield— to drive right past the small road theatre to some big town where a better company was playing. More grief for the road show producer and the road show theatre operator who played his attractions!

This was also the time in which vaudeville, taken over from the somewhat rowdy variety of earlier days, by Keith, Albee, and their United Booking Office, was being dressed up, cleaned up, and made a family amusement. Its theatres were newer and brighter, its entertainment obvious and undemanding, and its prices were far lower. Thousands of people found it an entirely satisfactory substitute for the legitimate theatre.

SHADOWS ON A ROLL OF CELLULOID

None of these factors, perhaps not all of them together, ever necessitated as many readjustments in the theatre as the arrival of the motion pictures, and this was a form of entertainment only as old as the Syndicate.

The motion picture, as a philosophical possibility, had been conjectured as far back as Aristotle, but the first step toward its materialization was not taken until Athanasius Kircher demonstrated his magic lantern, or Magia Catoprica, at Rome, in 1640. Still, nothing more was done about it until 1824 when the accidental passage of a horse and cart before the slits of a Venetian blind, gave to Peter Mark Rôget his theory of *The Persistence of Vision*, the principle of which is the basis of motion pictures. Publication of this revolutionary paper started a series of experiments which terminated in 1853 in the Zoetrope, or Wheel of Life, in which a series of hand drawn figures on the rim of a wheel could be projected by a magic lantern on a screen as a single moving figure. This was, in effect, the forerunner of the motion picture cartoon of the present day.

In the meantime, in the laboratories of Daguerre and Niépce, in France, photography had been developing since 1829. The marriage of photography to motion was conceived in the restless and indefatigable mind of Thomas A. Edison and brought to consummation in his laboratories in 1887. Because of his success with a similar device in the phonograph, Edison at first attempted to make use of a wax cylinder for his pictures, but found himself quite unable, with the knowledge and tools then at his command, to secure adequate magnification.

Edison then hit upon the method of feeding the recording material into his camera by a belt, but was momentarily balked by the lack of any substance both sufficiently sensitive to record the pictures and tough enough to stand handling. But while he was in the midst of these experiments, George Eastman, in 1889, brought out a photographic film with a nitro-cellulose base, and Edison was off on the trail again.

The first Edison Kinetoscope was a peep show, in which the audience was confined to one person at a time. Its first commercial showing was in the Kinetoscope Parlor, on Broadway, New York, in April, 1894. As such it was no more competitive with the theatre than a book. A year later, however, the first projection machine was exhibited by Major Latham, and suddenly the peep show could be viewed by a whole room full of people. The first motion picture show, in the sense in which it is commonly employed, was projected by a Vitagraph machine at Koster and Bial's Music Hall, on Herald Square, New York City, on the evening of April 23, 1896, the two hundred and eightieth anniversary of the death of William Shakespeare.

While a good deal of public interest had been aroused by this demonstration, the commercial development of motion pictures had to wait for several years while patent difficulties were being straightened out, and showmen were being developed who knew what to do with this ingenious toy.

It was not until the strike of the White Rats, the vaudeville actors' union, in 1901, that showmen realized pictures would make an acceptable substitute for actors and rescued them from the lowly position of chasers at the end of vaudeville shows.

Spurred by this success, the first all-motion picture house, The Electric Theatre, was opened in Los Angeles, in 1902. Its presentations were essentially screen vaudeville, but the idea of telling a story in this medium was in the air. The first feature film was *The Great Train Robbery*, produced by Edwin S. Porter, in the autumn of 1903.

It was in Pittsburgh, in November, 1905, and in a converted store renamed the Harris Theatre, that the first complete motion picture presentation was shown for a nickel. There was soon a rash of these store shows, which began to dot the face of the great cities.

The legitimate theatre did not for some time consider motion pictures as competition or even as a form of entertainment deserving study and concern. Its theatres were in the meaner quarters, its patrons were poor, often illiterate, many times unable to speak English, its exhibitors shop keepers and retail salesmen from the fur business, buttons and cloaks and suits. And so these men, unopposed and unappreciated by the theatre, obtained first experience and then control of the motion picture field. Some of them who made their start in this lowly manner now control the destinies of the great motion picture companies, and their social viewpoint, their business methods and ethics have influenced and colored the whole course of motion picture development.

It has been said that motion pictures have destroyed the legitimate theatre, but, although they have in many instances replaced it, that is not a wholly true statement.

Motion pictures have certain definite and, in the end, enormous advantages over legitimate theatre productions. Whatever the initial expense of production, and it often appears to be excessive, it is almost the entire requisite outlay. Thereafter, except for the slight cost of transportation and booking, it has no expenses. Every performance of a legitimate play is essentially a new production with continuing expenses for salaries, materials, transportation, and other things. The potential audience of a legitimate play is limited not only by the cost of tickets but by the size of the theatre in which an audience can see and hear and by the physical limitations of the cast. A motion picture, on the other hand, can be magnified and amplified to be shown to an audience of five or six thousand. It can be exhibited up to six or eight times a day and in hundreds of theatres simultaneously. And all of that can be done for a small part of what a theatre ticket costs.

As the theatre withdrew from the road in the decade after 1908, vaudeville and motion pictures moved in and took over its theatres. As they broke the links of the one night stands and made jumps longer and more expensive, the theatre contracted still more tightly upon the large cities. That process has continued and is still continuing.

But it is not only on the theatre side that motion pictures have hampered and restricted the legitimate theatre. By the payment of salaries which the theatre could not hope to match, they have drawn into their production web the best writers and actors of the country. Their seduction has been even more serious than that of the theatres and audiences which is the charge customarily leveled at motion pictures.

Certainly the pictures have acquired many of the patrons

of the legitimate theatre, particularly those who formerly tenanted theatre galleries. But it is likewise true that motion pictures, like tabloid newspapers and confession magazines, have created a whole new audience—one which had never known the theatre and which, because of price barriers and cultural differences, might never have known it. Even at the peak of its most prosperous season the theatre probably never attracted more than one-sixtieth of the number of people who wash into and out of motion pictures almost any week in any year.

ENTER THE ACTORS' EQUITY ASSOCIATION

As the road contracted and the managers' difficulties multiplied, the lot of the actors became wretched, indeed. Alone of all the groups in the theatre, they had no effective organization, no protection against the necessities, the cupidities, and the whims of their employers. In a falling labor market they shouldered the brunt of the theatre's misfortunes.

There was probably no one contract in which all of the abuses of the moment were met. But what was missed in one engagement was apt to be encountered in the next. And there was nothing to prevent the imposition of any of them at any time, except the good will and the good faith of the manager.

These abuses ranged the whole gamut of an actor's relation to his employer. It began at the moment of his engagement, when he would be required to sign a contract drawn by the manager or his lawyer, which bound the actor completely while leaving the manager free to make any adjustments he chose. It continued through an unlimited free rehearsal period, often requiring six or eight weeks for dramatic productions and up to sixteen or eighteen for musical shows. At all times, during rehearsal and after the play opened, the actor's tenure of employment was slight and subject to termination without cause and often without payment, either in part or in whole. Pay was irregular and not assured in any way; strandings were frequent; many items of costume were required of actors and practically always of actresses, which should have been furnished by the management; salaries could be cut at any time and to any extent. And finally there was no machinery for the adjustment of claims and disputes except the slow, costly, and cumbersome one of the law. Under the stress of these injustices and of others, the actors were angry and discontented, but felt that there was nothing they could do about it. The Actors' Society was impotent and growing weaker, and the efforts it put forth to negotiate a charter from the American Federation of Labor had failed utterly.

Its membership and morale dwindled to such a point that on December 22, 1912, a hundred of its representative members met in New York to decide whether or not it was worth while to attempt to continue its existence. The consensus of opinion was that the Actors' Society of America had outlived its usefulness.

But there were men at that meeting who felt that the fight must be continued, if not with that organization, with one that might profit by its mistakes. And so the final motion of the meeting was the appointment of a Plan and Scope Committee to formulate the outline of an organization concerned primarily with the economic difficulties of the actor. The original members of that committee were Albert Bruning, Charles D. Coburn, Frank Gillmore, William Harcourt, Milton Sills, and Grant Stewart.

Five months of arduous conference, conciliation, and negotiation culminated in a meeting of one hundred and twelve actors in the Pabst Grand Circle Hotel, New York City, on May 26, 1913, at which was formally born the Actors' Equity

Association, whose first president was the rebel actor-manager of a decade previous, Francis Wilson.

Equity came on the stage just subsequent to the conclusion of a truce between the Syndicate and the Shuberts, a truce which endured with minor intervals of sporadic warfare until the end of 1917. In this interval the Association made considerable strides in its membership campaign, and after a mild and inconclusive flirtation with the American Federation of Labor, negotiated a standard contract and Basic Agreement with the United Managers' Protective Association.

Almost as though that had been a signal for the renewal of the conflict, war suddenly flamed again between the Shuberts and Klaw and Erlanger, survivors of the Syndicate, a savage, country-wide struggle in the heat of which the combatants had little heed or care for a standard contract with their actors, and the United Managers' Protective Association no control whatever over its embattled members.

Equity's situation was tragic and desperate in the extreme, its very survival precarious. The country was becoming daily more engrossed in the prosecution of the World War; restrictions were constantly limiting the heat and light allotted to theatres; transportation was more and more diverted to the business of men and munitions. And now the managers were divided into two hostile camps with little thought but for each other's extinction at any cost.

Under these circumstances the interrupted negotiations with the American Federation of Labor were hastily resumed and this time pushed to a successful consummation. On July 18, 1919, the old White Rats—Actors' International Union charter was turned in to permit the issuance of a charter to a new international union, the Associated Actors and Artistes of America, in which Equity was the leading spirit, and of which it has retained the control.

But the issue had been pushed too far for peaceful settlement. The managers, too, had been reorganizing and drawing new alliances. Their new organization, the Producing Managers' Association, had come to an understanding with the Vaudeville Managers' Protective Association, the National Association of the Motion Picture Industry, which included both producers and distributors, and the Columbia Amusement and Burlesque Interests of America.

Backed by these groups, the strongest combination of managers in the history of the theatre, the Producing Managers' Association now notified Equity that it would refuse to issue the contract accepted by its predecessor, would issue its own contract, and would decline to deal further with Equity or to recognize it as the representative of its members. To their united might, they declared, the actors must answer as individuals: a troop of Goliaths demanding that David hand over that sling! To such an ultimatum Equity had no recourse but a successful appeal to arms, or go under as had so many similar actors' organizations before it.

War was declared on August 7, 1919, when thirteen companies in New York City walked out of their theatres at curtain time. The theatre was in the throes of the longest, costliest, and most desperately contested strike it has ever known.

The managers worked frantically to keep their plays running. Some of them returned to acting after varying periods of retirement; press agents stepped into breaches created by striking actors; non-members of Equity were offered large sums not to join; Equity members who could be persuaded, or coerced, were held to their contracts; the managers organized and financed a company union, the Actors' Fidelity League.

But the actors had strong and resourceful allies, also. Half a dozen unions with no direct quarrels with the managers came to their aid. Walkouts by stage hands and musicians closed several plays the actors had not been able to touch; transfer men refused to haul baggage and scenery labeled unfair; billposters declined to handle paper for productions not sanctioned by the actors; and other unions by resolution, expressions of sympathy, and gifts of money helped the actors' fight.

The strike lasted thirty days, spread to eight cities, closed thirty-seven plays, and prevented the opening of sixteen others, and cost everybody concerned in the neighborhood of three million dollars. At its end the actors had won all and more than they had sought at its beginning.

And yet the producing managers were not yet ready to concede that they had been beaten by superior force. As the Germans since 1918, they felt that they had lost through internal weakness and dissension—and indeed that had played no small part in the final settlement. And so they set themselves for a renewal of the fight at the expiration of the Basic Agreement included in the peace terms.

In the meantime they went to work to undo as much of Equity's victory as they might. The same terms were granted to all actors, whether Equity members or not. If anything, they went out of their way to see that Equity membership was a handicap rather than a help to actors.

These tactics soon made such inroads on Equity's paid up membership that the actors' association felt it incumbent to forge a new weapon to meet them. What it evolved was really a variation of the closed shop which is known to the theatre as the Equity Shop. Briefly it is an agreement between the members of the association and their association that in any company in which there is one Equity member, every member of the company must be an Equity member in good standing.

Although announced for the season of 1921–1922 in all companies except those controlled by members of the Producing Managers' Association, it was this organization which took up the challenge. Equity Shop, said the managers' association, though specifically exempting its members' companies from its scope, was really a form of coercion since, for the sake of engagements with other managers, it forced actors to join Equity who might not have been willing to do so, otherwise.

The issue was joined before Federal Judge Julian W. Mack as an arbitrator, on August 17, 1921. Ten days later he handed down a sweeping decision to the effect that Equity Shop was not only no violation of the Basic Agreement, but that it was not in violation of law or sound public policy.

There remained then, only one real question to be settled between the two associations: whether, at the expiration of the Basic Agreement, on June first, 1924, the Producing Managers' Association would accept Equity Shop without a fight; or whether it would take up the battle against it, again; and if it did so, who would win. Of all the issues that crowded the scene and appeared to clog the air, there was not one that could not have been settled in ten minutes, once this was out of the way.

What settled the matter eventually was the cleavage in the ranks of the Producing Managers' Association along the line of the Shubert-Syndicate fault. What of it, if of the Syndicate only A. L. Erlanger remained, his partnership with Marc Klaw at an end, and all the others either dead or out of the theatre? While Erlanger remained in the theatre, the Syndicate lived, and there could be no peace.

In the fall of 1923 the Shuberts and certain of the managers bound to them by ties of interest or affiliation, came to Equity and agreed to accept Equity Shop, with slight modifications, without a fight. There were negotiations and bickerings and times when nothing but a good rousing fight seemed adequate to clear the air, but in the end the Shubert faction seceded from the Producing Managers' Association three weeks before the end of the Basic Agreement, and signed terms of peace with Equity as the Managers' Protective Association.

The Syndicate die-hards, known currently as the Round Robins, went through the motions of a fight, but the defection of the Shuberts doomed it before it started. Seven plays were closed on June 1, however, and a legal fight dragged itself through several courts and lasted until the beginning of the new season. Then the managers capitulated, and shortly afterward the Producing Managers' Association turned up its contentious toes and retired from this world.

When the Managers' Protective Association had staved off a fight in 1924, it had fulfilled its real reason for existence. It never functioned very well or satisfactorily thereafter and was often in trouble with Equity. The latter, tired of its arguments and evasions, caught it in arrears in its agreement, and, although it was given another chance by an arbitration board, there was no real interest in saving it, and its members allowed it to go by the board rather than pay its debts. Its Basic Agreement was ended by Equity in July, 1933, and if it lives today, it is a shadowy and groundless existence.

THE THEATRE IN TEMPORARY ECLIPSE

Last of all the great countries, the United States was struck by the world wide financial stringency in 1929. With the country's economic collapse in the next five years, the theatre entered a period of temporary eclipse from which it has not yet emerged. When it does emerge, it will probably wear a somewhat different mien.

There are great cities which no longer have a professional theatre, or it comes to them irregularly and precariously. There are whole states, even provinces, from which the professional theatre appears to have vanished into thin air. A generation is growing to maturity to which the theatre and its people are only slightly less fabulous than the clipper ships that once dotted the seven seas.

All of that does not mean that these people have been deprived of entertainment. Motion pictures, somewhat uncertain as to how grateful to be for the gift of speech conferred upon them since 1927, wait around any corner, in any city. They, too, have suffered from the depression, however much they may protest to the contrary, but economically, intellectually, and emotionally they are more nearly within the reach of every person than the theatre was or ever will be.

Radio broadcasting, with television peering over its shoulder, pure speech, and *only* pure speech, is available in most homes for the mere twisting of a dial. Newspapers, periodicals, and books were never so cheap, so interesting, or so accessible as they are today.

The people who were drained off into these other channels of entertainment left a big hole in the theatre. But what remains is probably the finest and most intelligent audience the theatre in any land has ever known.

The theatre may as well face the fact that to reach this remaining audience it will need not only a new deal but new cards and new rules for the game. It may mean new types of plays, new methods of presentation—almost certainly a new alignment among actors, producers, playwrights, stage hands, musicians, scenic artists, press representatives, and audiences, both to themselves and to the theatre. It may entail a new theatre, so different from that to which we have become accustomed as to be almost unrecognizable to those who now work in it.

I do not suppose that all these groups, or their members, will understand the necessity for these changes or like them very much when they come. But I believe that such changes will come, nevertheless, and that the theatre can no more stay them by opposition than industry was stayed by the opposition of handicraftsmen to the introduction of machinery.

As long as our present economic system governs the theatre, the audience must remain an important factor in that new theatre. No matter how honorable the intentions of author, actors, or producer, or how ably they are realized, as long as the theatre is required to pay its own way, any play which does not yield an appreciable profit must be withdrawn.

In any theatre which is designed for fine and intelligent audiences, it will be necessary to eliminate the neck or nothing gamble in production, under which the theatre in this country has always labored.

It can be accomplished through the creation of subscription audiences or through the underwriting of theatrical seasons in road towns by groups of persons who love the theatre enough to determine to have it.

Symphony orchestras, art collections, and lectures, by recourse to this method, are able to appear in communities which would not support them if they merely moved in, opened up the hall, inserted a few perfunctory advertisements, and waited for audiences to turn up.

It is not to be expected that people in these road towns will subscribe to or underwrite productions sight unseen. But if the theatre, organized anew and motivated by a new spirit, will work out plans for one or more seasons in advance, it may look for the support its competitors in culture received and from much the same sort of people.

For the theatre is worth having and worth being made constantly more available to more and more people.

It is not only the medium which the greatest minds of all

ages have chosen for the expression of their noblest thoughts; it would suffice by itself, if no other traces remained, to re-create all the stages through which we have passed on our journey from eternity to eternity. Such an art is not to be disregarded lightly, or to be considered merely as a pastime.

Despite the confusion and uncertainty of the moment, I believe that there may yet issue a theatre greater and more splendid than any we have yet known. We have seen the theatre's first three thousand years. We shall never see its end.

AUTHOR'S NOTE

It must be apparent that any work of this kind can only sketch very briefly and hastily the main lines of the theatre's descent. It would be impossible to consider in such a limited space related branches of its family tree, which, even though they are great and complex arts, have not directly influenced the theatre we know. The theatre of the Orient is ancient and has been developed to a high pitch, but it has developed apart from and practically unrelated to our own theatre. And there are other national theatres throughout the world in the same situation.

All that I can hope to accomplish here is to explain how the theatre got to be as it is in our day.

Nor is it to be expected that any original research work could be done for such a study. I have taken what I have needed where I have found it. It did not seem desirable to interrupt the story continually with footnotes to other and more scholarly works. But they are there waiting to reward those whose interest may be aroused by the telling of the story in this form. In particular I am indebted to:

The Theatre—Three Thousand Years of Drama, Acting and Stage Craft, by Sheldon Cheney, Longmans, Green and Co.

The Business of the Theatre, by Alfred L. Bernheim, Actors' Equity Ass'n.

The Story of the Theatre, by Glenn Hughes, Samuel French.

Enter the Actress, by Rosamond Gilder, Houghton, Mifflin and Co.

The facts are theirs. The mistakes in interpretation are mine.

A. H.

Hastings-on-Hudson, New York, May 2, 1935

THE PRESENT DAY THEATRE

by

IRVING PICHEL

Irving Pichel, actor and director of stage and screen plays, lecturer, and author, was a charter member of Professor Baker's "47 Workshop." He began his career with the Castle Square Stock Company in Boston; and has directed little theatres in St. Paul, St. Louis, Detroit, Berkeley, and Santa Barbara. In New York, Mr. Pichel directed for the Shuberts and served on the advisory board of the Theatre Guild in its early years. Either as director, actor, or producer he has been concerned with over a hundred and sixty plays. Among them are: Pictures directed—*The Most Dangerous Game* (with Ernest Shoedsack); *Before Dawn:* Picture rôles—*The Right to Love; An American Tragedy; Murder by the Clock; The Cheat; Cleopatra; British Agent; Fog Over Frisco:* Plays produced for the first time outside of New York—*Beyond the Horizon; All God's Chillun Got Wings; The Great God Brown; Marco Millions; Liliom:* Other productions—*Wild Birds* (first production); *Dear Brutus; Mary Rose; Not So Long Ago* (first production, New York); *The Tragedy of Nan; The Faithful.* Also, his productions include the principal plays of Shakespeare, Ibsen, and Shaw. At present Mr. Pichel is directing Rider Haggard's *She* for the R. K. O. Studios.

THE PRESENT DAY THEATRE

by

Irving Pichel

These comments on the present state of the theatre should be prefaced by a clear warning to the reader that the factors attributable to the depression have been largely discounted. It might be argued, though not too safely, that last year's improvement is a clear barometer of an improved state of affairs. We want a farther reaching picture of the theatre's condition, however, than such a seasonal rise and fall can give. We want, if possible, to know what creative forces are at work, what product they have set before us, what characteristic residue will give the theatre of our period its color, after depressions, movies, and Broadway have done their worst.

First, I am compelled to the belief that a process much more inexorable than the creeping paralysis of our economic life has been at work in the theatre. To know it at its face value, it may be well to go back to the beginning.

Twenty or so years ago we became definitely aware that a great change was taking place in the theatre. From Europe came accounts of new and exciting ventures in stagecraft. We heard of the Moscow Art Theatre; we had accounts of a producer named Reinhardt; Huntley Carter wrote *The New Spirit in the Theatre;* Professor George Pierce Baker returned to Harvard from a trip abroad with accounts of performances, lantern slides of settings designed by Adolph Appia, Ernst Stern, and others, and he started at Harvard "The English 47 Workshop." In Chicago, Maurice Browne established a little theatre; in Boston, Mrs. Lyman Gale converted a stable to the uses of her "Toy Theatre."

From 1912 till our entrance into the World War, the country seethed with a new interest in the theatre. Little theatres sprang up all over the country; the Washington Square Theatre and the Provincetown Players began their work; a host of new playwrights were caught in the ferment. Stage setting and lighting advanced to a new position of importance. The director became a newly important factor in production. Acting steadily declined, and actors of note and great personal following in the theatre became fewer.

The war was an interruption, but no more; and, during the boom years that followed, the Theatre Guild sprang up, Eugene O'Neill became known through the world as our most important playwright, individual producers like Arthur Hopkins, Winthrop Ames, Brock Pemberton, Guthrie Mc-Clintic, and Kenneth Macgowan sprang up to preëmpt the place which David Belasco had held alone for many years, while one pair of players, Alfred Lunt and Lynn Fontanne (and a little later Katharine Cornell), shone star-like, where a few decades before a Mrs. Fiske, a Margaret Anglin, a John Drew, a Maude Adams, an Otis Skinner, a Sothern and Marlowe, a family of Barrymore, and many others had been able to fill theatres by the naming of their names.

The little theatres, too, multiplied and flourished, and some of them—in Pasadena, in Cleveland, in New Orleans—grew to institutional permanence. The designers—Robert Edmond Jones, Lee Simonson, Norman Bel Geddes, Jo Mielziner, Cleon Throckmorton, and others—had their names advanced from the bottom to the top of the program.

That all this process has slowed up is incontestable. The depression may tell some of the story. The fact that Macgowan is producing for the movies, that Hopkins is directing them, that John and Lionel Barrymore are acting in them tells more of the story. But most of the story is contained in the fact that those who had most to do with the renaissance that began in the early years of the second decade of this century have now passed the age of forty.

There was a tremendous conviction on the part of the young producers, directors, designers, and founders of little theatres that they were pioneering. They spoke with belligerent feeling of the theatrical syndicates and of the evils of the road system; they talked of creating an audience for better plays and were honest in their faith that a fine play indifferently done was better than an indifferent play perfectly done. They scored the ludicrousness of the old-fashioned scenery of painted perspective, read and quoted Gordon Craig, and quoted (without reading) Adolph Appia. They were idealists, and they worked in a medium so tangible that it forced upon them practicality and in time proficiency. From the beginning they had the service, both in the little theatres and on Broadway, of designers who were, however new to the theatre, professional in their training. In time, it might have been hoped, as their proficiency increased to match that of the designers, and as more writers rose to serve the "new movement," a vigorous, rounded theatre would have come into being.

As a matter of fact, the entire renaissance was, from the beginning, a decorative renaissance. The impulses which so remarkably refreshed the theatre were all visually actuated. The drawings of Gordon Craig, the scenic simplifications of Ernst Stern, the mechanical improvements which moved plastic sets readily—these were the kind of evidence of a new life in the theatre. It was not a new drama, a fresh stream of dramatic poetry, or a young generation of great actors. And on this slim base of visual reclothing of the stage was built an evangelism which promised our theatric salvation.

It is inevitable that even evangelists should become tired. Pioneers push into new territory in order to settle. Once settled they wait for younger pioneers to push on to a new frontier.

It is my conviction that the generation of pioneers which preached and labored so ardently twenty years ago has come to rest in its well settled new home, and that the frontier they fought to reach has simply proved to be no frontier at all. Middle-aged, they are waiting for the younger men to come on and push forward. It is part of the chance that rules the appearance in cycles of these impulses and generations that the renaissance has subsided. The Drama department of Yale and the Drama Schools at Carnegie Tec and Iowa State University and Cornell and the school of the Pasadena Community Playhouse have supplied no new pioneers to take the places of those who have grown tired or successful. The one playwright who was definitely a part of this recent movement in the American Theatre is Eugene O'Neill. He, too, was fascinated by the scenic renaissance and wrote for the redesigned stages of the time. But, with the serenity of his successful forties, he has produced the amusing and pleasant *Ah! Wilderness.*

None of this is to be decried; it is a process of nature. It puts forward an accounting for the "decline of the theatre" during the past few years, which may cut deeper than the depression.

Next in importance comes the influence of the talking pictures. I have put this in second place because, like many others of my time, I have embraced pictures. They have provided for those of us who lived embattled artistic lives, a haven of comparative security. And, fundamentally, there is no reason why the theatre as a whole should not embrace them. They are part of the theatre, employ the same talents, the same materials, and presumably give a degree of the same kind of satisfaction to their audiences. It is not so much that they have wielded a baneful influence on the theatre as that they are a part of the theatre which has not yet become first-hand. It is theatre recorded and *réchauffé*, though there is no reason, save juvenility, why it should not be theatre pure and simple. It has not yet learned to walk on its own feet. Its actors are trained in the theatre, then bought and borrowed from the theatre. Its plays are the plays of the theatre re-made. There is no intrinsic reason why it should not find, in time, writers who write expressly for the screen all the time rather than occasionally.

The screen has problems, some technical but mostly economic, to solve before it can explore more freely a field of its own and cease being a means of reproducing works originally created for another medium. When this comes about, whether or not the screen is to be all the theatre we know, it can provide most of the pleasures we seek in the theatre.

Its one lack, of course, remains the somewhat mysterious alchemy wrought by the contact between a living audience and living players. The performance of the living theatre is always conditioned by its audience, lifted to new heights of performance by generous response, depressed to dullness by audience apathy. The screen performance, being recorded, is unalterable, identical with each unreeling.

So we concern ourselves here with the theatre as we have known it, in which plays are freshly re-created, night after night, by living players.

The condition of the theatre today differs greatly from that of two decades ago. Despite complaints even then that we had no theatre as an institution, the industry of the theatre was definitely institutionalized, along wholesale merchandizing lines. New York was the center of play manufacture, and there was a nationwide market. Theatres in every major city were owned or leased by one of two producing and booking firms. So each city with a profitable audience was assured of two theatres in which appeared, competitively, the most popular actors in the most successful plays of the best-known playwrights. The system, artistically, was hit-or-miss, but it did mean a season of theatrical performances during the course of which whatever survived a New York test was bound to be seen elsewhere in the United States.

The tale of the break-down of that system has been often told. Today it has wholly disappeared. Four or five companies may now make the cross-country trek annually. The second and third and even fourth companies, playing a popular success, are no more. The stock companies which used, a season or two later, to reproduce popular successes, have vanished. During the past season, there were sixteen stock companies in operation in the United States.

In addition to this vestigial theatre which remains, we have two other busy activities which belong in the theatre—the so-called little theatre movement and the dramatic activities of the schools and colleges. A first rate account of little theatre organization and activity may be found in Kenneth Macgowan's *Footlights Across America*. Though the statistics contained in Mr. Macgowan's report were obsolete almost as soon as the book appeared, it remains a sound report of a general state of activity. The little theatres in America may be somewhat fewer and the budgets of all of them considerably curtailed, but the outstanding theatres are still at work, and there is the usual birth and death rate of new ones.

It has been a fault of the little theatres from the beginning, and remains the outstanding fault today, that they are no more creative than the professional theatre. From the beginning, they have fed, as the stock companies did, on the successes of the previous New York season. They made a somewhat different and better choice of plays than the stock companies, it is true. They even ventured to the point of producing New York failures. But they borrowed the plays of the Theatre Guild and the Provincetown Players, where the stock manager borrowed the plays of Messrs. Shubert, Woods, Belasco, *et al*. And they still do that. They ventured at times into the continental drama, into the revival of classic plays, and very, very infrequently into experiment with new, unproduced work. Hardly one of them has given the commercial theatre a new writer. They have gone along on the impetus of the scenic renaissance and have been fortunate enough to find a place made for them by the decay of the stock company, so that in many instances the little theatre has become the only theatre a city can boast. But in creativeness, in contribution to the art of the theatre or its literature, in the formulation of a craft sounder, more sincere, more skilled than that of the theatres they have supplanted, they have done exceedingly little. They remain definitely more juvenile than the movies. The amateurism which at first they cherished as a distinction has been permanently forced upon them by economic conditions, and save for one or two which have abjured amateurism from the beginning, notably the Cleveland Playhouse, under the direction of Frederic McConnell, little more can be said for them than that they have kept the theatre alive. In some places, particularly in Pasadena, the effort merely to keep the theatre alive has become little short of feverish. The Pasadena Community Playhouse group now operates four stages and produces fourteen or fifteen plays every month. A critical mind might suggest that they have the capacity to produce one play well each month.

On the whole, to be sure, this activity is a good thing, even if it is merely activity, since it keeps a theatre mechanism going and keeps an audience in the habit of going to a theatre against the time when a new creative energy is set loose and finds the mechanism and the audience at hand to use.

It is my conviction that this new period can be inaugurated only by a generation of writers. Scenic revivals have shown the utmost they can do. Actors without plays which require acting are helpless. We do not even know whether there are any actors who can act, they have had so long imposed on them the elaborate subterfuge of not acting at all. This is, of course, the fault of the writers. Their interest during this entire century has been in people whose tragedies arise from the suppression of emotion instead of its expression. There will, one day, be a rediscovery of the fact that crises in human affairs rise out of uncontrolled passions, not out of repressed ones. Then, actors will again be called upon for the displays to which, even in classic plays, audiences are so unaccustomed that they no longer know what acting is.

It appears that the universities and their theatres are the most hopeful places to look to for such a new wave of creativeness. This is not merely because their players and writers and technicians are definitely in a learning and experimental stage of their careers, but because the university theatres have consciously directed their attention, first of all, to the writer. This is largely due to the influence and example of one man, George Pierce Baker, who at Harvard and later at Yale taught playwriting. He taught it, to be sure, in a very special sense, knowing that, though a man may be taught to compose sentences in English or any other language, he must begin by having something to say. So, from the beginning of his work, the first requirement Baker made of a student who wanted to learn to write plays was the ability to write a play. He admitted to his very small classes only those who had demonstrated by submitting a play that they had something to say in dramatic form. Then, by acute criticism of his work, by study of the example of successful playwrights, and above all by the test of performance, the student was "taught." A queer, patient kind of teaching which must wait and wait for the student who has something to say. It was late in Professor Baker's teaching career before he was able to fulfil his ambition to have a fully equipped, functioning theatre ready for such students.

But his influence and example did a great deal, in fact, did everything to make the teaching of the drama as something more than a department of literature respectable in our universities. It led to the establishment of university theatres all over the country. Here the craft of the theatre is taught, and the art of the theatre may be learned by a gifted man. Princeton, Cornell, Michigan, Wisconsin, Iowa, North Carolina, Stanford all have theatre departments where, in varying degrees, the young playwright may try his wings. A score of other universities provide some degree of dramatic opportunity of a creative sort. Only Harvard, where Baker's work began, ignores the matter.

The picture here drawn is not a very heartening one. In comparison with the excitement of a dozen years ago, the theatre seems in a very low state. And so in fact it is. Where not a dozen players can command an audience on their own account, where only one or two institutional theatres have a reputation based on a consistent standard of achievement, where only a handful of writers serves the stage with skill and a degree of sincere devotion, where even the commerce of the theatre has been broken down by speculation to virtual bankruptcy, where its art is represented most numerously by unskilled amateurs, what is there to do but wait with a depressed patience? But one waits, nevertheless, if only because something keeps going on, and because the universities are there, with their hospitable stages and their far-seeing teachers whose whole life and profession are devoted to a patient service of the future.

PART TWO
PLAYS AND PRODUCTION

PLAYWRIGHT AND THEATRE

by

BARRETT H. CLARK

Mr. Clark, an international authority on plays, attended the universities of Chicago and Paris, but did not finish his undergraduate courses. He acted with Mrs. Fiske and lived abroad for two years. The following is a partial record of his activity: actor and assistant stage-manager with Mrs. Fiske, 1912–13; instructor in drama and speech, and dramatic director, Chautauqua, N. Y., 1910–17; instructor and lecturer, Columbia University and Bryn Mawr, 1928–31; member Board of Directors, Drama League of America, 1915–30; dramatic editor, Drama magazine, 1924–31; Dramatic Director, Camp Humphreys, Va., 1918; on Board of Directors, Provincetown Playhouse, 1928–29; Play Reader for Theatre Guild, 1930–31; Literary Editor, Samuel French, since 1919.

Author: *The Continental Drama of Today*, 1914; *The British and American Drama of Today*, 1915; *Contemporary French Dramatists*, 1915; *How to Produce Amateur Plays*, 1917; *European Theories of the Drama*, 1918; *A Study of the Modern Drama*, 1925; *Eugene O'Neill*, 1926; *Oedipus or Pollyanna*, 1927; *Professor Clark, a Memoir*, 1928; *Speak the Speech*, 1930; *Eugene O'Neill, the Man and his Plays*, 1929; *Eugene O'Neill, a Bibliography* (in collaboration), 1931; *The Blush of Shame*, 1932; *Maxwell Anderson the Man and his Plays*, 1933; *Paul Green*, 1928; *The Modern Drama* (ALA pamphlet), 1927; *An Hour of American Drama*, 1930.

Books edited: Walter Prichard Eaton's *Plays and Players*, 1916; *Masterpieces of Modern Spanish Drama*, 1917; *Jurgen and the Censor*, 1919; *Representative One-act Plays by English and Irish Authors*, 1921; *The Appleton Book of Short Plays* (in collaboration), 1926; Same, 2nd series (in collaboration), 1927; *Great Short Stories of the World* (in collaboration), 1925; *Great Short Novels of the World*, 1927; *Great Short Biographies of the World*, 1928; *The American Scene* (in collaboration), 1930; *World Drama*, 1932; *The American Theater Manuals* (in collaboration), 1928 ff.; *One Act Plays* (in collaboration), 1929.

Books translated and edited: *The World's Best Plays for Amateurs* (58 vols.), 1914 ff.; Hervieu's *The Labyrinth* (in collaboration), 1913; *Three Modern Plays from the French*, 1914; *Four Plays of the Free Theatre*, 1914; *Four Plays of Emile Augier*, 1915; *Lovers*, etc., by Maurice Donnay, 1916; Sardou's *Patrie*, 1915; Hyacinthe-Loyson's *The Apostle*, 1916; Curel's *A False Saint*, 1916; Brieux's *Artists' Families*, 1918; *Two Belgian Plays* by Vanzype, 1917; *The Fourteenth of July and Danton* by Rolland, 1918; *The People's Theater* by Rolland, 1918.

PLAYWRIGHT AND THEATRE

by

Barrett H. Clark

However it may be with other writers, most playwrights exist on excuses. How otherwise can the average maker of plays explain his years of futile effort to sell something to a manager? How support his self-respect until the day when, if he is the fortunate one in five hundred of his fraternity, he signs a contract and gets his advance check?

The playwright's excuses are a curious lot: if they were classified and printed in double columns they could fill at least four good-sized pages. The commonest of them are:

Managers don't read scripts. Managers lose scripts. Play readers are ignorant office boys and stenographers. The unknown author has no chance. Only dirty plays are accepted. "If I chose to be smutty, I'd be successful." No writer can sell a play without pull. "My plays are too good for the public." Ideas in plays are passed on to managers' favorite authors, who (slightly) rewrite them and claim them as their own. Agents deliberately prevent their clients' plays, for personal reasons of jealousy, from being read by managers. Managers can't visualize manuscripts; "hence they can't realize how effective mine would be on the stage." Managers buy good plays with the deliberate intention of delaying their production—for various reasons. Managers won't produce Radical plays. Managers won't produce Conservative plays.

I could easily extend this list, basing each excuse on what some playwright has written or told me during the fifteen years I have been reading manuscripts, as reader for a manager, as associate manager, as agent, critic, and observer of the theatre.

Though there are stupid and careless managers and unimaginative and irresponsible readers, though there is occasionally some basis to almost any alibi, the truth is that managers buy and produce the best plays they can find, and ninety-nine per cent of the trash remains unsold and unproduced.

Doubtless a fine play will occasionally have to await that peculiar combination of person, time, and circumstance that looks like destiny, but rarely if ever is any masterpiece lost to the stage.

I know of two great geniuses in the American theatre (whose work belongs to the past quarter-century), poets and playwrights who were said to be so gifted that no producer ever took it upon himself to buy and mount their work: the plays of one are printed by an obscure publisher, and the other's remain in manuscript. Both men have received high praise, from non-theatrical persons, who smile beatifically when you tell them the plain truth, to wit, that whatever other merits the plays may possess they do not belong in the theatre.

I know, too, of a few exquisite plays that are as yet unproduced, but I am reasonably confident that they will find their way to the stage; yet if they don't, I shall have to admit that my judgment was at fault. I wrote a play myself several years ago, and for some time I thought it was pretty good; so did the agent who sold it and the manager who bought it. It was tried out at last—thank heaven, not on Broadway—and when it became my duty to criticize it as a reviewer, I saw that it was a false and sentimental bit of claptrap, and said so.

Managers are, by and large, no different from other people; they are human beings, swayed by the same motives that affect you and me; they accept and reject plays because they like or dislike them, because they want to make money, achieve a reputation, be actively and pleasantly engaged in their chosen profession.

Generalizations used in connection with theatre managers are as accurate as generalizations about lawyers, doctors, or women.

The men who buy and produce plays for professional use in Broadway theatres range everywhere from hard boiled and uneducated speculators to cultivated gentlemen with Phi Beta Kappa keys and collections of exquisite paintings and rare books; they are Jews and Gentiles, men who come from the ghettos of Eastern Europe, from the cities and villages of Hungary and Germany, men of English, French, Irish, Italian, and Scandinavian heritage, native-born hundred per cent Americans, philosophers, business men, insurance salesmen, brokers, artists, some of them almost illiterate and some of the highest culture and breeding.

No one method of classification is properly applicable to managers as a class, because they are not a class. They are all engaged in the pursuit of manuscripts which they can turn into paying productions. Occasionally a man of wealth, like Winthrop Ames, buys and produces a play with little or no expectation that it will prove profitable; but a producer must pick the kind of play that does make money, or he will soon find himself out of the running.

His problem is to find a script that not only appeals to his own taste—a play he will take pleasure and pride in sponsoring—but one that will pay. John Golden has been especially fortunate in liking the unpretentious and popular sort of play which was for so long associated with his name. He once told me that while he admitted the artistic superiority of the work of Bernard Shaw and Eugene O'Neill to plays like *Turn to the Right,* he personally preferred the latter.

It must be clear that if managers are to exist at all, they must have a continuous supply of new plays. Burns Mantle tells us that during the season of 1919–20 there were about one hundred and fifty plays produced, including the musicals; during 1925–26 there were two hundred and twenty; and during 1931–32 there were one hundred and thirty-four, not including musicals. Where does the manager get them?

Luckily there is no one traditional or fixed way of buying and selling plays. You may, if you like, announce yourself tomorrow as a theatrical producer, rent an office, and send an announcement to the papers that you are looking for plays. The same day the manuscripts and authors will begin to flow in. You will not, of course, have a chance at Sidney Howard's new play, because Mr. Howard must first know what sort of manager you are, what actors and director you can get, how responsible you are as a business man; besides, he is probably under obligations to other managers with prior rights of refusal on his next two or three manuscripts.

But in time, provided you make one really good production (whether it happens to make money or not) you will have a chance to see most of the manuscripts that are going the rounds. Neither friendship nor influence will determine the quality or quantity of new plays that come to you; that will depend chiefly on your reputation.

Even before you become known for your actual accomplishments in the theatre, and solely as a result of the fact that you call yourself a producer ready to read plays, you will find a steadily growing pile of manuscripts on your desk, and you will have to get someone to read them for you. Most of these plays will be pretty bad, run-of-the-mill products, but they must be read. When I was play reader for the Theatre Guild, I had to go through and report on nearly a thousand scripts a year; when I was on the Board of Directors of the Province-town Playhouse, I read about three hundred a year; on an average I read from twelve to fifteen hundred full-length new plays annually; it is my business to pick those that may interest some manager sufficiently to make him sign a contract and pay a cash advance. If I let one such play slip through my fingers (and I have done so, I admit), I am not doing my job on a perfectly efficient basis.

At the Guild it was my business to make a written report on every play I read. This was sent to one of the directors; but in case a play possessed any quality above the average or showed any promise, I made out my report on a special kind of paper, and sent copies to all six directors, any one of whom —within a short period—might ask to see the manuscript.

As a rule most managers employ one or more readers to look over the bulk of manuscripts submitted to them and to return all that are obviously impossible, passing on to the manager the few that might interest him. If the manager likes the play, believes in it, thinks he can finance and mount it and can either pay expenses or make a profit on it, he is ready to talk business with the author or the author's representative. A few managers have courage and conviction enough to make up their minds on this critical matter without asking advice, but most of them have not. True (and this applies especially for the period since 1931) managers have partners—backers, so-called—who must usually be consulted in the matter of choosing a play; and most of them are anxious to know whether the manuscript has movie possibilities before com-mitting themselves, in so far as paying the customary (five hundred dollars) advance which secures the right to produce the play within a certain period.

Most backers are persons with sums of money varying from two hundred and fifty to twenty thousand dollars (or even more), which they pay to a manager for a "slice," or share, of the profits, and a good many are stage-struck men and women who want to have a finger in the pie. As a rule the backers must read any manuscript which the manager wants to produce.

Very few manuscripts are bought before they have been read either officially or otherwise by someone in the office of the story editor of one or more of the picture companies, or at least before the manager is reasonably sure that his manuscript will ultimately interest one of the picture companies. Nearly all of the smaller and younger managers submit scripts to persons affiliated with a picture company before they will seriously think of signing a contract.

If you don't believe this, try sending out a manuscript (a really good manuscript) to fifty managers on Broadway, and put a note on the cover stating that "The picture rights of this manuscript are not for sale." Most of the managers will refuse even to read the play.

Managers are not only anxious to get manuscripts, they must have them; in view of the sharp competition in the business they really do read them, and tell the authors or their agents in a reasonably short time whether or not they are interested. It stands to reason that no manager could exist very long who let manuscripts lie around gathering dust. The classic story about the manager who one day went into his closet and pulled out at random a manuscript from a vast pile, produced it and made a fortune is still told. I should like someone to show me the documentary evidence.

I have known playreaders who were office boys and stenographers. Two of these boys are well known producers, and one stenographer is an eminent and successful play agent.

Coming now to the next standard excuse of the unproduced playwright, namely that the unknown author is at a disadvantage in selling his wares, I am inclined to think that the exact reverse is true. Naturally, the manager who receives from Eugene O'Neill a new play will probably take it home with him that very night in preference to the manuscript by Nellie Smith from Arkansas, but I am not at all sure that there isn't just as big a thrill in opening the manuscript of a writer whose name is unknown. It is so with me.

I confess that after reading plays professionally for fifteen years, during which time I have probably read as many thousands of plays, I am more excited over the possibility of finding something new or extraordinarily fine from the hand of some farmer, shoe clerk, negro preacher, convict, or school teacher, than I am when I open a new manuscript by Martin Flavin or Elmer Rice, Eugene O'Neill or Philip Barry. And I believe that most playreaders and managers feel that way, too.

I am, among other things, a play agent. In submitting a play to a manager I feel that I am a better agent if I can tell him that I have a new and original play by an unknown writer than if I have a new manuscript by a writer whose earlier work is already known. For one thing, there are managers who definitely don't like X, or Y, or Z, but in the case of the unknown playwright, no such prejudice can exist. Besides, there is hardly a manager anywhere who doesn't like the idea of being the first to introduce a new author, if his work shows promise or merit.

So circumstances favor the newcomer. If his manuscript comes, either to the agent, or direct to the producer, unrecom-

mended and unheralded, so much the better. It is not necessary to know what the local minister or the college English
teacher thinks of it; the writer needn't send even a letter:
the play speaks for itself.

"Only dirty plays are accepted. If I chose to be smutty, I'd
be successful." If I hadn't heard this kind of thing from
otherwise sensible and talented playwrights, I could omit the
point as not worth discussion. Someone says it every season.
As if plays succeeded, or were good or bad, because they were
or were not "dirty"! As I have explained elsewhere at some
length, there is so much that is sensually suggestive *outside*
the theatre that I can't imagine anyone paying money to see a
play in which the lives and situations can't be half as exciting
as life itself, *outside*.

No, you may depend on it, this is a feeble alibi urged by the
author who, during a season in which one or two "spicy" plays
are doing good business, can't sell his own work.

As for "pull"—recommendations, letters of introduction,
and the like—the only pull that's worth anything to a playwright, is a good play. The less said *about* it, the better.

"Too good for the public?" Another alibi, with perhaps a
tiny grain of truth in it. In one sense, some of Chekhov's plays
were too good—for a time. But if a play remains unproduced
for any very long period, and is seen nowhere, there's something wrong with it.

Are ideas stolen? Can an author in submitting manuscripts
safeguard himself against theft?

Occasionally an idea *is* stolen, but I am inclined to think
that any idea which is so unusual and so peculiar to its origi-
nator as to be protectable in a Federal court under an intelligent judge, is not worth keeping or using. There are people
(I have seen them at plagiarism trials) who insanely believe
that men like O'Neill and Howard go about furtively reading

unproduced manuscripts and privately printed books, and set themselves the dangerous and extremely difficult task of building plays out of characters and plot ideas which they have not "invented." Sidney Howard tells us that, like Molière and Shaw, he took the fundamental plot of one of his plays from Wagner, who (incidentally) got it from a dozen earlier writers.

If your plot is so original that you fear someone will steal it, you will either be able to dispose of your play to a manager, or find a collaborator who can make good use of it.

If that doesn't work, then you might just as well give the idea away—if anyone else wants it. It isn't ideas (though without them you are nowhere) that make a play.

About agents. It is the agent's business not only to sell plays to managers but to draw up contracts, see that they are executed, and so long as the play continues its existence as a "live" property, get from it every possible advantage and use. Writers are, of course, able to sell their plays direct to managers, and it is not likely that scripts so offered are much if any longer delayed in managers' offices than scripts submitted by well known agents. It is, however, usually admitted that the agent is better able to deal with the many intricacies of business detail that must be attended to in the case of a successful play, than the inexperienced layman. Besides, the playwright should not waste good time and energy worrying over matters of business.

The charge that agents sometimes play favorites, or interfere with the sale of plays, has no reasonable foundation.

As for the manager's inability to visualize a play by reading the script, and the assertion that managers buy plays with no intention of producing them, some confirmatory proof *could* be brought forward. However, most managers with any experience can visualize manuscripts better than most playwrights can. As for the manager who holds plays without using them, very few nowadays care to spend money in advances unless they think they are going to make use of what they contract for. Fortunately, the Dramatists' Guild goes about as far as any such association can go in safeguarding authors against their own stupidity and ignorance.

This summary of conditions governing the present-day professional play market is susceptible of criticism on minor points. I have purposely oversimplified here and there to make a general statement rather than a detailed description. It must be admitted, for instance, that there are several good and potentially successful plays that have not yet been produced, plays that are well known to most if not to all Broadway managers. I could name at least ten such scripts, and I am inclined to attribute their failure in reaching production to blindness on the part of the managers and to certain material conditions that have to do with real estate and finance rather than anything else. There is also the case of Elmer Rice's play, *The Left Bank*, which was in no sense an experimental or unconventional oddity. That play went the rounds for the better part of two years, and this after the success of *Street Scene*. I believe that some fifty managers read the script and not one thought it either good or salable enough to take it. At last Mr. Rice turned the manuscript over to me, and I sent it to fifty of the best non-professional theatres in the country, offering it on the most reasonable terms. Not one would take it, whereupon the author turned producer, bought the play from himself and produced it on Broadway, where it ran longer than any other play of the season. There are a few such exceptions to my generalizations, yet if *The Left Bank* had not been produced by Rice, had it found no producer either here or abroad, in the professional or the non-professional theatre, say until 1940 or 1945, I might be forced to reverse my opinion on it as an actable as well as a well written and interesting play.

There are other instances which may seem to give the lie to my generalizations, but in the final analysis the process of disposing of play scripts to managers is a simple matter: the manager represents the play-going public; that public pays him to offer it the plays it wants to see and will pay for; the playwright's business is to write what the public will ultimately pay for. Our market is the broadest, most catholic in the world today.

When we speak of the theatre we mean—unless we go out of our way to modify the word—the show business that flourishes in one small district on Manhattan Island, confined mostly to an area bounded on the south by Thirty-eighth Street and on the north by Fifty-eighth; on the west by Eighth Avenue and on the east by Sixth. Almost without exception all the hundred and fifty to two hundred plays annually produced in that small area are financed by men who (1) do it solely in order to make money; (2) chiefly in order to make money; (3) primarily because they like to produce plays and must make or at least not lose money if they are to continue in business. I should like to add a fourth category: those who produce precisely what plays they like even though that may mean a continual loss, but such persons cannot long exist in any business conducted under a system that requires profit before all else.

So even the most idealistic producer, who asks the public to pay to see his plays, must conduct his affairs more or less according to the rules of the game.

Since the New York theatre (for reasons that are elsewhere well explained [1]) costs a great deal of money to run, the price of tickets demanded of the public is excessively high, as

[1] See Morton Eustis' *B'way Inc.*

compared to other forms of entertainment; almost without exception this theatre is patronized by the well-to-do, by persons who can afford to pay from two dollars and twenty cents to as much as twenty dollars each for tickets. This public is interested chiefly, therefore, either in those subjects and backgrounds with which it is familiar or, by way of novelty, in certain exotic themes or backgrounds primarily because they are different. By and large, the New York theatre public is a "class" public.

True, on Broadway we may see in any season a wider variety of plays, may hear more different viewpoints presented than would be possible in any other city in the world; neither in London nor Paris nor Moscow can the theatregoer attend so many plays, by so many different kinds of writers. We may complain, as we do, of puritanism and business methods and the defects we now recognize as due to the necessary appeal of our stage to its "class" audience; but Broadway is still the great mart, the show place of the theatrical world where one may in the space of a single city block buy tickets to see a tragedy by O'Neill, a flea-circus, a bawdy musical show, a brilliant comedy of manners, a slow-moving folk play, a German middle-class drama, a rebel's dramatic condemnation of capitalism and a Tory's defense of it. Let us be thankful that we have not yet fallen under any form of Fascism (whether it be in the interests of one party or another) that forbids the treading upon the feet of too many sacred cows; that for all its short-comings Broadway audiences will accept nearly any kind of play, provided it has enough of that indefinable something that may be loosely termed vitality.

And yet we all know that "Broadway," used in almost any sense you like, is not big enough, not representative enough, does not, by a long shot, give us everything that we want in our theatre. Yet until we can form a somewhat definite notion of what we require, it isn't possible to conceive an ideal theatre.

Until we know what we want, we can't very well tell whether what we are getting is good or bad, in the right or in the wrong direction. I feel that until we have throughout our country a much larger number of theatres, producing as many different kinds of plays as we want, we shall have no very vigorous or important drama. Since Broadway represents only a very small part of America, we cannot look in that direction for any large or inclusive body of plays to satisfy the need which all good plays must satisfy if drama is to fulfil in us its chief function, which is to move us emotionally to a full sense of the life about us.

Our professional theatre in New York (with certain necessary exceptions) appeals to the well-to-do; it is primarily a form of entertainment for the small minority of persons who pay income taxes or can afford lawyers to show them how to avoid doing so. There is no need of complaining that Broadway will not listen to arguments proving that proletarian clerks are sweated by capitalist employers; such clerks don't often go to the theatre, but their bosses do, which means that the bosses' viewpoint is more likely to be set forth and maintained. If Elmer Rice, who tells us he is sick and tired of Broadway, wishes to argue politics and economics (and there's no reason why he shouldn't), he must choose the right place and the right audience.

The Theater Union, with its plays of social protest, has left Broadway proper and begun to find an audience that comes from districts some distance away from Park Avenue; the Group Theatre, somewhere (figuratively speaking) between Union Square and upper Broadway, has to struggle hard to make ends meet and must, as in the case of *Men in White*, sometimes produce work that could just as well have been done by one of the regular producers.

We must, therefore, if we would have a larger, a bolder, a more vital theatre, move out into the country; decentralize; strike down roots in the provinces, where the financial difficulties are less serious; above all, we must seek new and different audiences, larger, simpler, less sophisticated; our theatre, throughout the land, if it is to be a living thing, must offer a hundred times as many plays as we can see in New York, plays of every kind, and at prices that large numbers of people can afford to pay. We know that at least half the entire population of the country can afford to patronize the movies and pay from twenty cents to a dollar a seat every few days.

I cannot imagine the theatrical managers of New York migrating to what they consider the howling wilderness north of the Harlem and west of the Hudson; for good or ill, the Broadway crowd will remain on Broadway and go on very much as they have gone on in the past.

But we have throughout America the road, stock, the summer theatre, and the great mass of non-professionals. The first three categories are mostly an extension of Broadway, depending upon the metropolitan professional show business.

As for the thousands of schools and lodges, churches and small dramatic clubs, I regard these as social phenomena, important chiefly as activities that furnish every community with a more or less necessary form of light entertainment; they do, no doubt, direct a certain number of young people toward the college and the non-professional Little or Community Theatres, and by and large they serve to create audiences.

It is about these last that I have a few words to add. I believe that here, in the numerically vast world of the amateur—or let us say the non-professional, since the word amateur has evil connotations—is the seed of a new growth; there is a little evidence here and there, among the more advanced Little and Community Theatres, and more particularly in the drama departments of a few colleges and universities, supporting my contention that an audience exists outside Broadway for the sort of play that only too often cannot maintain itself in the centralized professional theatre, either because it happens not to appeal to a large enough paying public or because those persons in the habit of patronizing New York theatres demand a certain finish and sophistication in writing, acting, or production.

Every season we see plays in New York which "fail" simply because there are not quite enough people to support them. It is absurd to think that one play can have a long run on receipts of twenty-five hundred dollars a week, and be regarded in the show world as one of the season's hits, while another takes in fifty-six hundred a week and closes in a short time, set down as a failure. I take these specific examples from the 1933–34 season.

There are a dozen plays produced every year on Broadway that might attract audiences in every state in the Union if they had a chance, and even make money—if they were produced in the non-professional theatre. There are many more that never reach production—plays, too, by well known writers—because managers can't afford to risk their capital, fearing that they will be unable to attract the necessary three to twenty thousand dollars' weekly gross. I speak here not of the earnest, honest but misguided attempts by playwrights without experience; there are plays by Elmer Rice, Eugene O'Neill, Maxwell Anderson, Martin Flavin, Lynn Riggs, Owen Davis, Philip Barry, Paul Green, and Kenyon Nicholson that have never seen the footlights.

And there is no telling how many plays, by the established

writers as well as by newcomers, are never even written, which will of course not be offered to any manager, on Broadway or off. As a rule playwrights don't go on writing unless there is a reasonable chance of finding an audience for what they write.

It is pretty well established that where a certain sort of theatre exists, plays and audiences come into being to fill it. Antoine started in Paris with two one-act plays and a stage, and in ten years he changed the character of French drama; Brahm began in Berlin with two or three plays, and in a few years he had done the same thing for Germany; the Abbey Theatre in Dublin had only to let it be known that they wanted new and original plays, and Synge and the others came; the Provincetown players invited O'Neill to join them, and he stayed with them long enough to experiment and learn some of the fundamentals of his business.

We have a great many young writers ready to work for the non-Broadway theatre, but except in a very few cases, that theatre is not ready for them; and meantime they either try to adapt their wares to Broadway or go to Hollywood. When Elmer Rice shook the dust of Broadway from his feet in the fall of 1934, there should have been a hundred provincial theatres ready to say to him, "We told you so! Now send us your new plays."

It is our problem to find some means of reaching an immense playgoing public that is not exclusively interested in the domestic difficulties of well dressed ladies and gentlemen, and cannot afford to pay high prices to see expensive reproductions of the interior of "Westchester" or "Long Island" mansions; a public which has here and there proved that it is willing to watch scenes and hear lines that might not attract so many thousands of New York playgoers as are necessary to pay the absurdly high rents and wages that must be paid there.

True, the non-professional theatre of our country is still ninety-nine per cent snobbish, timid, reactionary, intellectually dead; it is the existence of the one per cent that gives me some hope. The fifteen or twenty non-professional theatres that have already shown initiative are pointing the way; it is among these that we look for signs of a new theatre; already this theatre has its honorable record; already it has gone to the playwright, the known and the unknown, and produced such works as Paul Green's *Tread the Green Grass;* George O'Neil's *Something to Live For;* Eugene O'Neill's *Lazarus Laughed;* Albert Bein's *Heavenly Express;* Edgar Lee Masters' *Separate Maintenance* and *Andrew Jackson;* Virgil Geddes' *Mud on the Hoofs;* George Middleton's *Hiss! Boom! Blah!!!;* Maxwell Anderson's *Seawife;* E. P. Conkle's *Mayor of Sherm Center;* Martin Flavin's *Amaco* and *Sunday;* and Owen Davis' *Harbor Light.*

Is this evidence of something new, or is it the last flicker of an old order?

PRODUCER AND PLAY

by

Arthur Hopkins

Arthur Hopkins began his successful career in New York as a producer and director in 1912. Formerly he had been in newspaper work in Cleveland. He produced vaudeville sketches as a preliminary to his activity in the legitimate theatre. Recently he has produced the screen adaptation of Ronald Bennett's *Great Adventure*. In addition to his book, *How's Your Second Act?*, he has written numerous articles on the theatre.

Among his many productions are: *On Trial; The Deluge; A Successful Calamity; Wild Duck; Hedda Gabler; A Doll's House; The Jest; Richard III; Macbeth; Daddy's Gone a-Hunting; The Claw; Anna Christie; The Hairy Ape; The Old Soak; Hamlet; Romeo and Juliet; The Laughing Lady; What Price Glory; The Second Mrs. Tanqueray; Close Harmony; In a Garden; Paris Bound; Machinal; Holiday; Rebound;* and *The Passing Present.*

PRODUCER AND PLAY

by

ARTHUR HOPKINS

IN accepting a play for production the producer is at once confronted by his clamorings for revision. If he be too much of an egotist, he may lose sight of the author's intent and in his mania for improvement may impose upon the creator some very striking ideas which should find expression in a totally different play. It is not unusual for one good idea to give birth to a totally different good idea. Both may be good but unrelated.

This seeps over into dramatic criticism. Frequently critics quarrel with a play not for what it is but because it is not something else.

Therefore, it is imperative that the producer find and believe in the author's intent. If he cannot do both, he should not produce the play. He should save his ideas for a work of his own. While this is obviously true, it is not easy of accomplishment. There is something emotional about revision that subtly leads astray people of best intentions.

When the throbbing torso of a play is laid on the table, the dissecting instruments are not content with exploration. They go in for organic reconstruction. In the reassembling, the heart may be left on the table, the intestines may be left to wither, the torso may be distended with convenient undertaker's padding. The cheeks may be rouged and lips lifted into a beatific smile, but disintegration has set in.

It is a wise producer who knows how to find the author's path and shove ahead on those lines. If the author's path is misguided, the play should not have been accepted.

It is not unusual for an author to leave the path that he has laid down for himself. Some alluring by-path beckons him, and he follows full tilt seeing somewhere at the end a grand moment that does not belong to his play.

The old well built and forgotten French dramas that gave themselves up completely to the big second act curtain are camphory examples. Truth disappeared when the jockeying for the big moment began.

As anyone who has collaborated well knows, one idea invariably releases another dozen. It is in the selection of these that writers must be careful. So with a producer. If he be a person of even slight imagination, the author's ideas release in him a score of unsuspected clamorings which, if he is without compass, he will seek to impose. Each of them may have merit, and yet none of them be of the slightest value to the work in hand.

There is a Pandora's box of the mind that is better left unopened.

How are these pitfalls to be avoided? In the first place by the greatest hesitancy of the producer to tamper with a work which he has found upon first reading to have authenticity. In the second place by finding sympathetic contact with the author's work so that changes he may suggest are a furthering of the author's aim rather than a deflection of it.

It is not always necessary that an author be able to justify the trend of his play or the reaction of his characters. These can easily be right and still not susceptible of explanation. Anyone who has written at all knows well that characters sometimes have their way and frequently a way quite surprising to the author. The author who knows at all times exactly what his characters will say is unlikely to be the parent of anything remotely profound.

There is a mediumship in writing, and those who have never surrendered to it cannot possibly know the exhilaration of creative release. Portrait painters frequently find their subject taking on the most unexpected expressions, sometimes too evil for comfort, yet to all appearances the face has not changed. Writing is a form of portraiture. No one can foresee how deep the unrestrained pencil may pierce. It is not an instrument to be picked up lightly. The wielder must have the courage to pursue its lacerations.

The producer finds himself in the depths of portraiture. He, too, must not shrink at the sight of great terror or great grandeur.

Once the embarkation is made, the producer must be willing to follow the course, wherever it leads. Always he must have his eye glued to the readings of the author's intent. The minor details then fall away. Readings, gestures, movement have little import. Has the producer got firm hold of the author's idea? If he has, he will bring the play into safe harbor. If not, he will leave it foundering at sea.

PART THREE
STAGE DIRECTION

THE DIRECTOR

by

Brock Pemberton

Since 1920, Brock Pemberton has produced a number of unusually successful plays in New York. He served as a member of Arthur Hopkins' staff from 1917 to 1920. Prior to 1917 he was reporter for the Emporia Gazette, 1908–10; dramatic editor for the New York Evening Mail, 1910–11; and assistant dramatic editor for the New York World and for the New York Times, 1911–17. He is the author of numerous articles on the theatre.

Mr. Pemberton has produced: *Enter Madame; Miss Lulu Bett; Mister Pitt; Swords; Six Characters in Search of an Author; Loose Ankles; The Living Mask; White Desert; Strictly Dishonorable; Personal Appearance;* and *Ceiling Zero.*

THE DIRECTOR

by

Brock Pemberton

WHEN a play has been written, accepted for production, and players have been cast for its parts, it does not automatically translate itself to the stage. Someone must engineer the process of transmutation, and the one who does is called the director. It is the director's task to fuse play, players, settings, properties, and costumes into a homogeneous whole, to perfect a microcosm from intellectual, spiritual, and physical elements. The task is at once one of the most difficult and important assignments in the theatre.

It is only within the last two decades, in America at least, that the director has become a personage. In an earlier day, when the theatre was a more personal institution, managers achieved fame through the excellence of their productions, the skill of their players, and the quality of their plays, but since the physical accessories of stages were much less complex and the routine of performance more stylized, usually following a conventional pattern, the director was a sort of graduate stage manager and was more or less submerged.

When American critics of the drama discovered the director, they so glorified him that now half of the young men and women who annually descend upon the theatre aspire to become directors. Too many of them do, unfortunately for the stage, for while a few have some of the necessary qualifications, the majority have not the essential temperament, talent, or training.

In England a play is "produced" instead of "directed," and the one who performs the service is called producer instead of director. The English nomenclature is happier because it is more comprehensive. In America directors are divided into two general classes, producers who direct their own offerings and directors hired by producers. Since the director should have complete supervision over the script from the time it is delivered by the author till the curtain has been rung up and, for that matter, down, the felicity of the English terminology is apparent.

The adage that plays are rewritten rather than written may be hackneyed, but it remains true. The director should know whether a script is ready to be acted, and if it is not, he should be competent to assist in correcting its faults. He need not be an author himself, although some of our best directors are dramatists, and even if he has writing ability, it may not avail him anything because of the strict prohibition in the standard contract issued by the Dramatists' Guild of America, a contract governing the professional production of every play, against the change of a single word without the written consent of the author. This prohibition is zealously guarded by incompetent as well as competent dramatists. The wise author is willing to take good advice from any quarter, and the wise director is not willing to accept an assignment unless he believes the manuscript is ready or its creator wise.

Failure to determine these alternatives too often leads to disaster. Many plays are wrecked because of the misapprehension that they can be fixed at rehearsal, a critical period which finds the author either obdurate or incompetent. In the former predicament there is no hope; in the latter if he is

reasonable and the producing forces know their job, the necessary rewriting can be done. Infrequently a formidable producer rides roughshod over the dramatist and his protecting
contractural phrases, and again another may take advantage
of circumstances to make him listen to reason, as did the one
who called off rehearsals after they were under way until
the promised revisions had been made. But the rehearsal
period should be kept free for perfecting performances, a
difficult and sometimes impossible job if the text is not set.

There are two general schools of direction with almost as
many variations from the norm of each as there are individuals. In the one are those who visualize completely every
detail in advance; in the other, those who let the performance
develop itself at rehearsals.

The former will be considered first since a review of this
method will disclose the full activities of a good director.
Most authors interlard their scripts with stage directions or
business presumably to aid the director. In the case of imaginative or experienced playwrights the practice achieves
the desired result, but too frequently the contributions have
to be discarded as impractical or the opposite of what they
should be. This is particularly true of interpretative directions, for it is a curious fact that many authors can write a
telling scene on the stage. It is a fairly safe rule, then, to
delete all such arrows as "smilingly," "hissingly," and "with
great hauteur" before the parts are made and distributed to the
actors, because first impressions are often hard to eradicate.

The first business of the director, once the play has been
adjudged ready for rehearsal, is to select his cast. Some organizations have casting directors whose sole duty is to know
talent through performance or personal contact. A competent
director while not discounting expert advice from any source
should be a judge of acting, an appraiser of personality and

temperament. He should have a flair for visualizing the effect created by the bestowal of the endowments of an individual on the creation of an author. If he demands less than the best, his reputation will suffer.

With the cast corralled, his next session is with the scenic designer. This is extremely important, for many an excellent artist, if given his head, will sink a play with a millstone of scenery. Settings are sometimes so beautiful or elaborate that the ear cannot overcome the eye's distraction. This is especially true in the case of fragile comedies, which frequently of late, as the talent and skill of our designers have increased, have been smothered in beauty. Color is important. Dark lugubrious walls can blunt the wisest retort, and a chill, cold room can subdue the most passionate scene. Until a few years ago little attention was paid to modern clothes worn by actresses. The usual procedure was for the producer to budget their wardrobe and let them shift for themselves. The result was apt to be ludicrous and horrible. Nowadays experts reconcile line and color to personality, mood, and setting.

Even more important than these details is determining the ground plans, for until the floor space, the location of openings, the choice and disposition of props and furniture have been decided, no movement can be charted. The furniture must be practical as well as suitable and decorative. A divan must not be too squashy or too hard, too high or too low. The arms of a chair must be strong if an actor is to sit on them and not eventually on the floor. Since drama is conflict, conflict is action, and action is movement, the placing of the physical objects must be such as to allow visibility, freedom of movement, variety of grouping. The practicality of swift scene changes must be provided for. In these cinematic days tedious waits are apt to kill a play, and the wise director must know whether workable and adequate machinery is planned.

These preliminaries out of the way, the cast is then assembled for the first rehearsal, which is scheduled according to the date set for the opening. Under the standard contract issued by the Actors' Equity Association four weeks of free rehearsals are allowed for a dramatic production. This period may be divided into two parts by out-of-town performances if the New York première immediately follows the second period. Unless the play is complex or there are casting or rewrite problems, three weeks' rehearsal time is ample for the average play.

At the first rehearsal the parts are distributed; then seated around a table, and aided by the relaxation and freedom from self-consciousness that comes when one has a table top to lean on and to hide one's legs (however handsome), the actors read aloud. Some authors and directors claim the prerogative of the first reading. This may be the first time many of the cast have heard the play. Likewise it may be the best reaction the play ever gets. Certainly no subsequent audience will ever have as much at stake. So many trusting souls have been misled by actors' reactions that this superstition has become established—if the actors like the play inordinately, beware of failure.

The length of the reading period is arbitrary. It may be brief, or the players may be kept off their feet several days. This is the time to catch word repetitions or other minor faults in the script, to standardize and correct pronunciations, especially of proper names or foreign phrases, to set inflections and readings.

The actors then walk through the first act. Stage braces form the outline of the set; the pickup pieces of furniture consisting of wobbly chairs and Leon Errol-legged tables which haunt the wings of any stage, stand where the real furnishings will later repose. The general movements have been included in the parts, and reading these frequently aloud between their dialogue, the actors stumble through lines and movements.

As quickly as possible the actors memorize their lines so that they may put down their typed parts. By the time they are able to give the act from memory, the business has been pretty definitely set; movements, positions, groupings, and postures have been registered, and the players are ready to concentrate on their characterizations. The director now deserts the stage for the auditorium, and once the act has begun to flow, he desists from interrupting to counsel or criticize, and instead takes notes to be given at the end of the act.

When the players are fairly glib, which should be at the end of a few days, the same process is followed with the second act. The first is by no means dropped, but as it approaches completion, less time is devoted to it and more to the new material. The third act follows in turn, till toward the end of the second week, in the ordinary schedule of rehearsals, parts are out of the players' hands, and they are ready to put the finishing touches to their performances.

The time when hand props are introduced and the performance is placed within the settings depends on the producer's ability to afford these luxuries. Among the unfair rules of labor which have fastened themselves on the theatre during the ascendancy of union labor in the past thirty years is one that a crew must be held under pay after a setting has been put up through the whole period of its use, and another that property men must be paid whenever hand props or the regular furnishings are used.

At some point, however, if only on the day of the opening, a full performance should be given. Before this event the director must see that the scenes are properly hung, set, and dressed, that the lighting conforms to the time elements of the play, preserves its moods, and achieves the highest pictorial values without sacrificing playing ones. Cues for light changes must be rehearsed, and care taken to have the proper intensity of light on playing areas. This is accomplished by having someone move through the focal points and assume the various attitudes of the players. Modern stage lighting is a complex science and a highly developed art that can add mightily to a production.

When the lighting is fixed, make-ups are tested, and a costume parade proves whether the wardrobes harmonize with themselves and the background. A time-saving process, especially if props and settings are a last minute luxury, is to jump through the play for action only, omitting all lines that do not carry movement. Whether to leave a door open or to close it after an entrance or exit, where to find a match for the ubiquitous cigarette, how fast to ascend to have steps and speech synchronously carry the speaker off, how to sip a drink and not delay the action, to eat your cake and have your speech—these and countless other bits, heretofore ghost motions, must be blended with the physical reality of things. Settings help the player visualize the play, and some of the less imaginative seem to understand what it is all about for the first time when they find themselves within the scene. Few of them have any difficulty in adjusting themselves to their new surroundings. The ability to "suit the action to the word, and the word to the action" and to handle props is by no means universal, since bodily coördination, one of the requisites for good acting, is a rare gift.

The dress rehearsal has arrived. The curtain ascends, and unless an emergency presents itself, the act is run off without interruption. The director, swallowed up somewhere in the dark reaches of the auditorium, pencil and pad in hand, scribbles wildly as points new and old present themselves to ear and eye. Most of them are probably old, either incurable faults or those the tension of the occasion has uncovered. After each act or perhaps at the end of the performance there is a huddle, notes are given, impressions exchanged, enthusiasms inflated. This is the pep talk before the game for dear old alma mater.

With variations this is the routine of one school. The principal difference in method of the other is that the director has not developed his details in advance. He has done little more home work than the actors. The extreme exponents even eliminate the full reading. Given the general geography of the settings, the players are allowed to find their way about as instinct or inspiration suggests. The director is the referee, and when the effects that strike his fancy transpire, he selects and registers them. The burden is not always passed entirely to the players. If the director is not an absolute charlatan without sincerity, industry, or resourcefulness, he will anticipate as well as edit the results. The one pitfall to be avoided is not to relinquish authority by allowing points to be debated or decisions questioned.

A line might be drawn in another direction to divide directors into two other groups. The inhabitants of each would then be characterized as the good and the bad, the craftsmen and the fakers, the sheep and the goats. The good director has been described. The interloper is usually one who sells his services. The incompetent producer-director cannot long survive because of the inexorable law of diminishing bankrolls. If the faker is merely a hired man, he may flourish indefinitely, as often he is a consummate actor. His performances usually coincide with the visits of his boss. He is the survivor of the old megaphone school of directors. He browbeats his actors, goes into trances better to feel their auras, demands pear-shaped or orchid tones, and performs similar tricks calculated to annihilate with envy an ordinary exhibitionist. A crossbreed of this type is the producer who contributes a couple of inflections and poses as the director.

It is impossible to impose any more rigid classification because every director is a law unto himself. The results may be equally good whatever the method since the sum total is compounded largely of human emotions, personalities, and temperaments. A good play can be heightened by good direction and may survive bad direction, while a poor play may be made less poisonous but can scarcely be saved by good direction. Generally a good director shines if play and players possess quality; if the play is meretricious, both players and director are apt to be considered inadequate. It is a fact that few people not of the theatre can unscramble characterization, performance, personality, direction. A fair actor in a well-written part rightly placed is hailed as a genius, and a star in a badly written rôle is made insecure from head-shakings. Only those who witness the unfolding of a play from typed part to full-blown performance can know the director's contribution, can guess the boundless energy, patience, enthusiasm, and imagination he contributes.

MY METHOD OF DIRECTING

LEGITIMATE NOTES ON STAGE DIRECTION
IN THE ILL LEGITIMATE THEATRE

by

MELVILLE BURKE

In addition to numerous productions in New York, Melville Burke has directed stock companies in the principal cities of the United States. He was director of the Art Theatre, St. Louis, 1915–16; managing director of the Municipal Theatre, Northampton, Massachusetts, 1916–18; general director for the Stuart Walker Company, 1923–25; managing director of Elitch Gardens, Denver, Colorado, 1925–29; and with the Fox Film Corporation, 1929–31. During the summer months Mr. Burke is managing director for the Lakewood Summer Theatre, Skowhegan, Maine, and for the Newport Casino, Newport, Rhode Island.

Among his New York productions are the following: *Episode; Excess Baggage; Precious; Tonight at Twelve; Just to Remind You; A Saturday Night; A Perfect Marriage; A Church Mouse; Privilege Car; Adam Had Two Sons; Queer People;* and *Al. Rights Reserved.*

MY METHOD OF DIRECTING

LEGITIMATE NOTES ON STAGE DIRECTION
IN THE ILL LEGITIMATE THEATRE

by

Melville Burke

The theatre is ill, acutely ill, less from new disorders than from those chronic ailments it has suffered through its longevous, diversified, and complex existence. Delicately perceptive, since its development from early religious ceremonials, it always has paralleled the public state of mind, reflecting its strength and weakness through the physical and mental aspects of civilized progress. It has ever emerged from infirmities, stronger, more productive—Promethean; and it will rise up from its present sick bed, wiser, richer, finer, for having been purged again of the germs of incompetence, mediocrity, and over zealous psychiatry, the cultures of economic depression.

The most serious result of the present theatre depression, other than the hardships endured individually and collectively by members of the profession, is the practical annihilation of all media for the proper training of young directors, actors, and technicians. The theatre, with the exception of various amateur groups, has ceased to exist beyond the limits of a few of the larger cities. That most practical of all training schools, the stock company, for reasons obvious enough, no longer functions, while the dramatic school, frequently operated by inexperienced theorists, never has been fully credited with practical instruction. There remains only the New York production which theoretically should be closed to the inexperienced; unfortunately, in times of depression, it is not. The shrewd, established manager cuts down production rather than face almost certain losses; good plays are hard to find, as even the skillful playwright is influenced by temporal destitution. Theatres are dark and rents are low. Responsible managements retire in favor of petty promoters who with little financial backing, a poor play, and a cast of players who are willing to work for practically nothing, flood the production field. Here is opportunity for inexperience. Because they ask little in compensation, many talented, ambitious, and hopeful apprentices find themselves in positions which they are not qualified to fill. They move from one failure to another, uncomplaining and content, gaining confidence and assurance through what they think is recognition but hampered by the fact that they do not know their business, regardless of how innately sensitive they may be of it. Acting and direction may be an art, but two-thirds of each is craftsmanship.

Craftsmanship! The foundation upon which is builded proficiency in any art. Essential to the actor, it is this mastery of mechanical skill which is the structural basis of stage direction. Varied in scope, it includes a knowledge of the limitations of the stage, a first hand acquaintance with stage lighting, scenic design, the proper preparation of the manuscript, theatre administration, and the technique of acting and casting, an acute development of the power of visualization, the ability to convey direction to the actor with clarity and brevity, and an understanding of all the devices, tricks, and conceits used for effects in the theatre. This technical knowledge is a necessity before the director can bring adequately into usage his creative imagination faculties, the emotional approach to the theme, the mood and the interpretation of the play. These qualities establish the grade of the director, that instinctive feeling for or sensitiveness to interpretation, but I doubt if anyone has reached a lasting recognition without a thorough technical background.

A director must guide rather than propel his actors through a performance. Someone has said that a play is a sort of glorified prize fight, and so it is; the director is the referee, whose job is to see that the rules are observed and that the performers keep up their foot work. The actor must have latitude and initiative to be held in check only when his attack is destructive to the unity, coherence, and emphasis of the director's and the author's design. An actor's creation of character may be excellent as a unit but destructive in its relation to other characters in the play. His interest is in playing one part—his part—and he is incapable of judging his relation to the whole structure. He must be guided not arbitrarily but suggestively. His interpretation of the lines must bring out the exact meaning which the author intended through requisite emphasis, inflection, phrasing, and pausing; this is reading. His feeling for the eloquence of the pause must result rhythmically from the emotional reaction which establishes his mood. Tempo and rhythm are extremely important principles in the projection of a scene. An action establishes a tempo, slow or fast, which, in turn, sets a rhythm to accompany it. Change the tempo, and the rhythm adjusts itself to the new time. A director can regulate an actor's tempo without difficulty because it is a purely mental process, but rhythm is emotional and rests largely within the actor's impulse. Climaxes must progress slowly so that their force is not spent before they reach their peak, and the director must be ever watchful of contrast in playing so that the performance is projected in light and shade.

There are various methods of direction, none necessarily better than the other, all dependent upon the individuality of the director. Only result matters.

The first task of the director after reading the play, provided his reaction to it is favorable, is to discuss it carefully with the author and producer so that all are in mutual agreement relative to its interpretation. Ideally he should never consent to stage a play unless he is sympathetic to it, but unfortunately Fate has usually tossed his ideals on the fires of his youth where they were consumed. All changes in manuscript should be made before putting the play into rehearsal; of necessity there will be minor changes during rehearsal, additions here and deletions there, as it is practically impossible to space scenes rhythmically without seeing them in action. The next step is casting, and this should be done most carefully to obviate changes during the early period of rehearsals. A director will pencil in, opposite the names of the characters, the names of players whose talents and type make them suitable considerations. The practice of interviewing large numbers of actors is a frightful waste of time. It is better to select a capable, intelligent, and responsible casting agent, requesting not more than three names for each character, choosing from this list and his own a tentative cast. After the necessary interviews and the discussion of business agreements with the manager, the final assignments are made. The director is now ready to discuss with the scenic designer, from the ground plans laid out by the former, the designs for the settings, the properties, and the trimmings. The designer, who is (or should be) familiar with the manuscript, will have constructive ideas, many of which the director will accept gladly. The settings are merely the atmospheric backgrounds of the play, should be in key with it, and should never become conspicuous as scenery. As most scenic designers expect to have a hand in the lighting, the wise director will insist on the approval of the lighting set-up. The designer is concerned with a lighting which will present his setting most favorably, and the director with one which will bring out the values of the play. The whole subject of stage lighting is too exhaustive to be even sketched in a chapter of this nature, but it should be said that the modern trend toward overhead and spotlight zoning wherein the stage is a variegated mass of brilliant light and stygian shadow is a very trying medium for both actor and audience and seldom has aided in the success of any play.

With these preparatory but important arrangements completed, the director is now ready to study in detail his manuscript, visualizing the action of the play, planning and plotting the movements and mechanics of the actors, seeing the play unfold itself as in performance, keeping all in the key and mood of his interpretative design. A director should be thoroughly conversant with his manuscript before his first rehearsal, but there are several directors of reputation in New York so delicately balanced emotionally that they must face their first rehearsal free from all preconceived concepts, giving the play but a cursory reading and relying upon their exalted and extraordinary inventive capacity to bring their play into flower. It may be added that this method of dramatic horticulture requires the liberal use of fertilizer.

The first rehearsal should be devoted to the reading of the play by the actors, rather than by the director or author, because it is well not to suggest readings or interpretations which the actor, in his desire to please, may imitate, and because it is difficult to hold the undivided attention of the group to readings of this sort. It is important that all members of the company, regardless of the importance of their parts, should know the entire play.

Several successful directors believe in prolonging this reading through a period of ten days or more. The weakness in this method is that the anticipated absorption of the play, the amalgamation of actor into character, is seldom accomplished, and the coördination of the action to the word is too long delayed. Tone, vocal light and shade, tempo, pace, can be accomplished more easily in action, all being irrevocably related. It is not unusual to find actors whose readings are satisfactory while seated about a table, who become hopeless when they begin "to walk." Excellent interpretative readers often fail utterly when obliged to coördinate physical movement and emotional registration with speech. A successful platform reader is not necessarily a successful actor. The method leads to unnecessary delay.

Progress in rehearsal depends on physical, mental, and emotional balance, and it is logical to consider them in sequence; in the second or third rehearsal get the play into action, laying out the mechanical movements, and the physical aspects of the performance. This has been planned precisely and mathematically by the director whose chief care has been to see that no movement is made without proper motivation. The practice of unnecessary movement to animate dull scenes is dishonest and emphasizes bad writing; nor are the skillful devices of stage trickery successful antidotes to poisonous scenes. If the author is unable to remedy the fault, the safe procedure is to "star" the scene, to force it in relief rather than to try guiltily to slur over it, as this method immediately exposes its weakness. Scenes should be gone over and over until the mechanics are set and the whole play has been covered. During this period the director is not concerned with readings or interpretations of character, but the attention is centered solely on movement.

A method dear to the hearts of youthful experimentalists or to managers and producers who feel they have "an ear for direction" is to leave the mechanics and business of the play to the actors, whose mood will subconsciously guide their movements more subtly than the prearranged plans of the director, which cramp their impulse and disturb their intuition.

"Where shall I go?" asks the actor of Mr. —— on his entrance.

"Where would you like to go?" says Mr. ——.

"Well—I don't know," responds the puzzled actor.

"Don't be absurd. You have just returned from your office after a trying day. You wearily enter your own living room. Why ask me where to go? It's your home; you are thoroughly familiar with every object in the room. Go where you please." This, from Mr. ——.

The actor in an agony of indecision moves to below a table wondering what he will do in the ensemble scene soon to follow, or if he is an actor of skill and assurance, he will select a spot which will put him at a definite advantage over his confrères on their entrance. The actor instead of concentrating on the immediate scene is appalled at the prospect of the ensemble scene with ten players all moving about on impulse. The weakness in Mr. ——'s theory is that the living room is not the actor's but that of a character which he is interpreting, and he is not thoroughly familiar with it, despite the detailed word picture Mr. —— has drawn of it. It's Mr. ——'s room; he has created it with the able assistance of the author and the scenic designer. Regardless of how skillful Mr. —— may be in his descriptive style, he will find that the actor's picture of the setting is a somewhat hazy blur, limited to approximate entrances and the positions of a few pieces of workable furniture. Most actors, and good ones, too, are thoroughly amazed when they first see the completed scene. The actor may not feel like moving at all, as the business in his part specifically states that he is weary; so he decides to sit down, where he feels justified in staying until he makes an exit or until the curtain drops. What this decision may do to the other players is obvious. A director of this school, in a recent Broadway production, suddenly became conscious of an artful juvenile who had managed to plant a chair in the center of the stage and himself in it.

"Harold, what are you doing with your feet?"

"I don't know. What do you want me to do with them?" asked the outraged youth.

"Well, I don't know what I want you to do with them, but I don't want you to do that," was the helpful and withering response.

It was this same director, who, dissatisfied with an actress's reading, asked her to say "North Dakota." This she did in a variety of keys, when suddenly the director cried, "That's it. That's the tone I wish you to use throughout the play."

It is apparent that this method of direction produces performances with no variety of action, no shift of stage pictures and vitality. It entails a frightful waste of time, as the actors, finding themselves in utter confusion, spend hours of needless discussion in an attempt to find a way out. But the devastating argument against the whole theory is the fact that the method admits of the realization of a dramatic composition and ignores the limitations of the theatre. No play can be realized—can be a real experience. It is a painting, rather than a photograph, deliberately devised for definite effects, high lighted and exaggerated to suit the devices of the theatre. Poetically, it is an expression of life translated into the terms of art. As the play is written and prepared for presentation with deliberate design, in the same manner as a musical composition, the director should have the same constant control of the actor as has the conductor of the orchestra of his musicians. Imagine the havoc of this method in orchestral interpretation. It is the function of the director properly to visualize the "natural impulse" for action suggested by the scenes so that the performance will be lighted and shaded with a variety of movement and action rhythmically suited to the moods of the actors. The actor's freedom must be limited to the director's plan as a whole; this the actor cannot know, and the unlimited freedom of this method leads inevitably to the actor's overstepping his limitations. The method is illogical, leads to confusion, delays progress, and puts a burden upon the actor he never should be expected to bear.

The mechanics set, the director can best conduct rehearsals from the auditorium where he may view the play from the proper perspective and see it through the eye of the audience. Characterization, readings, tone, rhythm in playing and in line, emphasizing values, building for effects, timing of lines and business, tempo, necessary alterations in mechanics, demand his watchful eye and ear. Any attempt to set pace must be delayed until the performance begins to take form. It is now that the actor should be given his greatest freedom, being checked only when he is in error and guided in his own development as inconspicuously, yet as forcefully as possible. The director must be ready to back his suggestions or his demands with logical reasons and should have the faculty of simply and clearly explaining his ideas to the actor. No actor can execute effectually critical suggestion unless he has fully understood it. To be sure, there are actors who, in their zeal to please, get the idea before the director has expressed it, a well meaning but annoying trait. It is not enough to tell an actor to do this or to do that; he must know why the request is made. The ability to convey ideas speedily and lucidly is one of a director's most valuable qualities. The method of playing varies greatly with the style of writing; the psychologic or realistic play demands an infinitely more subtle attack than does the theatric play constructed for situations and effects. In the one, the playing is largely for the ear—in the other, for the eye. In comedy and tragedy, situations arise through character—in farces and melodrama, situations are devised for effects and have little or nothing to do with character; so quite obviously the manner of playing is greatly divergent. One is a drawing from life, and the other is a cartoon of life.

Actors are of two kinds. One accomplishes his effects through mental processes which he projects through a well planned, skillful, technical attack, while the other relies on his instincts and his emotional reactions to situations to mould his characterization. The performance of the first, while accurate and forceful, must be watched in an effort to soften the precision of its mathematical structure; the second, motivated by purely emotional urge, may go overboard. The greatest actors never have been intellectuals; they have been simple, primitive persons untroubled with inhibitions, instinctive, uninterrogative, but delicately sensitive to tremendous depths of feeling, and capable of holding the audience completely under their spell.

Actors must believe in the play. It is possible to give a moving and gripping performance of a tawdry drama if the actors' faith in it is unchallenged. The same play, performed by technicians who see its every defect, is a glaring exhibition of its weaknesses. The sincerity resulting from wholehearted faith may not be able to move mountains, but it will move audiences. The revival of the primitive and the elemental appeal in the theatre would go a long way toward retrieving an interest in it.

Assuming that the performance has reached the stage where it has taken definite form, it is time to set its pace, its rate of progress as a whole, slow or swift, depending upon the character of the play. In the psychologic or realistic play it is slower, of course, than in the artificial play of situation. It is a restless and impatient age in which we live, and rapidity of pace is almost stylized. Speed allows an audience little time for thought, and as the ear is much slower to function than the eye, many a dull play has been vitalized in this way. But the character of the action alone should determine the speed of playing.

A few days before the dress rehearsal, it is an illuminating practice to ask the ladies and gentlemen of the company to be seated and to devote quietly an hour or so to cool reflection on the seemingly unimportant events and situations occurring off stage during the action of the play, which so frequently are the causations of the effects that occur on. The actor largely concerns himself only with what he has to do while on the stage, and seldom gives a thought to what he is doing while off. He enters and exits on certain cues because it is so written in his part or because he has been directed to do so; but why he enters at that precise time or what he was doing before he enters seldom seems worthy of his consideration. Now the function of this exercise is to force the actor into a more comprehensive understanding of the character he is creating, and to ask him to pretend to play his part before his entrance and through all periods when he is off the stage. He instantly and exhaustively rounds out his performance and fully explains to himself his actions and reactions while on. Inconsistencies and discrepancies in the writing will often be exposed. Let us imagine by way of illustration that the play opens revealing a handsome library, the focal object, other than the vast rows of books in cases along the walls, a massive desk at the left of the stage. A door opens upstage and a butler enters carrying a bowl of phlox which he tenderly, almost reverently, places on the desk suggesting that it is a daily ritual. He is lost in the sheer enjoyment of the ceremony as the mistress of the house enters and surveys him with annoyance.

The Mistress: Collins, I've repeatedly told you I can't stand the sight of phlox. Take them away immediately.

Collins: But the master is so fond of them that I thought—

The Mistress: You are not here to think, Collins, but to obey. Take them away.

Collins: Very good, madame. (*Regretfully he exits with the bowl of phlox.*)

It is obvious from this scene that the play deals with people of means, that the room revealed is a favorite haunt of the Master and that the relationship between husband and wife is not altogether congenial. But there is more to it than this, for the opening scene is related to what has happened before the curtain rises and possibly to a number of scenes which follow. If the actor playing the butler is asked why he entered the door, right center, he will usually respond because he was so directed. As the response is inadequate, the director will supplement his first question by asking the actor where he came from. This usually elicits, "From off stage." It is then explained that the house is a large one, the stage setting but one room, and that it is possible that other rooms have a definite bearing on the action that unfolds in this one, and that the butler has a definite and varied relation to each section of the house. It is important that the actor know where the butler was before he entered the library. Through persistent interrogation it is finally agreed that he was in the butler's pantry, arranging the phlox in the bowl, having gathered it with his own hands in the garden, that the housekeeper reminded him that the Madame had warned him never to put phlox on the Master's desk, that a wordy quarrel ensued in which the housekeeper threatened to tell Madame of his intolerable behavior, the result of which was the realization that he stood alone in his loyalty to the Master. Not all these facts are apparent from the opening scene, but let us assume that they could be deduced from other scenes in the play. It is perceivable that the manner of the butler's entrance with these facts clearly in mind would be vastly different from one in which he merely held the thought of an entrance right center with a bowl of flowers. In this manner the questionnaire continues with every actor in the play, revealing details of "off stage" character and situation, expanding characterizations, clarifying situations, and materially augmenting the players' understanding of the story. It takes a good play to stand up under this minute examination.

With the dress rehearsal the director's task is almost complete. He is eager to perform the play before an audience to determine whether its reactions will be what he expects them to be—what he has planned they should be. He is frequently disappointed as there are scenes that do not play, comedy that fails, climaxes that are static, curtains that are flat, and innumerable other unexpected reactions. It is customary to arrange such trial performances either by booking the attraction out of town for several weeks or by giving a series of invitation performances at the theatre where the play is to be presented in New York. These are vitally essential as no director can be certain of audience response, and it is during this period that he is striving to make its reaction what he wants it to be. So, through persistent experiment in performance, changes are made in script and playing, until the proper audience reactions are assured. Especially is the tryout period necessary in farce, melodrama, and comedy. So fine is the line of distinction that melodramas have been received as farces.

Directors are accused frequently of deliberate obscurity of method, of pompous exhibitionism, of bombastic fads and fancies, of being "full of sound and fury, signifying nothing," of employing fantastic affectations and conceits with the ostensible purpose of focusing attention upon themselves. These accusations usually come from actors who desire completely to fill the public eye and seldom from managers or critics who are profoundly impressed by them. There is in business and in most professions what is called "the professional manner," a mode of personal expression designed artfully and profoundly to impress the world with the importance of one's occupation; it is not necessarily damning to one's capacity or competence; it is merely a form of salesmanship; but it requires the greatest perspicacity in its use. It can make one ridiculous.

The director who tells the actor, "You are giving it to me green and I've told you I want it yellow," or the one who asks for "pear-shaped tones" or he who sits with his head buried in his hands while an actor makes repeated entrances through a door, shouting, "I don't feel you. Do it again," or the one who asks the company to stand facing a stage wall with heads bowed and eyes closed for five minutes' concentration, or he who asks the actor to stroke a piece of velvet before making an entrance, or the one who answers every question with, "What do you think, darling?" or he who telephones his directions to the stage manager from a complicated tower rising from the center of the auditorium—these gentlemen have lost their perspicacity; they have become comedians.

Despite the fact that every American theatre-goer is a con-

scious critic, he has vague and erroneous views of the function
of a stage director. Because he is unseen and unheard, he becomes unimportant and uninteresting. If the play is well
directed, the theatre-goer will not think of him, as good
direction never obtrudes itself any more than good acting
becomes deliberately conspicuous. If the direction is bad, the
audience will sense it; if it is good, the audience will have no
apprehension of it at all. Fine direction is forceful and compelling, seemingly intuitive, never prominent.

Plays of expansive atmospheric background, spectacular in
character, permitting large casts and striking scenery are
looked upon as directors' holidays. A firm discrimination to
preserve balance and proportion is necessary to prevent the
director from losing himself and his play in a welter of
atmospheric verisimilitude; the temptation to "star one's
self" is too great to be resisted, and very frequently, fine,
intimate, and delicate plays have been buried in the director's
atmospheric ingenuities. It is only on rare occasions that a
play demanding stylization permits the hand of the director
to be seen consciously at work.

Great plays make great directors just as great parts make
great actors; or possibly a better way of putting it, great plays
make successful directors, as great parts make successful actors.
The skill of the director is shown when he gives a bad or
commonplace play the attributes of a good or distinctive one.
Few experienced and intelligent theatre-goers, including the
expert critics of the press, are able to separate the technical
and artistic skill of performance from the quality of the material which makes up the play. A prominent producer has
said that the percentage of success is fifty per cent play and
fifty per cent skill in performance. This is refuted in the light
of the great number of successful amateur and semi-profes-
sional performances, whose play committees invariably have

the acumen to select fine plays. Good plays are easy to stage because they progress psychologically through proper motivations, and it would take a bad director indeed who could stifle this progression. A man with creative imagination, a cultural background—although it is said that men with inhibitions more often reach the truth—good taste, dramatic instinct, and a thorough mastery of the technique of play production should make a skillful stage director. He is the vigilant watch dog of the theatre.

MY METHOD OF DIRECTING

by

BERTRAM HARRISON

During the past few years Bertram Harrison has directed nearly fifty successful productions in New York, several of which have been presented under his direction at the Garrick and Savoy Theatres in London. For several seasons he devoted his attention to comedies and farce comedies. He has also directed a number of musical comedies, and recently has done dialogue direction for several motion pictures. Preceding his personal direction Mr. Harrison spent ten years with Henry Miller, who was for many years not only one of America's foremost stars but also an active producing manager and director.

With Jessie Bonstell as co-director he organized the first Municipal company in America at Northampton, Massachusetts, and operated it for the first five years of its existence.

Among the numerous productions that he has directed are the following: *The Best People; Grounds for Divorce; Heavy Traffic; Partners Again; Little Women; The Love Child; The Masked Woman; Lawful Larceny; The Man's Name; Ladies' Night; The Girl in the Limousine; Up in Mabel's Room; No More Blondes; Tumble Inn; Betty Lee; Hold Everything; Treasure Girl;* and *Singin' the Blues.*

He has also acted as co-director on dialogue for the motion pictures: *The Laughing Lady; The Big Pond;* and *Fast and Loose.*

MY METHOD OF DIRECTING

by

Bertram Harrison

THE matter of stage direction is so interwoven with details of production, selection of artists, and decisions as to "sympathetic" theatres that I find it necessary to think for a moment of the best way to attack the subject.

Perhaps the solution would be to ask the reader to visit and accompany me through a production period, share with me the depressions and optimisms of the different stages of the work up to the fall of the curtain on a first night. It's a lot of fun, a lot of hard work and satisfaction—this staging of plays. Frankly, just how hard the work is depends on the temperament of the director and his honesty. By honesty I mean that I believe the principal qualification for successful directing is satisfaction in one's material. In several years' experience in the theatre I have never accomplished work that was gratifying to myself unless I was in complete sympathy with the material to be produced. The question of judgment does not enter into the matter. A number of good producers have produced bad plays. If a director believes in his material, he will usually do a good job of the staging; and should the play fail, he will get his reward in the hereafter for at least having been honest.

I believe in a healthy realization of one's limitations and the inadvisability of accepting an offer, because of exceptional auspices, when the subject matter is beyond one's knowledge. I have, I will admit, on one or two occasions been persuaded to stage a play that I did not believe in, but never without first having expressed my lack of faith in the outcome, and even though there has resulted a measure of success, I have never gained any personal satisfaction in the result.

Well, it is time that the manuscript should be in our hands for reading. Here it is now, by grace of a Western Union boy, and accompanied by a note from the producer, who has assured us over the telephone that he is still under the spell of its greatness. All right, we've read it, like it, and see ourselves doing it. Yes—again over the telephone—four o'clock will do very nicely to meet the author, to smile at and size up each other. Having reached the producer's office and being a nice person, I am sure you won't mind if after a brief introduction I leave you alone in a corner to listen to the discussion.

I would like to pause for a moment to remark that the conditions under which the play is to be produced affect, in quite some measure, the amount of preliminary work to be done. If the producer be an important manager, he will have very definite ideas as to the cast, in fact may have some artists under contract whom he desires to exploit. If the manager is one whose judgment has been proved good, the work and responsibility of the director are considerably lightened. The condition of using people who are under contract usually necessitates some readjustment of the manuscript on the part of the author.

Occasionally a director is offered a play by an enthusiastic newcomer in the theatre, who is more than willing to leave all matters of selection of cast to the director and the author. This means more responsibility but also greater freedom, and the responsibility can be lightened by insisting that the manager shall express his opinion freely during the early stages of rehearsals and agree or disagree with the cast selections.

A sense of humor and much patience are required frequently when a producer has definite ideas as to casting. One producer for whom I have staged many successful comedies has an unshakable belief in the value of youth. In the main he is right, but it means long hours of rehearsing to obtain results from glittering but inexperienced graduates from the Follies, in parts that the average young actors could handle easily. Such selections are frequently justified in literally the "long run," but I have been exasperated at times by seeing a charming young graduate from musical comedy cast for the part of a comfortable middle-aged housekeeper.

Let us assume that this is a production with a Wall Street backing and a consequent feeling on the part of the producer that he is best off by leaving everything to the author and the director. The first joyous reaction of having one's own way is mitigated by a slightly bereft feeling at the lack of the usual managerial suggestions or decisions. However, if one is honest and truly more concerned in the successful presentation of the play than in the financial recompense, the difficulties are not overwhelming.

Well, come on, let's go! Our conference is over, and together with the author we leave the office. Full of enthusiasm we walk to the elevator exchanging brief suggestions and addresses with an appointment for a meeting the following day and a promise on our part that we will have read the manuscript again over night. We rather like this author, and our brief talk has told me that he will be helpful in a practical way, and that he is not one of those writers who is so tied up with magazine work that he will only be able to drop in occasionally at rehearsals to remark, "You don't need me, do you?"

Having now reached the point of rereading the manuscript from a producing standpoint, I'll part company with you, go home, and after dinner send the family off to the theatre so that I may concentrate on my reading without the usual bridge and radio distractions of the average evening.

I believe implicitly in a very complete study of the script. An uncertain director is apt to result in a confused cast. A lack of understanding of his material on the director's part inevitably invites suggestions from the members of the company, and nothing is more contagious than a desire to be helpful—and nothing more upsetting. I do not mean by this that a director should be arbitrarily set on stage business and character interpretation. I believe he should have an open mind as to the playing of certain scenes for the reason that an accomplished artist should never be hampered or forced to play in a manner foreign to his nature and feeling. The director, however, who has made a thorough study of the play is in a position to advise the actor and to give him adequate reasons for his beliefs. He must certainly have a definite idea of how the play should come across in its entirety, and of the mental attitudes of the characters toward each other and to the situations of the play. Quite often the actor, after a sensible discussion of a scene that has perhaps bothered him, can bring something to the director that is very definitely helpful. Should the director and the artist come to a deadlock with the latter either unable or unwilling to carry out the director's ideas, then it is better for all concerned to make a change in the casting of the part. A director who allows himself to be overruled in his final convictions is at sea, unable to control the other members of the cast, and obviously unable to give a proper interpretation to the play.

It is also very necessary for the director to have a clear mind on two definite matters. One, the physical positions of the characters on the stage, and the other, a general idea of the tempo and its variations according to the writing of the manuscript.

Positions should be studied in advance so that a tiresome repetition of playing may be avoided. A change of the positions of the characters and background is a relief to the audience and also helps to create a variety of stage business. The laying out of business—by that I mean natural physical reactions and the handling of properties—is particularly important with a play in which the action takes place in one setting. The matter of tempo is similarly important in that a fast or slow delivery of lines maintained for too long a time becomes tiresome. The experienced author usually understands this and constructs his play so that scenes are of varied tempo and afford contrasting time in the playing.

The preparatory work on the part of the director includes the laying out of the furniture and the planning of the entrances and exits. He will naturally have been in consultation with the scene designer. Furniture should be so arranged that the characters are gracefully and advantageously placed for the playing of their scenes. Where a couch is used, it should be so situated that two characters seated thereon are both well in line of sight of the audience. I dislike a setting that is cluttered with unnecessary furniture, but I do like, and think very essential to the natural playing of a scene, little properties placed with discretion and good taste about a room so that the artists are provided with things to handle as one does in real life.

A magazine may, even during an intensely dramatic scene, be of inestimable value in helping one of the people concerned to appear unconcerned. A lighted cigarette may be used advantageously to express either complete ease or intense nervousness.

In the design of a stage setting, windows are to be considered carefully. As a general rule a window does not provide a good background. The outside perspective is apt to be distracting; and when a window is placed in a back wall, little use can be made of it legitimately for the lighting of faces. A stage setting is usually ten or twelve feet in depth. A scene of any length is seldom played at the back of the stage. A good old rule of the theatre is that the nearer one can be in the foreground, the better. This is particularly true with comedy. There are, of course, exceptions to this rule regarding background lighting, but my preference is for side lighting effect. If the time of playing be at night, lamps and wall brackets should be so placed that the supplementary light coming from spotlights would seem to be the result of the fixture lighting.

I am not in favor of settings that are more than twelve feet in depth, particularly when entrances are played in the back wall. When a dramatic scene is concluded, it is usually with the characters well in the foreground; and should the scene be followed by the exit of one of the characters, a walk to the exit is apt to destroy the effect of the scene.

There are naturally many physical conditions to be considered in the dressing of a stage setting. The height of chairs and couches is most important. It is impossible for the actor of average height to rise from a low seat gracefully. Should an armchair be used and the business of a scene call for one of the participants to be seated at some time on one of the arms, care must be taken that it is so constructed that he may do so comfortably and with no feeling of uncertainty and self-consciousness.

Floor covering is very important. If a hard wood floor effect be desired, care should be taken that rugs are so placed that the noise of heels is not distracting in scenes where concentration of the audience is required. Rubber heels can be used by the men to overcome the sound but not by the women.

I am not a believer in exterior settings and try to avoid them when possible. To me they are seldom convincing. If a garden setting be essential for the action of the play, I like to make it as intimate as possible by backgrounding the characters with a high hedge, the dark green of which provides a restful and effective backing for the characters, and gives the feeling of seclusion that is so essential to the playing of scenes of a confidential nature. When it is necessary to use an exterior, I always, if possible, set the time of the action at night as the moonlight effects soften the harsh material that must be used for the representation of foliage.

If I seem to have encroached too much on the scenery department of producing, it is only because stage settings and acting are interdependent.

I would like to illustrate this with an experience I had a few years ago when I was producing one of the successful Avery Hopwood farces. (As a rule, farce comedy is one of two forms, a case of mistaken identity or a chase. I will mention *Charley's Aunt* as one of the former. The chase variety is one in which the action is concerned with the finding of a missing article that must be recovered in a certain time to avoid serio-comedy disaster.) In the play to which I refer, the final act was laid in the garden of an elaborate estate on Long Island. With all of the farce comedies produced by the manager of this particular one, the many successes written by the author, and the several that I had directed, we did not realize until the opening performance that a chase farce could not be played convincingly in an exterior setting. A great part of the action of any farce consists of the "just at the right moment" escape of one character from another. Let us say that one of the cast must get out of a room hastily. He starts for a door, hears the voice of someone approaching from the other side. He starts for another door and sees the handle turn. He rushes to a French window, and just as he reaches it, voices come from the garden. There is nothing left for him to do but to hide in a grandfather's clock. In the exterior setting that was provided for the play I mentioned, we had planned on the use of shrubbery, gate posts, and the like for hiding places. The consequence was that the situations were completely lacking in conviction. The reaction of the audience was one of wonderment that the character did not rush away from the scene of danger. Eventually we were forced to discard the effective out-of-doors setting and take the cast back to the interior of the house.

With this second reading of the play ideas begin to formulate for casting. Some years ago I compiled a casting book with divisional lists of stars, featured players, character, and juvenile people. This book I keep up-to-date by notes of newcomers to the theatre and of recent performances and the availability of players.

Also, when I have seen or heard of actors who have made favorable impressions in small parts I make a memorandum of their performances, the plays and their dates of production. I make it a rule to read through this book on the occasion of each new production with which I may be concerned. In this way I frequently realize that some artist whom I might not otherwise have thought of would bring an unsuspected value to a part in the play. Having made a list of several names for each part, I then arrange to meet the persons either directly or through one of the recognized agents.

I give the more important people to be engaged a brief outline of the play and of their particular part, and being assured of their interest I provide them with the manuscript requesting that I hear from them on the following day regarding their reaction. The principal characters should be cast first, by the way, so that when it comes to engaging the less important people, a proper contrast of personalities is assured. It would be manifestly unwise to have all the women in the cast red haired.

Salaries are usually discussed only in an informal way and then only so that I may advise the producer what his salary expense may be. The producer usually engages a business manager whose duty is to attend to the matter of salary adjustments and contracts. There are of course many matters of contract details, such as a guarantee of a certain number of weeks' employment, and precedence in advertising matter. The Actors' Equity Association takes excellent care of many contract details of the minor members of a company and affords them ample protection in salary advances and other ways.

The Equity contract permits four weeks of rehearsal for a dramatic production and five for a musical comedy. Personally, unless a play presents unusual difficulties in the technical departments, I prefer to rehearse only three weeks. I have frequently found that a company becomes stale with a fourth week, and some enthusiasm has evaporated. Also I believe the knowledge that a play is to have only three weeks of rehearsal is an incentive to intensive and concentrated work. There is further a material advantage in the three weeks' arrangement in that the producer is thereby allowed a week's cessation of playing without salaries, should cast or manuscript changes have been found necessary after the opening of the play.

I am not a believer in the directing method that has developed in the past few years of devoting the first week of rehearsals entirely to a series of readings of the play. I believe certainly that a comprehensive knowledge of the manuscript in its entirety is very necessary, and I make it a rule to devote time to at least two readings. I never read a manuscript to a company myself, and unless the author is gifted with a musical power of expression and a sense of characterization, I prefer that he should not read his play to the company. It requires about two hours to read the average manuscript, and listening attentively to one voice for that period of time requires too much sustained concentration.

I prefer to have typed a careful description of each character and its relationship to the other characters. These descriptions I write myself and check carefully with the author to be sure that we are in complete accord. Each member of the cast is given his or her description before the reading of the play. A complete list of the characters is read to the company, and the name of the artist who has been selected for each part is mentioned. Having assembled the company, given out the parts, requested that the cleaning women who are working in the front of the theatre—that is, in the auditorium—proceed as quietly as possible, I then read the description of the setting so that the cast may have something of the feeling of place in which the action occurs. The lines are then read by the members of the cast with a realization, of course, on the part of the director that he can expect only a semblance of characterization and practically nothing in the way of tempo.

The Equity contract permits of seven days' probationary rehearsing, which I have always found to be a generous allowance. The careful description of each part and an explanation of any character quality that may seem obscure is of great help to the actor, and in turn gives the director the right to expect a semblance of the actor's portrayal and qualification for the part within two or three days after rehearsals have started. I am usually satisfied by that time as to individual suitability. I have always found that actors are appreciative of an early decision as to their retention. Where there are parts—or rather characters—that do not appear until late in the play, I usually postpone their engagement until a day or so before rehearsals of their scenes commence. Otherwise after the first and second readings of the manuscript those who are playing only in the latter part of the play are idle for ten days or more, and may, when the director reaches their scenes, prove to be unsuited to the parts, or experience disappointment through changes that may have developed as necessary during the early period. Each party being contractually bound, the arrangement may very well work out as a hardship to either or both of the parties. Should there be a reason for making all the engagements before starting rehearsals or should a producer have done so without giving thought to the matter, I then appoint a day toward the end of the first working week for a rehearsal of those latter-part-of-the-play scenes.

Now as to my method of directing. I have always made it entirely flexible and dependent on the quality of the play to be directed and the personalities and temperaments of the principal players. Drama depends to such a great extent on the emotion of the characters that its development lies in the absorption of the character and the acquisition of the lines to be spoken. I have worked with certain stars who at the end of two weeks are still stumbling in their line delivery, but have at the same time inspired confidence in an ultimately fine performance. It would be obviously unfair to demand arbitrarily that a sensitive temperament—as in the case of an artist who in years of experience in the theatre has developed a method of gradual development and acquisition of a character—commit to memory words as words.

I am usually satisfied if by the commencement of the final week of rehearsals all parts or manuscripts have been discarded by the actors, and allowing for a day or so of line hesitancy, I feel confident of a satisfactory result by the end of the third week.

My experience in the theatre has been so varied that I have found it necessary to employ different methods for different plays. I have directed many farces and comedies. Farces being quick moving in action and delivery of lines require the utmost security of line delivery. Being built primarily for laughing purposes, they depend greatly on audience reaction. Two or three performances of a farce before responsive audiences do more than an additional week of rehearsing. For this reason I always ask for a quick study and complete security of delivery by the end of the second week of rehearsing. In fact I like to be ready at that time to feel that the company could give a fair performance if it should be necessary. The third week I then devote entirely to approximating laugh lines and to rehearsing the entrances and exits that are so important in the average farce. On an opening night, which with farce should be before an out of town assemblage or if in New York before an invited and non-professional audience, I instruct the actors not to wait for laughs that we are uncertain of, but to keep the pace going. After a first performance I have a fairly good knowledge of what the important laughs are and how the comedy situations are to be humored.

The first two weeks of rehearsals will doubtless prove tiresome to the non-professional visitor; so I will not blame you if I find that you are slipping out of the theatre now and then for a cigarette with a whispered "I must telephone and explain that I'll be a little late coming home." It is a tiresome period; so let us jump beyond the days of rehearsing scenes over and over again and come down to the commencement of the third week. I like, when it seems safe to do so, to give the members of a cast Sundays for study without rehearsal restrictions. I usually exact a promise of intensive home study and intimate that the question of evening rehearsals will depend during the final week entirely on the progress that has been made by the actor himself at home. The getting away from the theatre is, too, a good thing for the director, who, if he is wise, spends the day playing golf or indulging in whatever may be his favorite pastime. On the Monday of the final week I look for a commencement of a nervous tension that is born of the fact that in just one week the curtain will be rising on the first performance. With an admonition that I expect everyone to stand by, take up cues and entrances, we start rehearsal. Something has happened!! The actors have begun to live their parts. The scenes begin to grip. The leading woman suddenly plays the big scene which she has heretofore garbled. The author, who has been giving signs of suicidal tendencies, rushes over to the director; the manager, who has been sitting at the back of the house, nods enthusiastically. Even the cleaning "ladies" in the balcony have stopped work and stand in their various places among the rows of seats looking meditatively at the stage.

So far so good. But now commences real work. There is much to do. Timing principally. The big scene sounds fine, but don't let us forget that we are rehearsing in a large theatre, and we are booked for an intimate house. Voice quality must be adjusted. There are many matters that a director realizes must be taken care of in the last week, with a good allowance made for the approaching first rehearsal with scenery and properties. No matter how carefully the settings have been described, there is always someone who will say, "Oh, is that where the door is? I thought it was farther over." With the average play I like to have at least one good mechanical rehearsal of the production so that the company may become completely at home in the settings, and in the handling of properties, and accustomed to the change of feeling that accompanies a completely lighted setting after the period of rehearsing on a bare stage with only a dim overhead light. With the accomplishment of this private rehearsal, we are ready for the final dress rehearsal and the attending comments, favorable or otherwise, that come from invited friends. And this is when the director must keep his head. Not only must he listen to—and consider—the friendly suggestions that are made directly to him, but he must as well be prepared for the author's last minute reactions and give consideration to the nervous manager's list of suggestions jotted down on the backs of envelopes as they have been given to him by well wishers. In the case of an out of town opening another dress rehearsal is held on the Sunday night before the first performance. This is largely to see that the local stage hands in the various departments handle the scenery, lights, and properties smoothly. I prefer on the day of the opening to work the company as little as possible. Should the rehearsal of the previous night last into the small hours, I call them at two in the afternoon for a quick line rehearsal. I have a very definite attitude toward a first performance in New York, and even out of town I think it wise for the members of the cast to feel that their best efforts are expected. Naturally the director expects this for the important opening in town, and the actors know themselves that the length of the engagement depends upon the successful New York opening; so that feeling is automatically taken care of. Out of town there is perhaps an attitude that after all this is not the performance on which they will be judged, and consequently there may be a feeling that if something should go wrong—should a line be missed—everything will be smoothed out during the week.

On the opening night in New York I make it a point to call at each dressing room and chat briefly with the members

of the cast, talk of the general news of the day, and assure
the more nervous members that if they will only give half as
good a performance as they did on the preceding Saturday
night in Atlantic City, the play is sure of running the rest of
the season. It is, I think, the duty of the stage director to stand
by during the first performance. Not that he can do anything
in regard to the actual performance after the curtain has
risen, but should anything go wrong, he can be of great help
to the actor affected by assuring him that the matter is trivial.
I remember that on the opening night of *Berkeley Square* at
the Lyceum Theatre one very excellent actor lost his lines
completely for a moment in the first scene. When he came off
the stage he was trembling, and even under his make-up I
could see that his face was white. He stumbled over to me
and said, "Wasn't that dreadful? I have never done anything
like it before." I asked him what he meant, and when he spoke
of having lost his lines, I said, "Why I thought you paused
purposely. It was very effective." I believe this served to restore his confidence. At all events, the remainder of his performance was as secure and steady as one could wish. I did
not, by the way, direct *Berkeley Square* but was interested in
its successful opening as I was under contract at the time to
Gilbert Miller, who produced it. My friend, Marc Connelly,
did a magnificent job of the direction. I recall our mutual
admiration on the opening performance for the star, Leslie
Howard, who was the victim of one of those first night accidents. A chair which should have been placed on the stage
for a very important love scene was overlooked. There was
not the least indication on his part that he had ever played
the scene other than in a standing position, and his quick readjustment of business, which did not in the least affect his
tender and charming feeling in the scene, was one of the most
admirable exhibitions of self-control I have witnessed in the

theatre. Also, he abstained from any show of quite justifiable temperament when he made his exit.

Such accidents are frequently tragic in their results on first nights, and I must admit that sometimes I have a feeling that I have no right in the theatre as I have an inordinate delight in seeing the unexpected happen. I do not, of course, mean where it may affect a play materially, but in cases where it perhaps amuses an audience at the momentary expense of the actor. Some years ago I staged a production for William A. Brady, called *Carnival*, written by Compton Mackenzie. The third act setting of the play was a dreary kitchen in a Cornish farmhouse. As the setting stood for both the third and fourth acts, I realized that its drabness would have a depressing effect on the audience. The people whose home was represented would hardly have employed an interior decorator, but I felt that an accidental warmth was advisable and could be obtained by the use of copper cooking utensils on a rack above the huge kitchen stove. The stove itself had been so constructed that a red light placed inside would gleam naturally through the openings. There was a long window at the back, and I had the property department provide about a dozen pots of geraniums for the window ledge. At the first performance in Toronto I remained on the stage as there were innumerable light cues to be watched. The second night, however, I saw the play from the front of the theatre. When the curtain rose on the third act, everything was apparently in place. Outside of the window the snow was falling, the wind was howling, the rosy light of a substantial fire gleamed through the chinks of the stove, and on top of it were—twelve pots of geraniums. My realization that they must remain there for three quarters of an hour, and my anticipation of the effect on Miss Grace George when she caught sight of them, remains one of the joys of my experience in the theatre.

I like to do at least one musical comedy a year—preferably
in the spring when one is apt to be a little "mad" anyway.
Almost anything is permissible in a musical comedy. If the
builder hasn't provided a door where one was expected, it is
perfectly easy to bring the chorus ensemble on through a fireplace without tiresome comments from an audience.

Will I be forgiven if I tell one more amusing experience,
one which is connected with the presentation of a musical production? The last act took place in a garden setting. It was in
the days when the general formula for musical comedies consisted of starting in a boarding house in Hoboken and ending
up in Versailles. The first part of the act was devoted to a fancy
dress party with every member of the cast, including the
members of the chorus, appearing as an individual character.
Henry the Eighth, Adam and Eve, the Knave of Hearts, The
Spirit of Times Square, and many others. At a certain point
the little star of the company—a delightful dancer and a
charming actress—appeared at the head of a flight of stairs and
floating down did a beautiful ballet number. At its conclusion
the company drifted off the stage leaving the star to play a
final love scene with the young plumber to whom she was
engaged. We found that some device was necessary to help
the exit of the sixty-odd guests. Colonel Henry W. Savage,
the producer, had the inspiration of bringing down from above
a quantity of balloons. Our second out of town performance
happened to be in Bridgeport, Connecticut. For an hour before the performance we all joined forces in blowing up the
balloons that had arrived on order from New York. The inflated balloons were then placed in a large cloth so looped that
it provided a container that stretched the full width of the
stage above the garden. At a given cue one side of the cloth
was released, and down floated the balloons. Zelda Sears,
who wrote the "book" of the comedy, had a further inspira-

tion and suggested that, as they left the stage, the members of the company should bat the balloons out into the auditorium. The consequence was that the final love scene was performed to an accompaniment of aerial football played by the front row members of the audience, who were delighted to enter into the proceedings.

For the evening performance we decided that the projection of the balloons into the auditorium should be eliminated. Still breathless from our pre-matinee inflation efforts, we left the property man to take care of the supply for the evening performance. Being a conscientious property man, he set to work immediately after the matinee to inflate the hundred or so toys, placed them in the hanging cloth, and went home to recover as best he could from his solo effort. That evening Miss Sears and I sat together in the audience to watch the performance. At the finish of the dance the guests of the party applauded; so did the audience, and down came three barrels of what appeared to be garbage. The balloons had all deflated, and the stage was littered with green peppers, banana and tomato skins.

Not the least of the pleasurable by-products of stage direction is the contact with many interesting people—writers, artists, and musicians. I recall clearly my interest in the books of adventure by Richard Harding Davis. He was the author of one of the plays produced by Henry Miller, with whom I had all my early training in the theatre. It was indeed a thrill to be invited to visit him at his home in Marion, Massachusetts. I remember taking a walk with him one day on the beach of his property, accompanied by his eighteen dogs, and his remark that they had eighteen different ways of being bad. William Vaughn Moody, whose *The Great Divide* will always be to me one of the great American plays, was a most interesting associate during the production of the play. Mr.

Moody was, of course, a purist as far as English was concerned, and Mr. Miller, while he had the greatest respect for an author's writing, had not a particular capacity for a quick study of lines. Engrossed with production details as well as with the learning of his part, he, for the first two weeks of rehearsals, only approximated the lines. Mr. Moody's kindly but constant interruptions regarding the exact wording of speeches proved irksome to Mr. Miller. One day he confided to me that it would be impossible for him to get the production open on scheduled time unless Mr. Moody were "disposed" of. Together we devised a scheme to get him away by suggesting the importance of obtaining authentic properties used in the play. The action being laid in Arizona called for many western properties, Navajo blankets, pottery, *et cetera*. Mr. Moody, impressed with the value of having only the correct appurtenances, offered to go to Albuquerque to obtain them. When he returned, we had arrived at the dress rehearsal stage of the production. On unpacking the two immense cases he had brought back with him, he found that a Mexican saddle he had purchased had been omitted. In great consternation he reported this to me. "Don't worry," I told him, and we jumped into a cab and drove to a shop known as The Indians' Exhibit Company. One look about the place showed him that everything he had acquired in New Mexico could have been obtained in New York. He said nothing, but his quiet look of amusement told me that in a second he had realized the trick that had been played on him.

I believe I left you on the stage waiting for me while I made my round of the various dressing rooms. The half hour warning of the rise of the curtain has been called by the stage manager or his assistant, then the fifteen minute-call, and at last "first act—everybody ready." We either go to the front of the house or decide to stay within call, and stroll up and down the street near the stage door concealing as best we can our nervousness. If the play is a comedy and the laughs from the audience begin to grow, we are lured back to the stage to listen. Good or bad as the reaction may be, we reassure the company at the fall of each curtain that all is well. If the play is truly going with good effect, we mean what we say, and if it isn't, surely the reassurance does no harm. The final curtain falls. The friends and well wishers who have been in the audience begin to crowd the stage and dressing rooms, and we wend our way out into the night. Shall we go somewhere and talk the evening over? Perhaps we may even decide to stay up and see what the morning papers have to say —I mean about the play, of course.

MY METHOD OF DIRECTING

by

PRIESTLY MORRISON

Priestly Morrison has been active as a director of New York productions since 1917; but it was in 1894 that he entered the theatre as an actor. For eight or ten years he devoted the major part of his time to acting with an occasional engagement as a director. Before 1917, Mr. Morrison directed mostly in stock companies which included New York (at the Murray Hill and the Fifth Avenue Theatres), Chicago (Civic Repertory), Cincinnati, San Francisco, Boston, Kansas City, Atlanta, Washington, Cleveland, Indianapolis, New Haven, Los Angeles, Columbus, Milwaukee, and Des Moines. He spent two seasons, 1908–10, in Australia and New Zealand, as the general stage director for the J. C. Williamson interests.

The following are some of the better known plays that he has directed: *Mamma's Affair*; *Fascinating Widow*; *Queen Victoria*; *The Piker*; *Easy Come, Easy Go*; *The Jealous Moon*; *Earl Carroll Vanities*; *Nightie Night*; *Like a King*; *Alias, the Deacon*; *The Barker*; *One Man's Woman*; *Smilin' Through*; *Thumbs Down*; *Courage*; *Best Years*; and *All the King's Men*.

MY METHOD OF DIRECTING

by

PRIESTLY MORRISON

To THOSE who are even slightly familiar with the routine of the theatre back of the curtain-line, it may appear that I have included in this chapter details of procedure which are so manifestly matters of course that mention of them would seem to be unnecessary; but in view of the fact that the apparently obvious things are so often overlooked and neglected, I have made a point of calling attention to some of these plainly visible but unobserved pitfalls that beset the path of the stage director.

It is not to be inferred that the method of stage directing hereinafter outlined is claimed to be the *best* method, but it is the one I have used for a number of years—the gradual development of practice adopted after many and devious experiments along many and devious lines—and I have found it to be the best method for me.

From the viewpoint of the stage director, the theoretical ideal in play production contemplates first, a complete and perfect play, and next, a company of actors of superlative talent and unsurpassable suitability to their respective rôles. In practice, however, only a reasonable approximation of such perfection can be hoped for, or realized; for almost certainly the play will need more or less revision and change, and a few, perhaps many, of the actors will fall short of the requirements of their rôles; in view of all of which it will be rightly surmised that the director will frequently find it expedient and necessary to "temper the wind to the shorn lamb."

These and countless other reasons combine to make the staging of a play a task which involves an almost unbelievable amount of careful planning and painstaking effort, not the least of which is the extensive preparatory work on the play prior to the commencement of rehearsals, the necessity for which cannot be too heavily stressed. It might seem that the need for this work is so self-evident and imperative that it would never be disregarded, but it is a regrettable fact that all too many of the plays produced today receive absurdly insufficient preparation.

Times without number a play which possesses real merit and many of the potential elements of success, is hastened into rehearsal because, perhaps, of its fancied "up-to-the-minute" timeliness, or because of the over-anxiety of its sponsors to reap the harvest of commercial profits. It may be, as is usually the case, that some part of the play, a scene or perhaps an entire act, is admittedly inadequate, lacking in interest or effectiveness, and painfully in need of careful and well-considered revision, despite which it is incontinently rushed toward production, in the hope that sometime during the rehearsal period the author (or the director) will be divinely inspired to reconstruct and rewrite the inferior portions of the play, to rectify all errors of commission and omission, and thus to transform imperfection into perfection. Infrequently is this desired objective achieved, for more often than not the quality of this hurried work unmistakably demonstrates that that exalting, creative urge which, for want of a better name, we call inspiration, is a timid, elusive Muse and has refused to answer "Here!" when paged, with the sadly frequent result of failure for a play which, with more careful and intelligent preparation, might well have scored a success.

I am by no means alone in the opinion that this quality of inspiration is seldom, if ever, manifested in any work of art except at the time when it is conceived and born in the mind of its creator. An artist's original idea of a great work may have been (or *must* have been) highly inspirational, but in the operation of the various processes necessary to transmute that mental concept into tangible, discernible form, so that it may be apprehended and appreciated by others, there can be but little, if anything at all, of inspiration. The actual mental and physical work of material construction demands, in most instances, extensive research and study, deep concentration, patient and sometimes laborious experimentation, added to all of which it requires the unceasing application of that quality named in Carlyle's oft-quoted definition of genius: "The transcendent capacity of taking trouble."

The stage director, in his first reading of the play, should assume a mental attitude which approximates, as nearly as may be, that of the prospective audience. No sense of technical criticism should be permitted to obscure his recognition and appreciation of whatever dramatic or narrative value the work may possess. I find it a good rule to defer reading the author's description of his characters, until after the first reading of the play; the information is better secured in the way in which it must be conveyed to the audience—that is, from the dialogue of the characters themselves, by which the story of the play is developed.

The first reading should be unhurried but rapid and continuous, and the impressions gained therefrom should be deliberately fixed in the mind so that they may be remembered and considered in the later stages of rehearsal and production.

Further readings, many of them, are now in order for the purpose of gaining a comprehensive familiarity with the various phases of the play's form and structure; the plot and story; the intent and purpose; the motivation, cause, and effect; the sequence, progress, plausibility, and consistency.

The people of the play are then considered, first, one by one, in order to note their individual characteristics; then collectively, to determine their relation to one another, their development, and their bearing on the story.

At all times during the preparation of a play for rehearsal and production there should be close and understanding contact between author and stage director, but at this period such contact is particularly to be desired, for if structural or otherwise important changes in the play are necessary, now is the time when such necessity is likely to be discovered. With author and director in congenial accord, such changes can be intelligently discussed, agreed upon, and made, with a minimum of friction and delay.

It will be understood, of course, that much of the preparatory work mentioned herein will be, in the very nature of things, of a tentative character, and this fact should be borne in mind while the work is being done, and ample elasticity provided for change and revision.

Especial care should be taken to free the text from ambiguities and contradictions of any and all kinds; to make clear to the fullest extent any passages which may seem to be obscure or perplexing; to observe duly the element of climax by arranging the dialogue to the best advantage, not only as to its meaning, but with a view to its relative dramatic importance. For instance, such a sentence as:

"No! No! a thousand times *no*, I say."

will be changed so that the strongest and most effectual emphasis will fall upon the last word:

"No! No! I say, a thousand times *no*."

This matter might seem to be one best left to the author

and his climactic conscience, but the director will do well to give it his serious consideration.

One of the more important of the preliminary processes is that of devising or creating that part of the necessary stage business of the play which the author has not already specifically designated in the text. By stage business is meant the physical motions and actions of the characters, such as walking, sitting, lighting a cigar, shaking hands, fencing, fighting, dancing, *ad infinitum*. These actions are sometimes as essential to the play as the dialogue itself, but often their function is merely to emphasize or to amplify the spoken word. The ingenuity and resourcefulness which the stage director brings to this work serve in some respects as a standard of measurement of his ability and artistry.

With the ground plan (of which more hereafter) close at hand for ready reference, the director will scan the manuscript many times, line by line, in order to arrange the grouping of the characters, their movements and actions, the time and place of each entrance and exit; to fix upon the specific cues for the mechanical effects, light changes, music, and all the other minutiae of stage business down to the smallest detail; and finally to coördinate all these features so that they will take place at the time and in the manner most to be desired for pictorial and dramatic effect.

Following is a page of play-manuscript,[1] typical of the above mentioned treatment.

(A marginal notation, a diagram, or a descriptive mark or symbol should be set down in the manuscript to indicate and/or explain all of these various items of stage business, except those which are of very little importance or are virtually automatic in character.)

[1] Taken from *Strange Gods*.

READY
LIGHTS

Jason: (*Casts a quick look at* ZILLAH, *then hangs his head and plucks at* SAM's *sleeve*)

Sam: Well, what it is?

Jason: Sam, jest lem'me go and put on my shoes; I won't be but a jiffy.

Sam: Them shoes! God's mercy, ain't yuh run around yere barefoot all yore life—cep' Sundays fer church? Shoes!

Mrs. W.: (*Crosses to* ZILLAH *who rises to meet her*) Wah'd I tell yuh? The boy's clean crazy.

Jason: Miz' Ca'inton, haven't you tole me nevah to appeah befo' ladies in mah bare feet?

Zillah: I may have, Jason, but it doesn't matter now. Answer your brother.

Sam: Straighten up lak a man and look at me. Hold on yere— what's that yore hidin' behin' yore back?

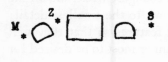

Jason: None o' yore buz'ness.

Sam: I'll soon make it my business. Hand it yere. (*They struggle;* SAM *swings* JASON *around into chair L of table.* MRS. W. *sinks in chair R of table;* ZILLAH *goes to back of table*)

Zillah: (*Holds out her hand*) Give it to me, Jason. (*Reluctantly, with averted head, he hands her the volume of poems*) Why this is what you were studying—Tennyson's poems. (*He nods dumbly*)

(SAM *goes up L and lights lamp*)—

LIGHTS
UP.

All of these details should be memorized by the director. This requirement may seem to be rather a large order, and so indeed it is, but it is really essential to the best results. When the director's lack of familiarity with the play makes necessary over-frequent reference to the manuscript for the purpose of refreshing or verifying his memory, especially as to the smaller details of stage business, the effect upon the actors is not only disquieting and distracting, but it tends to create an unpleasant sense of irritation, and makes for indecision and uncertainty with a consequent lessening of interest in their work.

Early and careful consideration must be given to the play's physical requirements—the scenery, properties, lighting effects, and costuming, with a mind to the demands of fitness, practicability, and artistic effect, and not forgetting the matter of cost in relation to the budget.

When the general character, style, and form of the setting for each scene and act have been decided upon, there is drawn (preferably by the director) a scaled ground plan of each of the settings, upon which is shown the position, dimensions, and as nearly as possible the shape of the doors, windows, stairs, rocks, trees, furniture, and such other of the larger articles as are component parts of the settings. In addition to the ground plan there is made a scene plot, which consists of a more or less detailed description of the settings, together with whatever measurements and other features and characteristics cannot be indicated on the ground plan.

When the settings are elaborate and complicated, it is usual to engage an art director, whose duty it is to design and supervise the making and assembling of the entire physical production, and to furnish whatever blueprint drawings of the scenery and its appurtenances may be required by the builders and scenic artists. In such cases, however, the director should not neglect to make his own plans; for they are most useful for reference when mapping out the stage direction and other particulars of the production, and for the use of his assistant during rehearsals and performances.

A satisfactory method of drawing these ground plans is first to make a scaled drawing in pencil, and then to trace with stylus and carbon-paper, as many copies as may be required, and finally to run them through the typewriter for the necessary lettering.

Next comes the making of an itemized and classified list known as the property plot, in which are specified all the various pieces of furniture, the carpets, draperies, decorations, ornaments, books, and all other articles of whatever size, kind, and description which are used in the action of the play, with the exception of the scenic, electric, and costume equipment. These articles, technically called properties (or props), are described in this plot, with what detail may be necessary, including such things as style, form, color, texture, and dimension.

AS HUSBANDS GO

Property Plot

Place: Paris and Iowa.   *Period:* The Present

Prologue

The corner of a smart, new café in
Paris, 4.00 A. M., September.)

Table C.
Chair R of table.
Chair L of table.
High-back bench back of table (built in).
Small serving-table R.

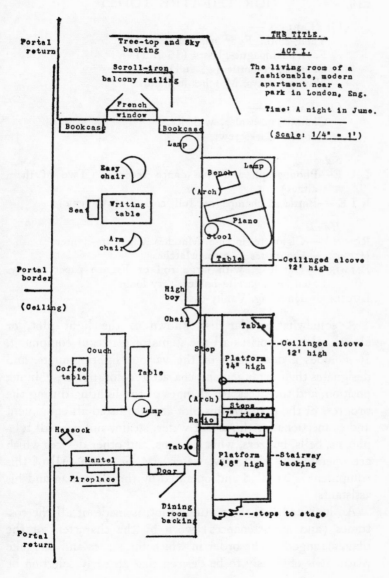

THE TITLE.

ACT I.

The living room of a
fashionable, modern
apartment near a
park in London, Eng.

Time: A night in June.

(Scale: 1/4" = 1')

247

On TABLE C—
  Table-cloth. Four napkins.
  Four champagne-glasses (½ full)
  Champagne-bottle (½ full)
  Two ash trays. Matches in stand.

On TABLE R—
  Champagne-cooler, with ice.
  Napkin. Corkscrew.

Side:
L U E—Phonograph and five dance records. (Two of them
    waltzes)
R I E —Bottle of champagne, full, corked. (WAITER)

Hand:
RONNIE —Cigarettes in case. Matches. Cigarette-lighter.
HIPPIE —Cigarettes in case. Matches.
EMMIE —Handbag, with large roll of French paper money.
    Extension cigarette-holder, very long.
LUCILLE—Handbag. Vanity-case.

A somewhat similar list, known as the light plot, or
electric plot, comprises all the items of electrical equipment.
It includes a description of the various lighting units, and
designates their arrangement, character, color, power, volume,
position, and the necessary changes of the lighting during the
progress of the play. In this plot are also listed all equipment
and connections for the use of water, steam, and gas; all telephones, bells, buzzers, whistles, fans, and other devices which
are operated by electricity, water, gas, or steam. All of this
equipment is handled and operated by the electrician and his
assistants.

An itemized list, the costume plot, is made of all the costumes (and appurtenances) worn by the characters of the
play, arranged in the order in which the scenes and acts take
place. It is obviously to be desired that an early selection be

made of the style, color, and other details of each costume, so that unpleasant or incongruous contrasts or similarities may be avoided. In the case of a modern play, the costume plot is usually called the dress plot.

Other lists and plots, such as music cues, extra people plot, program copy, will be made whenever needed.

Copies of the ground plans and plots will be distributed to the heads of the mechanical staff, with complete sets being retained by the director, and the stage manager.

It will be seen that in order to construct these plans and plots, the director will have been obliged to read the manuscript many, many times with the most painstaking scrutiny. It is a task which often becomes tedious and wearisome, but it has a two-fold value—not only does it yield the desired information as to the production's physical requirements, but it almost automatically familiarizes the director with those requirements to the smallest detail; and such familiarity is a necessary condition precedent to orderly and systematic progress toward rehearsals and performances.

The selection of the actors (the word actors is used herein to designate both sexes) who are to interpret the characters of the play—technically called casting—is an all-important step in preliminary preparation; and it is many times a most dubious one, for so many factors must be considered that sometimes its successful accomplishment seems hopelessly impossible. The actors' ability, fitness, personal appearance, temperament, must be judged in comparison—and often in competition—with others, which makes the process difficult and delicate, not to say dangerous.

Casting a play in the good (?) old days was simplicity itself compared with that task today. Then, the actors' lines of business were clearly differentiated and firmly established; and

in the writing of plays—submissive to time-honored custom—
parts were fashioned for leading man, leading woman, heavy
man (villain), heavy woman, first old man and woman, gen-
teel and low comedians, ingénue, soubrette, and so on down
the line to walking gentleman and general business—few
playwrights of the day having the temerity, or the inclina-
tion, to depart from traditional practice.

But oh, how different it is today, with the old lines of
demarcation almost, if not wholly, obliterated, and with casts
calling for perhaps ten men and one woman; or six women
and one man; or *all* men, or *all* women; or, as in a play now
in rehearsal in New York, four grown-ups and twenty-one
children ranging in age from twelve to twenty. Under such
conditions the bugaboo, *type*, persistently obtrudes itself.
Casting to type is the term applied by the theatrical profession
to the practice of engaging actors who look the part, with little
or no regard to their experience or ability. This kind of casting
is often carried to absurd lengths, but with every wish to
cognize the fact that competent actors are highly adaptable,
and capable of successfully portraying characters which bear
no small resemblance to their own personality, nevertheless,
in casting a play today, it is almost inevitable that of the actors
under consideration for a certain character the choice will fall
upon that one who (all things else being equal) most nearly
approximates that character in size, coloring, and general appearance.

The author should be a more or less active participant in
the casting of his play; for not only it is his privilege, by virtue
of his contract, to disapprove one or all of the actors selected
for the cast, but it is eminently wise and proper that the person who has created the play should be consulted as to the
fitness of those who are to interpret his creation. In this respect, as in other departments of the production, it is of para-

mount importance that the relations existing between author and director should be those of mutual understanding and helpfulness.

Before giving voice to his own ideas and opinions, the director should earnestly and honestly try to see with the author's eye not only the larger intent of the play, but also the particularized details of the manner and mode of its unfolding; and if then he should feel it necessary to recommend changes, he must be so sure of his ground that he can define clearly and explicitly his reasons for such proposed changes, and their purpose.

With the cast complete, the manuscript in as nearly perfect condition as seems possible, and the stage director so completely familiar with every detail of the play, in all its phases, that he feels able to answer any question pertaining to it that may be asked by author, actor, manager, or anyone else concerned, the company is called for rehearsal.

It has become the custom—an excellent one, I think—to have the principal actors of the cast read the play prior to rehearsals; and when this is done, the reading of the play to the company by the author or the director is usually (and in most instances, happily) dispensed with.

At the first rehearsal a table is placed in the centre of the stage close to the footlights; a semi-circle of chairs is placed a few feet from the table. The director sits at the table, on which is his prompt-copy of the manuscript, and the members of the company sit in the semi-circle of chairs facing him. The stage manager sits at the table with the director. The first two or three days, perhaps more, are devoted to the reading of the play by the actors from their individual manuscript-parts.

Early in the course of these readings I observe the reaction of the actors to the play and to their rôles; if any of them seems at all uncertain as to the meaning of any particular passage or scene, I take the time, then and there, to make all such points clear.

During the first of these readings a few suggestions (or even corrections) may be made as to emphasis or inflection, but as a rule it is better not to attempt much in the way of directing until the actors have had time to find themselves, to some extent, in their rôles.

When it is felt that as much has been accomplished by the readings as is reasonably possible, it is time to get the actors on their feet, and to begin the slow and sometimes rather dispiriting work of perfecting them in the stage business of the play—when and where to enter and exit, where to stand or sit, when to change positions, and all the other minutiae of physical action and movement.

The actors, at this point, will be materially helped in their work if each act is rehearsed two or more times before going on to the next one. The immediate repetition tends to fix the business of the act more firmly in their minds; in addition, it aids them in memorizing their lines by associating speech and action, so that the spoken word suggests the corresponding action, and *vice versa*.

The grind of daily rehearsals—and what a grind they *can* become when permitted—is more than likely to abate somewhat the first, ardent enthusiasm not only of the actors, but of the director, and even of the author, himself. At times there comes a peculiar, insidious form of abstraction, or mental staleness, which manifests itself in a desire for change; a desire not prompted by the conscious wish for improvement, but merely an instinctive urge for something different and new. It is almost wholly due to the fact that constant repetition has dulled the appreciation of material which at first teemed with vitality and interest but which now seems stale, flat, and unprofitable.

A rather amusing illustration of this peculiarity is the case of a well known manager who was about to produce a play which he admired with almost rapturous enthusiasm. He was present at every rehearsal and followed the progress of every scene and act with the most intense and delighted interest. This continued until toward the end of the third week of rehearsals, when he called the stage director to him and the following conversation ensued:

Manager: P., there's something gone wrong with the climax at the end of the second act.

Director: Indeed? I hadn't noticed it. But tell me what's wrong with it, and we'll try to make it right.

Manager: Well, I don't know just what it is, but I know that *something* is wrong with that climax.

Director: Why are you so sure?

Manager: Well, it doesn't thrill me like it did at first.

Fortunately, the director, aided and abetted by the author and the actors, succeeded in convincing the manager that the loss of his beloved thrill was due to his daily attendance at rehearsals and his consequent over-familiarity with the play, and the second act climax remained unchanged.

The point of the story is that the director must not allow his closeness to the play to blur his perspective, or to dull his recollection and appreciation of the values he first detected in it. He must resist to the utmost the temptation to make ill-advised or unconsidered changes, either on his own initiative or upon the suggestion of others, no matter from what source such suggestions may come.

Throughout every stage of rehearsals and performances there should be kept constantly in mind the fundamental fact that in the acting of a play, nothing should be said or done for which there is not a specific, explainable reason—every word, every move, every thought should be motivated by some definite intent and purpose. Hence it follows, that for a full and comprehensive enjoyment of a play, the audience must not only see what the actors are doing, and hear what they are saying, but must understand why they are doing it and saying it; and this will be impossible, of course, if the actors themselves do not understand the reason for their words and actions. Observance of this plain truth makes for clarity and directness as opposed to ambiguity and vagueness. *Vagueness* is as crafty an enemy as ever lay in wait for the unwary director, or author, or actor; it assumes various disguises, masquerading as suggestion, or impressionism, or symbolism, or what not; but whatever its form, it is always a menace to the positive, lucid expression of thought. Therefore it behooves the wise director to analyze with great care his development of the play's thought, speech, and action so that he will not fall into the error of thinking that because *he* understands the matters in hand, it must necessarily follow that they will be clearly conveyed to the audience.

Sheridan, in his play *The Critic*, amusingly illustrates this error, and at the same time satirizes the self-sufficient type of stage director.

Mr. Sneer is watching Mr. Puff, a stage director, conduct the rehearsal of a tragedy, in the course of which the character of Lord Burleigh enters, walks down to the footlights, folds his arms, and solemnly shakes his head, then turns and makes his exit without having uttered a word. Whereupon, the following dialogue ensues:

Sneer: . . . Now, pray what did he mean by that?
Puff: You don't take it?
Sneer: No, I don't, upon my soul.

Puff: Why, by the shake of the head, he gave you to understand that even though they had more justice in their cause, and wisdom in their measures—yet, if there was not a greater spirit shown on the part of the people, the country would at last fall a sacrifice to the hostile ambition of the Spanish Monarchy.

Sneer: The devil! did he mean all that by shaking his head?

Puff: Every word of it—if he shook his head as I taught him.

The fact that *The Critic* was written a hundred and fifty years ago, indicates that the vanity of vagueness is not a strictly modern development.

At a time best determined by conditions and circumstances, the members of the cast are notified that on a certain day they will be expected to know their lines, and to rehearse without the manuscript-parts in their hands; and it is to be fervently hoped that when that day arrives, and the perfect or near-perfect rehearsals begin, the actors, and the director, and the author will have come to agreement as to the desired interpretation of the various characters of the play.

The actor should be allowed great latitude in the conception and characterization of his part. The arbitrary insistence of the director upon a rigidly specified interpretation of each part as it is visualized by him is, in my opinion, short-sighted and unwise. It invariably has the effect of dulling the keen edge of the actor's interest and enthusiasm, for it not only belittles and suppresses his creative faculty, but it most unfairly limits the expression of his individuality.

On the other hand, the actor must not be permitted to project his personality, or individuality, to the extent of detracting from any of the values of his rôle or of the play. Some actors, even conscientious ones, seem to regard their part in a play less as a character to be interpreted and developed in the best and most effective way for its own sake, than as a sort of stepping-stone to self-aggrandizement. In most instances, I believe, this mental attitude is a subconscious one, but it must be watched for, and when detected, squelched, forthwith.

When the actors begin to rehearse without their manuscript-parts, there will come to the director a most hopeless feeling of utter chaos. The actors will seem to have forgotten nearly all of the stage business, and any idea of characterization will appear to have been thrown to the winds; but this condition is not so serious as it seems—it is simply that in the intense concentration on the words of the part everything else is disregarded. At this stage nerves are on edge and tempers ever ready to explode; little irritations assume an importance out of all proportion to their real significance, and the very atmosphere seems strained and tense. During this crucial period the few directions given (and they must be *very few*) should pertain only to the movements of the actors, and rarely, if ever, to readings or characterizations; and in a comparatively short time (if the director has been heroically patient and tactful), the words will commence to flow freely and smoothly, there will be more of crispness to speech and action, a most welcome resuscitation of interest will become apparent, and the play will begin to assume some semblance of its ultimate form and shape.

From now on the director will conduct rehearsals from the vantage-point of the auditorium, and as they take on more of the mental (or, if you like, intellectual) character, they will become correspondingly more interesting to everyone concerned.

As the time for the opening performance draws near, the different scenes (particularly the comedy ones) should be rehearsed at a tempo or speed considerably faster than that at which they will eventually be played. The reason for this is the virtual impossibility of exactly setting the correct tempo until the last few rehearsals; and as it is much more difficult to quicken the pace of a scene that has been repeatedly rehearsed too slowly, than it is to slow the pace of one that has been rehearsed too fast, the value of the expedient is obvious.

During all this time the physical production must not be lost sight of. Its progress must be frequently checked and verified to insure complete readiness for the dress rehearsal. A day or two before the dress rehearsal, a practice which results in the saving of much time (and incidentally, expense) is that of devoting a day to the rehearsal of the scenery, lights, properties, and effects. It serves materially to shorten the time of the dress rehearsal and adds to the probability of a smooth first performance. At the same time there can be held a dress parade, at which the actors (the female ones, in particular) will try on their costumes, check their correctness, and become a bit used to them before having to act in them. The cast should not be *rehearsed* on this day unless the time required for the mechanical rehearsal and the dress parade is so short that it may be thought wise to hold a quick rehearsal for lines, with an irreducible minimum of direction or comment by the stage director.

Every effort should be made to have the dress rehearsal start at the appointed hour, but on no account should it be begun unless there is a reasonable assurance that it can be completed without interruption. Under no ordinary circumstances should a dress rehearsal be stopped, except perhaps at the end of an act, and not then unless it be for the purpose of taking flashlight photographs, or for some other equally important matter. Furthermore, the actors should not be distracted and harassed during the progress of the rehearsal by corrections or criticisms. The author, manager, and director should make notes of all mistakes, inaccuracies, or other points to be considered, and they can be discussed and the necessary corrections made after the rehearsal is over, and in the time intervening between this rehearsal and the opening performance, which, it is to be hoped, will be not less than two days, for many times the dress rehearsal uncovers the need for much corrective work.

When the opening day arrives, the director will spend most of it in the theatre. With the stage manager and the mechanical staff, he will check those items of scenery, lighting, properties, effects, *et cetera* that are most likely to be overlooked or neglected. He will arrange for some means of communication between the front of the theatre and the stage (house-telephone, messenger, or otherwise) so that throughout the performance he will be able to establish quick contact with the stage manager, in case of emergency. He will see that a previously arranged list of curtain calls is posted on the call-board backstage. As curtain time draws near, he will make sure that every member of the cast is in his or her dressing room making ready for the performance; he will thank each and every one of them for their hard work and coöperation and wish them the success they deserve; he will give one last apprehensive glance at the stage and its appurtenances; then he will proceed to the front of the house, but will pause in some dark corner long enough to offer up a short but fervent prayer for a smooth performance, an interested audience, an early final curtain, and a long and prosperous season for everyone concerned.

It has been found difficult to classify satisfactorily the following observations on practice and procedure; so, with little thought as to their orderly sequence, and little concern as to the probable charge of their being self-evident and trite, I offer them—not as injunctions, but as hints—in the hope that they may serve to make a little less irksome and laborious the way of some aspiring young stage director.

Make haste slowly, particularly in the earlier stages of rehearsals. Plan your work with care and deliberation—let it be comparatively easy at first; then gradually increase the pressure until it becomes, toward the last, more and more intensive and exacting; then at the end a period of relaxation, to ward off staleness and over-training—all very much in the fashion in which an athlete is conditioned for a physical contest.

Don't try to accomplish too much at one time, especially by means of prolonging rehearsal hours to the point where the actors, or you, yourself, are over-fatigued in mind and body; for when that point is reached and passed, no matter what you may do in the way of direction, or how carefully you do it, by the next day the actors will have forgotten the greater part of it, and it will have to be done all over again.

Do not, at rehearsals, permit yourself to be drawn into protracted or heated arguments with author, actor, manager, or anyone else, on the subjects of changes in the play, or characterization, or interpretation, or on other matters pertaining to the play and its production. When differences of opinion arise (as they most certainly will), if it is found that they cannot be reconciled amicably at the moment, let each person concerned make notes of his ideas on the point or points at issue, and let all these ideas which are at variance be discussed calmly and at length at the proper time—which is *not* during the hours set apart for rehearsal, or in the presence of the members of the cast.

When calling attention to the mistakes of actors at rehearsal, never, *never* resort to personalities, to sarcasm, or to ridicule. This rule should be rigidly observed, if for no other reason than that of policy; for the use of such boorish expedients is not only certain to wound and humiliate the actors, but is almost as certain to arouse in them feelings of anger and resentment; and it is an oft-proved fact that theatre folk (like most other folk) accomplish most when in the best humor, with the mind undisturbed and at ease, instead of being inflamed with anger and bitterness.

Many years ago a stage director of some prominence at the time pronounced to me a precept which he doubtless considered as highly instructive as any gem of philosophy culled from the deepest Meditations of Marcus Aurelius. "Son," said he, sententiously, "there's only one way to handle actors: give 'em Hell, and *never* admit you're wrong."

That he was not alone in this view is evidenced by the fact that a deplorably large number of the directors of his day were swaggering, loud-mouthed martinets, who sought to hide their abysmal ignorance of the real requirements of their calling under a cloak of malignant sarcasm and profanity. This type, as such, no longer exists; it "strutted its brief hour" and passed on, to be succeeded, to some extent, by a type which made itself ridiculous by silly affectation, and the assumption of profound erudition. Directors of this order have been known to demand that some parts of the dialogue be delivered in tones not round, but "pear-shaped"; and to request that the actors characterize with more reaction to their "color vibrations."

Both these types—"drest in a little brief authority, most ignorant of what he's most assured"—have been or are rapidly being superseded by directors of vastly more intelligence and efficiency, many of whom have been equipped for their work by specialized courses in universities or colleges, and whose influence for good in the theatre is being increasingly manifested.

In my own experience I have never felt it necessary to assert my authority in the fear that if I failed to do so it would be minimized or mitigated. When I find myself in the wrong (an occurrence of greater frequency than I should care to have shouted from the housetops), I acknowledge my mistake and at once seek to remedy it; and I am quite certain that in so doing I have never forfeited one iota of authority or respect.

Be constantly on the alert to detect false stress, misplaced emphasis, and all other forms of incorrect or careless reading. There are actors (sometimes even of the better class) who seem frequently to forget or to ignore the fact that emphasis, inflection, stress, are to the speaker what punctuation is to the writer; that they constitute his only means of differentiating the more delicate shades of meaning, and that their intelligent use imparts variety to the spoken word and serves to make clear and vital, phraseology which without them would many times seem obscure and lifeless.

Disregard of so elemental a fact is sometimes due to a faulty method of study, whereby the actor commits a rôle to memory by fixing in his mind an almost photographic picture of the printed words, rather than by the process of analyzing and defining each thought intended to be conveyed, and learning those *thoughts* (with the corresponding words) in their proper order and sequence. Or the error may be the result of a sort of mental indolence; or perhaps of sheer thoughtlessness or inattention. But no matter what its cause, the director must correct it, firmly and persistently, by precept or illustration, or both.

Josh Billings, that whimsical humorist of a bygone day, by means of a sly misquotation demonstrates how the original meaning of a phrase may be substantially changed, if not completely reversed, by even a slight alteration in punctuation, or oral stress.

The immortal Shakespeare affirms:

> There's a divinity that shapes our ends,
> Rough-hew them how we will.

Josh Billings opines:

> There's a divinity that shapes our ends *rough,*
> Hew them how we will.

Don't give orders at rehearsals! Direct by suggestion, whenever possible, rather than by arbitrary commands, so that the actors will receive the impression of acting on their own initiative. The results measured in willing, cheerful work amply justify such a course.

Confine your direction to the larger and more complex points, leaving the actors to work out the more obvious ones for themselves; but be ready at all times to help them when they need it, with suggestion, advice, and demonstration.

If it becomes necessary to criticize adversely the work of an actor in order to correct it, let both the criticism and the correction be made as quietly and as unobtrusively as is possible under the circumstances.

Be very sure that you know precisely what you want an actor to do before you ask him to do it; and on no account undertake to correct him unless and until you are prepared to explain to him exactly not only where, how, and why he is wrong, but what to do to be right. An actor is entirely excusable for being irritated and resentful at being told merely that he is at fault, without being told where the fault lies or how to remedy it.

In staging plays of the genre type, dealing with familiar characters and conditions, the director should take care not to incorporate in the stage business too many minutiae of the inveterate daily routine of the specified environment. Most of the customary practices and incidents of everyday life are sadly humdrum and commonplace, and almost wholly devoid of any element of dramatic interest or value. Of such details only those should be selected which are not only distinctively characteristic of the people and the situations of the play, but which will aid in its progress and serve to emphasize and amplify its meaning.

The lamest excuse for the presence in a play of features that are weak, dull, depressing, lacking in conviction, or otherwise undesirable, is that they are "true to life."

Percy Hammond, one of New York's ablest dramatic critics, in his review of a play produced last season, comments with seeming—but *only* seeming—contradiction on this subject:

It was my impression last night that the story of the play was known to the author to be a fact, and because she knew it to be a fact she over-estimated its value, both as Truth and as Drama. Many playwrights stray likewise. They feel that simply because things have happened they are true; which is not always the case.

From time immemorial there have been held heated discussions on a highly controversial question pertaining to the art of acting. The exponents of one school maintain that the actor must *ever feel* the character he plays, even to the shedding of real tears and the actual experiencing of all the emotions he portrays; while the advocates of the opposing school contend that the actor must *never feel* the part, nor even for a moment lose himself in the emotions of the character.

To the stage director who is called upon to uphold the contentions of one or the other of these opposite schools of thought, I commend the view of the matter voiced by Mr. Joseph Jefferson, one of the greatest and most intelligent actors of his time. Mr. Jefferson said:

Others will act with more effect no doubt by adhering to their own dogmas, but for myself I know that I act best when the heart is warm and the head is cool.

In this aptly terse statement I most heartily, and most humbly concur.

During the rehearsals of a play there arises such frequent necessity for the director to criticize the work of the actor and to correct it with such exasperating persistency, that it might be thought there would be erected between them an insuperable barrier of animosity and hostility, but this is rarely the case; and in the few instances where such feelings have prevailed, I am constrained to believe that the fault was more probably that of the director and his methods, than of the actor.

The theatre is exacting in its demands upon its devotees. Much of the work is difficult and arduous, taxing to the utmost the powers of concentration, self-control, and mental (and sometimes physical) endurance. With this in mind I earnestly try to do my work at all times and under all circumstances in a spirit of modesty, goodwill, and forbearance; and it has been my happy lot to know that by far the greater majority of my fellow-workers are more than willing to meet me halfway on that highroad of friendly relations.

Actors, no less than others, are subject to the foibles and frailties of humanity, and acting is a profession which, by reason of the intensely personal character of the estimations and criticisms of its workers, is peculiarly provocative of the smaller conceits and jealousies; in spite of this, however, an experience of many years in the theatre leaves me with the profound conviction that the followers of no other calling possess more generally or in larger measure than do actors, those lovable qualities that form the basis of firm and loyal friendship. Warm-hearted, companionable, generous, sympathetic, steadfast—they go their ways buoyantly and bravely; always giving a little more than they receive of good cheer, of happiness, of love, and exemplifying in their lives and works an abundant spirit of the Golden Rule.

The respective functions of author, actor, scenic artist, mechanician, and the other almost innumerable agencies incident to the production of a play, are separate and distinct, and often widely apart. The true province of the stage director, as I see it, is to foster all of these various agencies to the fullest development of their usefulness; to arrogate to himself no one of their functional rights or duties, but with helpful, constructive guidance, so to coördinate and unify their activities as to achieve the closest possible approximation of perfect performances.

Seneca, the Roman philosopher and dramatist, in a letter to his friend Lucilius, wrote:

> Life is a play upon a stage; it signifies not how long it lasts but upon how well it is acted. Die when or where you will, think only on making a good exit.

In somewhat different phraseology, but in philosophy no less sound, an outstanding writer and actor of a later time, George M. Cohan, expounded much the same doctrine, when in a song written earlier in his career as a successful comedian, he cautioned his fellow-entertainers to:

> Always leave 'em laughing, when you say Goodbye.

I fear I cannot follow Cohan's advice unless the laugh be at rather than with me; but I can, and hereby do, accept Seneca's suggestion, at least to the extent that, be it good or bad, I make my exit.

PART FOUR
STAGECRAFT

SCENIC ART

by

Cleon Throckmorton

Mr. Throckmorton, one of the busiest designers in New York since 1931, is the owner and manager of Cleon Throckmorton, Inc., theatre supply house and builders of stage scenery. During 1934 he designed and built several portable theatres for the government. Some of the plays for which he has designed sets are: *The Emperor Jones*; *Porgy*; *Outside Looking In*; *All God's Chillun Got Wings*; *The Old Soak*; *The Hairy Ape*; *East Lynne*; *In Abraham's Bosom*; *Beyond the Horizon*; *Tampico*; *After Dark*; *Suppressed Desires*; *The Blue and the Gray*; *Man With a Load of Mischief*; *Red Rust*; *Torch Song*; *Six Characters in Search of an Author*; *House of Connelly*; *Brass Ankle*; *Springtime for Henry*; *The Silver Cord*; *Napoleon*; *Diff'rent*; *Greenwich Village Follies*; *Eight Bells*; *Peace on Earth*; *Sing and Whistle*.

Mr. Throckmorton's organization has executed settings for: *Miracle at Verdun*; *Roar China*; *Romeo and Juliet*; *Reunion in Vienna*; *Green Grow the Lilacs*; *Hotel Universe*; *Alison's House*; *Sea Gull*; *Cherry Orchard*; *Pillars of Society*; *Getting Married*; *Garrick Gaieties*; *Three's a Crowd*; *Ziegfeld Follies*; *An American Tragedy*; *Pygmalion*; *The Great God Brown*; *Desire Under the Elms*; *The Doctor's Dilemma*; *Strange Interlude*; *Dynamo*; *Peter Pan*; *Major Barbara*; *Cradle Song*; *Game of Love and Death*; and many others.

SCENIC ART

by

CLEON THROCKMORTON

A LONG discourse on settings is not intended in this chapter. Suffice it to say, that excellent scenery was created for the theatre of the past, just as it is created for the modern stage of today. We are interested in that past period, only as it concerns and influences the work of today.

As a matter of fact, the history of American scenic art has not really become important until within the scope of the last twenty-five years. Then, through outside influences from Europe and inside influences due to the entrance of engineer artists into the theatre, came the birth of a desire to go at the problem of creatively staging a show, throwing traditional and accepted methods to the winds; and at this point the appearance of our stage began to change.

The chief European influence was a gentleman by the name of Gordon Craig. Craig made a series of designs that caused great discussion among theatre lovers. Even to this day some of our foremost writers are branding him as impractical and calling him a dreamer and a visionary. Thank God for that. Why can't we realize that that was just what was needed—a young fresh outlook, the setting up of ladders that would never be possible to climb; but in the very attempt to scale them, new heights have undoubtedly been reached.

The inside forces at work came from the artists forsaking their easels for a broader field and from the artist engineers who began to filter into the theatre, principally through underground routes, such as, for example, the little theatre. Before their entrance, we find all stage decoration resolving itself into traditional forms, which consisted of a set number of planes, spaced six feet apart, called wings, of borders, and of drops upon which were painted standardized interpretations of any given interior or exterior. It was quite customary to find a simple kitchen set forty feet wide and twenty feet high, and think nothing of it. I remember a director who rehearsed his entire company for weeks to make an entrance down the steps of a grand staircase, to be set in the center of the stage. At the dress rehearsal, he was all prepared to go ahead; he called the stage manager. "Where is my staircase?" he asked. The stage manager pointed and replied, "There it is, sir," and there it was. Painted on the backdrop! Tradition excused everything.

In a recent production of *After Dark* in Hoboken, these methods proved very amusing. In the great rescue scene of the fair lady, who was neither "maid, wife, nor widow," from a watery grave, the only bad feature was that the hero continually complained from behind his canvas ocean, that the wheels of his boat squeaked. But it was a traditional boat, and so it did not matter.

But the new men discarded all rules of production, and went at the problem with fresh vision. When they wanted light, they had light; and when they wanted concentration on smaller areas, they built themselves controlled spotlights and had it. I'll admit that the modern stage sometimes goes too far in controlling lights. An old actor said to me not long ago, "In my day we said, 'Up with the foots and on with the show.' " And, in some respects, he had grounds for complaining, for at many a production today have I hunted vaguely about the stage, trying to see what was going on. Well, perhaps there wasn't anything going on.

I confess, myself, to often saving some undistinguished scenery by the simple expedient of just not letting any light fall on it, so that the imagination of the audience went to further distances than my wildest dreams could lead them. Norman Bel Geddes managed in his production of *Hamlet* to make all of his scene changes without lowering the curtain, by the simple expedient of concentrating his lighting and action on the forward part of the stage, and thus allowing his changes in the rear to go on entirely unnoticed.

We have many fine designers in this country, but I doubt whether there is one who could be called perfect. It requires the understanding of too many professions, and too much general knowledge. The designer has first of all to be an artist at heart, with feeling and an open mind; he then has to be an engineer of high ability, for what good is a grand piece of decoration, if it cannot be assembled rapidly and taken apart, and another set up as the play may demand? He should have a familiarity, from contact, with all countries of the world. He should also be a finished and practical architect. Lastly, he should be a diplomat of high order, to guide his brain children safely through the shoals of the producer, the author, and the director (who usually each have their own ideas about the production); then the backer of the show who always has his; and far more terrible than these, the wives and relatives of the aforementioned gentlemen. And, last but not least, the star! When she enters the picture, the diplomacy of a Disraeli becomes necessary!

Lee Simonson had not only to be an artist in the staging of *Roar China*, but a plumbing engineer as well. For the star Chinese boy who had to drown in the tank absolutely refused to drown nightly, as well as at matinees on Wednesday and Saturday, unless the water was heated. Mr. Simonson designed an installation of steam pipes throughout the tank to heat the oriental "Davy Jones' locker."

However, in some cases, the scene designer gets more credit than he deserves. I remember reading Heywood Broun, then a dramatic critic, on the original production of *The Emperor Jones*. He said that he had never seen such entrancing clouds as drifted across the sky of the Provincetown stage. "Clouds," said I, reading his notice, "I didn't have any clouds in the production." Nevertheless, I went on to the stage, and turned on the lights, and lo and behold, there, to my great surprise, was the grandest cloud effect you have ever seen. I went back to see what caused all this, and found that a stage hand had put his foot through the gelatine covering the floodlight, letting out a spill of light that landed on the sky dome, and there were my clouds. This same production of *The Emperor Jones* was largely illusion, and the giant, forbidding trees were merely chunks of old scene canvas hanging on lines from above, and if enough light did not hit them, they were perfectly satisfactory. But one night, Charles Gilpin was going through his famous lines, "White rock, where are you? White rock ah knows I left you roun' here somewheah!" Crossing to the wings, he said in a hoarse whisper, "Throck, wheah's mah white rock? It h'aint theah!" And it certainly was not, for I had left it out. So I said, "Charlie, I've forgotten it," and he said, "Is that so?" and returned to the stage, where he took a beautiful revenge by vigorously kicking all my massive trees up by the roots and leaving them hanging there. Well, perhaps a lot of the scenery was a bit of a fake, but if it had come out all right, no one would have cared. On the opening night, I had forgotten one scene entirely, and so we pulled everything off, leaving a bare stage, and nothing but the blue sky dome. The next day, Kenneth Macgowan, in his column, remarked that never in his life had he seen such a symphony of dark flesh against a throbbing tropical sky. So you see from time to time the element of luck comes in very helpfully.

Robert Edmond Jones, a real artist, once made his lighting fixtures out of beer bottle tops and Christmas tree decorations, and built the Hall of Mirrors at Versailles out of cooking pot aluminum, and everyone was happier, though no wiser!

Many have been the heartaches and the struggles between the designs you see upon paper and their realization upon the stage. The holding on to an ideal, the engineering ability to make the designs practical, and the endless experimentation with lights to get the desired effect, apparently so simply visualized in two dimensions by a clever stroke of the brush—all this has to be considered; and again, some of the best designs for settings have been mere scratches on waste paper or backs of envelopes, with a definite intelligence behind them.

This country has produced a splendid group of artists that know their theatre; know not only the mere business of making an idealistic sketch, but the hard work necessary to its complete fulfilment on the stage. They know its possibilities and its pitfalls, and above all, realize the great unexplored field yet to be conquered.

Turning from the cheerful aspect, let us examine new and damaging roads.

We begin to find interior decoration making its appearance; we behold many a designer realizing his setting upon the stage through the employment of good reference books, together with the assistance of an able architectural draftsman. He forgets that the stage of the theatre should be supremely theatrical, that his decorations should be wrought of the things that belong to the theatre—illusion, creative design, the building up of super-reality by suggestive unreality and imagination.

Meticulous and exact reproductions of cornices, mouldings, and other such architectural frostings are utilized frequently, when actually, a more satisfactory feeling of solidity could be achieved by intelligent suggestion. It is similar to the thought that raising the letters of a book an eighth of an inch in height and giving them three dimensions, would enhance the value of a piece of literature.

In a recent New York production, I built an entire interior out of solid wood and painted the backings on canvas. The director came in and said to the producers, "Why did you go to the expense of building the backings out of real wood, and then make the set out of canvas?" And he was right. The painted pieces on the stage looked more real than the actual wood. But they had not been painted by an old fashioned rule-of-thumb scenic artist. They had been painted by a craftsman who was an artist, who felt the grain and texture of the wood as he painted it.

Scenic art should be an art and not a text book of traditional procedure. Many of our foremost men in the field are merely architectural organizers who take the sets verbatim from reference and research books and plank (and I can find no other word as expressive as plank) them in their entirety down on the stage. A moulding five inches wide remains a moulding five inches wide, the door eight feet high remains a door eight feet high, and so on. They do not realize that the illusion in the audience's mind of length, bulk, weight, and distance is what counts, and not the actual physical presence of architectural elements.

To make actors look large merely requires making the scenery small, and conversely to make them look small means making the scenery over size. The most unreal thing on any stage is a real tree. The Italians have what we call life-sized marionettes which are as a matter of fact about two feet six inches high but seem to be life-sized. This effect is produced by the ingenuity of the scenery, which is not only scaled down in size, but in which the illusion is heightened by painting each successive receding plan of the setting in diminishing perspective.

This discussion of scenic art as practiced by the designer is written with the hope that scenic art in the future will be approached by men with completely open minds; men who not only will profit by the contributions of the modern designer but who will eagerly seek and select all that is valuable in the way of illusion since the days when Michael Angelo designed scenery; who will, moreover, make the most of the advantages of all the modern mechanical and lighting devices for the creation of illusion, which have been perfected in recent years.

Scenic art should be approached always remembering that the theatre is a place of beautiful illusion, created with as many brushes and colors as can be found. And above all, let the artist remember that scenic art, though it may be composed of many elements, still must be a complete art of its own.

TECHNICAL METHODS

by

CLEON THROCKMORTON

TECHNICAL METHODS

by

CLEON THROCKMORTON

THERE are as many methods of producing scenery in the theatre as there are individuals. In this chapter I will discuss only the generally accepted methods which can be embroidered upon to one's heart's content. It is my intention not to lay down any laws which might interfere in any way with such creative ingenuity as may be contributed by the individual himself. We will therefore divide this chapter roughly into the following sections: designing, construction, painting, assembling the whole on the stage with consideration of light, which cannot entirely be left out, and some methods of making stage changes.

In the technical end of designing scenery, assuming that it is well in hand, naturally the creative idea comes first. A general discussion between designer, director, author, and producer is often very helpful in arriving at the approach or the attack that is to be made on the given play. When everyone has a general idea of what the other person is thinking, the designer then prepares rough sketches which can be discussed, or makes more finished drawings which can be presented in entirety, or uses the more complete method of making a scale model. This last is perhaps most satisfactory, as it indicates every piece to the scale of one to two inches to the foot, the color it is to be painted, the relative proportion of the component parts, and the position in which they are to be placed. This can be examined and mulled over carefully, and such changes as are necessary can be made either on the model or in the last step of design procedure, which consists of making carpenter working drawings, and color sketches for the painter. This having been completed, we are now ready to take up the next step, which is construction.

In all construction lightness is the one factor to keep in mind continually. Another feature to keep in mind is that no scene should be built that cannot be assembled in five minutes or taken apart in five minutes. Another standing rule is that no piece of scenery should exceed five feet nine inches in width. This rule comes apparently from the fact that freight car doors will not admit anything above this dimension, but more practically from the necessity of the scene shifter to gain leverage on the piece, and anything larger than this (which by the way is the approximate height of the average man) will become unwieldy. Scenery should be built out of the best grade of clear pine and should be covered with a fireproof linen or duck. Linen has been chosen by some of the leading scenic studios principally because the paint dries much faster when applied to its surface, and as space and time count in professional productions, it offsets the added cost, which is nearly twice that of the duck. Wherever possible, it is desirable to mortice and tenon the corners and joints of all pieces and reinforce them with a three ply block called a corner or a key.

The flat surfaced wing is the basis for most interior settings. To this is added other three dimensional pieces such as doors, windows, fireplaces, pilasters, steps, and the infinite variety of characteristic pieces necessary to create the identity of the set.

Exteriors may be made with such things as drops, cut drops,

legs, borders, and wings, and sky cycloramas in combination with set pieces, either flat or built for the whole exterior, or may be achieved by taking up all the stage space with pieces of scenery indicative of the occasion and practically eliminating the sky entirely. This last method often tends to intensify the acting of the play but on the other hand seldom calls for the usual round of applause, and oh's and ah's of the audience when the curtain goes up on a large expanse of electrically lighted blue sky.

Scenery is as a rule painted with water paint of various colors, which is mixed with a glue size to hold it on the canvas. This kind of paint is used because of its ease in handling, its cheapness, and its brilliance and range of color flexibility, and to some extent its fireproof quality. Ordinary whiting forms a base for most of the materials, and this is tinted with the more brilliant colors. Many effects can be achieved by painting the canvas in one tone (usually a warm one) and over this, scumbling, spattering, rolling with a rag, sponging, or dragging slightly cooler and lighter colors. This has a tendency to give the canvas a more solid surface with texture and ability to reflect the various colors of light which are generally used.

It is impossible to speak about technical methods of scenic art without a brief consideration of the relation of the element of lighting. After the parts of the settings are finished satisfactorily to the designers, they are assembled, and the arrangement of lights is then brought into play to complete the picture.

Generally speaking, lighting consists merely of having a certain amount of light of a given color in a desired place. The main trouble about lighting, however, is knowing how much light, what color, and where you want it. However, assuming one knows what one wants, this is best accomplished by the use of separate units that can be used to throw light in the areas one desires, and not in the places where one does not want it. They should be controlled if possible by some dimming system to get the desired volume and should have the color supplied by means of mediums. Enough of these units are suspended or placed to the best advantage, and the rest is up to the creator of the desired atmosphere.

The principal methods of shifting sets are as follows: The old stand-by, and perhaps the best for general use, is the rigging system of flying sets, drops, wings, and other pieces of scenery into the space above the stage and lowering to the stage level when needed. Since the recent error of bulk versus brain has entered the theatre, many new ways have had to be devised. One is the revolving stage borrowed from the Japanese by way of Germany, in which all the papier-mâché rocks, two ton trees, and four ton castles, are put on and spun about. Then there is the wagon stage on which the set is assembled complete, and pushed on while another wagon is kept ready. Sometimes this wagon is kept in the cellar and is brought to the stage level by means of an elevator, usually at the government's expense.

The Jackknife stage is the old reliable of the wagon stages and consists of two castered platforms, one on each side of the stage at right angles to the footlights, with pivots in the corner next to the ends of the footlight troughs. A set is placed on each of these and swung up as needed. This works pretty well when two very realistic sets only are used and fast changes are necessary, but becomes a bit of a juggling game when more sets are needed and changes have to be made in the dark while one act is in progress. These, and combinations and variations of these in general, take in the usual means of shifting settings, but hardly a week goes by that some new scheme is not invented by a new genius, and although it may not add much to the aforesaid methods, it at least contributes to very necessary self-expression for the artist.

It is hoped that this brief summary of technical methods for scenic art will give only fundamental, tried, and true ways and means of achieving results from the theatrical end. It has been intentionally kept in this mood so as not to impose any definite ways of how to do scenery upon the individual artist. It is merely to present those few things that have always proved satisfactory and to allow the individual to go as far as he likes in any direction. There is no such thing as abstract right in the theatre. New methods are born with each artist who enters the field.

THE PROCEDURE FOR LIGHTING
A PRODUCTION

by

LOUIS ERHARDT AND S. R. McCANDLESS

Upon completing his graduate work in architecture at Harvard University, Stanley R. McCandless held the Sheldon Traveling Fellowship for the year 1923–24. From 1924 to 1925, he practiced architecture in the office of McKim, Meade, and White, New York. He has been associated with the theatre since the summer of 1925, when he was technical director of the Neighborhood Playhouse. During the same year Mr. McCandless was appointed lighting instructor and technical consultant for the Yale Theatre. He was made associate professor of lighting in 1933. In addition to his work at Yale, he was lighting consultant for Bushnell Memorial Hall, Hartford, 1928; Salvation Army Headquarters, New York, 1930; Severance Hall, Cleveland, 1929–30; and Rockefeller Center, New York, 1932–33. He has published *A Glossary of Stage Lighting*, 1926; *A Syllabus of Stage Lighting*, 1927–30–33; and *A Method of Lighting the Stage*, 1932.

Louis Erhardt was an assistant in lighting at the Yale Theatre, 1932–34. In 1930, he was technical director of the summer session of the New York Theatre Assembly, and in 1933, he was lighting consultant for the Washington and Philadelphia Programs of Visual Accompaniment of the Electrical Research Products, Inc. In the fall of 1934, he worked out the lighting for the Broadway productions of *Anything Goes, The Farmer Takes a Wife, Gold Eagle Guy,* and the Philadelphia Opera Association productions of *Tristan and Isolde, Carmen,* and *Rosenkavalier.*

THE PROCEDURE FOR LIGHTING A
PRODUCTION [1]

by

Louis Erhardt and S. R. McCandless

Production is the process of coördinating the visual and auditory elements of the stage, whereby the producer conveys the playwright's ideas to an audience dramatically. Lighting is one of the most useful of these elements, yet so little understood, that its full potentiality is seldom realized. It should be more closely coördinated with the traditional means of expression, i. e., acting and scenery, to be consistent with modern production. Assuming that the playwright and the producer have taken advantage of the dramatic use of light, the problem of application falls to the designer. He is responsible for all of the visual effects, although he may depend upon the costumer, the scene technician, and the electrician to execute the details. The use of light is an exceedingly selective process. Both limited equipment and meager knowledge of how to use it often prevent the execution of many excellent ideas, which are projected without considering these limitations. More and more, the playwright, the producer, and the designer must

[1] The application of light to each production presents so many individual problems that the following material should be considered only as a guide. It should be read through to grasp the relationship between the various steps and then used as a reference or check-list in planning the lighting for a particular production. The reader is urged to consult the sources of information mentioned in the bibliography for the details of technical apparatus.

understand the functions of lighting, and further, they must learn to think in terms of the practical and possible.

Although the consideration of lighting begins more or less unconsciously in the mind of the playwright when he visualizes the surroundings and the atmosphere in which the various scenes are to be played, it becomes so obscured that the problem of reconstructing these original ideas in practical form is difficult.

The kind of play, and the style of production expressed as functions of the direction, the design, and the lighting are the indications which will be pursued in this analysis. When the production staff is agreed on these basic aspects, they should be developed as far as possible in notes and drawings, before the staff launches into the practical work, such as line rehearsals, building and setting scenery, making costumes, and hanging the lighting instruments. When all of this preliminary work has been completed, it must be coördinated in technical, lighting, and dress rehearsals. Although this may seem a logical and simple procedure, the interest of each member of the production staff in his own problem, and his ignorance of the problems of the other departments, present differences in point of view, which must be eliminated before a completely harmonious result can be expected.

THE PLANS FOR LIGHTING AS INDICATED
IN THE MANUSCRIPT

While plays differ widely from each other in subject matter, the dramatic material or kind of emotional expression can be classified as tragedy or comedy. A different *mood* pervades each of these types of plays, and it can be suggested by the visual elements in the production, as well as by the meaning of the spoken words.

Plays likewise differ in the style of writing and production. *Mourning Becomes Electra* by Eugene O'Neill, and the original Greek trilogy have essentially the same mood quality, but the method of presentation visualized by the playwright in the first play is personal and realistic, and in the second it was detached and formalized. *Uncle Tom's Cabin* written realistically would receive a style of production today quite different from that of *Rain*.

Style deals, on the one hand, with material which when viewed objectively may be arranged in accordance with some formal pattern, while on the other hand, from a subjective point of view, complete freedom in the treatment may hold. Hallmarks for the determination of these styles in lighting are the *composition* of the stage picture and the expression of *locale*.

The type of play and style of production determine the extent to which the lighting can serve in creating emotionally an atmosphere or *mood*, and pictorially a visual composition and a suggestion of the time and place or locale of the drama. The functions of lighting interlock and co-exist to such an extent that although they may be separated for purposes of discussion, in actual practice it is impossible to dissociate them, one from the other. The most obvious function is the creation of *visibility*. These four functions, visibility, locale, composition, and mood serve as the objective and definition of stage lighting.

A special application of each function of lighting should be planned to fit the type of play and style of production. To do this, the functions must be translated into lighting possibilities which exist through the use of available instruments. Lighting instruments are designed and controlled to provide approximately the range of an individual's sensitivity to light. The eye can distinguish accurately and distinctly great ranges of *intensity;* hues, tints, and shades of *color;* sizes, shapes, and positions of *form;* and changes in each of these in terms of *movement.* The functions are carried out through the expression of combinations of these four qualities of light.

The sensation of vision or seeing can be analyzed in terms of the qualities of light. The painter dramatizes a static relationship between objects and localities by a composition of forms and colors in pigment. The abstract beauties of architecture and sculpture depend largely upon the relationship of forms. Intensity is interpreted in the brightness or darkness of colors (by the painter), in shades and shadows, in space (by the architect and sculptor), but only in the motion picture and on the stage are the rhythm, harmony, and sequence of movement in visual form available to the designer.

In summary, the designer plans the functions of lighting to express the type of play and the style of production visually. The application of each function suggests itself almost automatically as a certain combination of the qualities of light. They, in turn, are created by available instruments and control apparatus, and must be coördinated in rehearsal with the other elements of production to give a finished performance.

THE TYPE OF PLAY

Although the types of plays correspond most directly with the different expressions of mood in lighting, the other functions contribute to the creation of a definite emotional reaction. The diversity of conditions presented by each type of play necessitates the simplification of the following suggestions into something like general principles, which can be treated with great latitude in application. Most plays have a dominant tragic or comic mood and are so classified, but there may be elements of both in each for the sake of relief or contrast. Such emotional expression as might be contained particularly in fantasy, melodrama, or what is called serious drama—other types in addition to the first two—can be classified broadly under tragedy and comedy. They are simply ramifications in the way of whimsy or exaggerated emotions in essentially serious or humorous material.

Tragedy—"Tragedy arises then, when, as in Periclean Greece or Elizabethan England, a people fully aware of the calamities of life is nevertheless severely confidential, of the greatness of man, whose mighty passions and supreme fortitude are revealed when one of these calamities overtakes him." [2]

Visibility may be low to medium, often with great contrast, as this is consistent with tragedy. The actor's facial expression and the important features of the setting should be most visible since a goodly portion of the emotional content of the drama is carried by these two factors. Backgrounds, not too clearly seen, will be suggestive and tend to enhance the illusion, to create suspense.

Those things which are considered under *locale* are important only in so far as they suggest tragedy. Unnecessary material should be avoided because it confuses the audience and detracts from the more important subject matter. This simplification, however, must be followed with great care, to avoid having it become a formula for the accomplishment of tragic locale. The dominance of the forces of nature permeates the fatalistic drama. Natural phenomena tend to advance the emotional meaning of the play; for example, change in time of day, the approach of a storm, turning out the lights in a

[2] Joseph Wood Krutch in *The Modern Temper*. Harcourt, Brace and Company.

room, and the rising of the moon. These elements may be utilized to their greatest extent, but care must be taken to provide adequate visibility.

Localized lighting gives emphasis to the tragic element, either a character or an object. The composition of the stage should aim to picturize the significance of the plot at any given moment. If a character is enacting complete desolation, he must not seem to be intimately connected with everyone and everything around him, but should be cut off and alone. On the other hand, broad effects correspond with the magnitude of the dramatic sweep of the play. Strong contrasts in light and dark, in color, in form, and in movement, promote emphasis when the climax approaches, and arbitrary changes in the lighting assist in the building or fluctuation of strong emotional situations.

The dominant effect of the lighting should be heavy, somber, oppressing, or awesome. If the other aspects of the preparation of the lighting have been properly carried out, this result will be achieved without conscious effort on the part of the lighting designer.

Comedy—The material of comedy is more varied in outward aspect than that of tragedy; for example, high comedy, satire, farce, and burlesque. Comedy is usually light, amusing, or humorous—basically the opposite of tragedy. Where seriousness is the keynote of tragedy, levity is the hallmark of comedy. It may have elements of the tragic, but there is a dominance of the gay and lighthearted. In this brief description will be felt a distinctly different attitude toward the staging of comedy, quite opposed to the previous handling of tragedy.

Bright light of a warm and cheerful color is the point of departure for the lighting. The *visibility* should be medium to high. The degree on this scale may be determined by the necessity for seeing critical detail. The more sophisticated comedy demands that the audience see every slightest expression of the actor. If it is a farce executed in broad strokes, the scene need not be so bright, but more color may be used.

Pleasant places suggest comedy; so this type of play should be set in a *locale* that is at once both light and happy. In selecting the details of the place and time of day for humor, one need not be guided so completely as in tragedy by their meaning in the play. If it is a pleasing or an amusing aspect, it may be included for this reason alone.

In comedy, as in tragedy, it is best in *composing* the stage, to picturize the humorous. Whether this will best be done by a soft, delicate composition or by a contrasting use of lights and shadows or colors, will be indicated by the broadness or delicacy of the humor. Comedy of the Restoration demands brilliance, while a classical satire can be done in contrasting colors. In composition, as well as locale, anything that can be done to enhance the lightness or comic nature of the play is justified.

Regardless of any other consideration, the *mood* of the play must be bright—it must be gay. In comedy, as nowhere else, the lighting designer is completely justified in altering any or every other purpose to attain this end.

THE STYLE OF PRODUCTION

The term *style* signifies the "emanation from the prime-symbol of a great culture" and is therefore organic, having an "inconspicuous beginning, a slow growth, a brilliant moment of fulfilment and a gradual decline," [3] or simply a series of conventions, sometimes fads, which grow out of the conditions of any period.

[3] Oswald Spengler in *The Decline of the West*. Alfred A. Knopf.

Style implies a distinctive or characteristic *method* of expression, whether the expression be a mass feeling, or individual. In the development of a style, a form is achieved which is usually a group expression; it is detached and objective. This style is *classicism*. The succeeding step is personal and subjective. It is improbable, adventurous, and romantic, from which it derives its name—*romanticism*. The revolt against the unreal leads to materialism and *realism*. A final attempt at purification causes a denial of all that is real, and strives for a direct emotional expression, and this is called *expressionism*. The style of a production is indicated in the manuscript, and in simple terms the adherence to, or departure from, *realistic* form and detail comprises the range and is expressed visually in the design of the production. There can be no dogma to replace understanding and taste, but a few suggestions as to treatment may be valuable to the student in developing this appreciation. Style has been subdivided into only four groups, but it must be realized that an unending subdivision might be made. The styles flow freely from one to another with infinite gradations.

Classicism—To this style of production is sometimes applied the term "Formalism," for it is based on a very strict form. Realistic motifs are stripped of all unnecessary adornment, and arranged in an ordered manner. The Greek drama is an excellent example, since it has as its essence a definite and well ordered structure.

Locale is suggested only for the sake of orientation. There is only a suggestion of realism. If the place or the time of day has a bearing on the action of the play, it must be indicated, but from this point the composition becomes all important.

The composition is stately, often symmetrical, and simplified. It is the formal aspect that carries the stature of the play to the audience. It consists of understandable elements occasionally designed to have a symbolic significance. It calls for the use of light in an abstract form, to speak directly to the intelligence or emotions of the audience. The stately character of the lighting design is in harmony with the measured rhythm of the line and the formal structure of the drama.

Romanticism—Growing contrastingly out of classicism is the form which carries the individual into the realm of the imaginary, adventurous, ideal. The real is suggested, but treated with so personal an attitude as to lose in the subsequent expression, its original connection with the material. It is glamorous, colorful drama removed from factual reality.

Time and place may be freely interpreted to represent an ideal locale. Moonlight is no longer a shaft of light, integrated into the form of the composition, but a silvery beam casting colorful shadows, stealing into the drama to reveal to the audience the emotional meaning of the players' words. The color effect is often exaggerated toward sensuous beauty, and all natural phenomena are treated with heightened fancy.

Composition is based entirely on the idea of gaining an idealized pictorial effect. It is not a formal arrangement of visual patterns, but rather a guide to mystery, romance, and the freedom of the individual character, searching for the expression of himself and the world as he would like it to be.

Realism—This drama says factual, photographic material is more moving than the imaginary. The degrees of reality are easily discernible, ranging from naturalism to a highly selected realism. The former is usually defined as photographic realism, but this must be qualified to a certain extent, since photographic realism is neither possible nor desirable. It is rather realism that has been selected for dramatic content and altered only as far as need be for adaptation to the limitations of the stage. It should seem to be real.

The motivation for all sources of illumination is naturalistic to such an extent that the movement and positions of actors must be carefully studied to secure proper visibility, for what is acceptable in daily life is insufficient in the theatre. In fact, it will probably be necessary to add many additional instruments to obtain a sufficient visibility, but these must be so well handled that they seem to the untutored observer to come from some lamp, wall bracket, or other recognizable source. There must be a strict adherence to the realistic factors of locale since the playwright has chosen to write in this style, indicating his belief in the inherent drama of the place and the time of day.

Composition must appear perfectly natural. It must grow artistically out of the necessity imposed by sunlight through a window or such other motivation as may be indicated. This is derived by the process of the selection of the essential detail and the exclusion of all else that does not aid in the artistic representation of the real scene. Selectivity is, however, the modern mode in playwrighting. It is the real subtly altered for dramatic effect.

Motivation prevails as a rule. Visibility is provided, but often at the expense of natural effect, and locale lighting may be somewhat exaggerated to offset the arbitrary result given in providing visibility.

Composition is free in the interests of artistry and dramatic emphasis, but the arrangement of the visual elements should convey a realistic effect.

Expressionism—Expressionism is the negation of reality where all of the elements have an emotional significance. The real is distorted until it loses defining characteristics and becomes a symbol. It is an effort to appeal directly to the emotions of the audience without the qualifying analysis of a mental examination.

Locale is lost. There should be a careful avoidance of anything suggestive of time or place. The drama is supposed to have a universal application which is not dependent on its place or time for understanding.

Composition becomes very important. All the visual elements should have a direct effect in emphasizing the emotional reaction through their symbolic meaning. The lighting should picturize the emotional relationship of things and actors on the stage. There are no general tendencies in the composition. It is highly individual and should be treated as a clarifying factor. Where the play seems to demand symmetry, the lighting designer must provide it. Where it is free, he must be guided to an execution that is harmonious.

These are slight indications of the treatments of the styles in the interest of a unity of the visual and auditory elements in production. With the picture of the desirable arrangement of visual elements in mind, the designer is ready to translate to the stage.

THE INTERPRETATION OF THE MENTAL PICTURE IN TERMS OF LIGHTING

The application of each function of lighting requires the use of a combination of the *qualities* of light. The light patterns by which the eye is stimulated determine the mental picture. Therefore, the designer can create the desired dramatic effect visually only by the proper application of each quality. The qualities of light can be expressed by the technical elements available to the artist, but because of the limitations of instruments and control, it is only through a definite technique or method that he is able to produce the best results.

Visibility—When the illumination of the stage discloses

actors, properties, and scenery in *proportion* to their importance dramatically, then good visibility has been provided. It should be as selective and heightened as are the chosen words of the actor in comparison with ordinary speech. High visibility of the actor's facial expressions and the movements of his mouth generally promote understanding. Low visibility on objects or large spaces that do not require concentration often stimulates the imagination to add details that are not present, and tends to create more illusion than where all things are seen equally well. Everyone is cognizant of the power of silhouetted figures in an emotional picturization. This is an example of an apparent, not actual, visibility, that impresses the audience with the emotion to a much greater degree than the complete revelation of the most delicate facial expression. The manner in which each quality contributes to the creation of this range of visibility is discussed in the following paragraphs.

Intensity is the amount of light reflected or transmitted by objects to the eye. The pupil opening determines inversely the amount of light needed to give the effect of brightness. The amount of light required is generally proportional to the visibility desired, particularly up to normal, at which point the intensities possible in the theatre usually end. On a bright, sunny day, the intensity is from ten to twenty times the maximum possible on the stage, so that only glare, occasioned by contrast, need be considered. Light sources in the line of vision, blackouts, and too fast dimming give this effect and should, therefore, be used with great care.

Color is expressed in terms of the *hue*, the degree of *saturation* from neutral to full color, and the *brightness* of the light reflected or transmitted to the eye. Visibility is best under tints, rather than saturated colors, and greater in the greens and yellows than in the reds, blues, or purples. The saturation of a color seems to increase with decreasing brightness, so that in a dim scene colors need not be so strong as in a brilliantly lighted one.

Form is the pattern of light and shade in color that the distribution of light makes on the retina. Reasonable contrasts promote visibility. Broadly speaking, visibility of details is inversely proportional to intensity. It is also affected by the arrangement of intensities and colors on the various objects in the field of vision. If a three dimensional object be lighted in equal intensities, and the same color on all sides, it appears to be two dimensional. The muscular action of focusing the eyes registers the space relationship of forms to some degree. We perceive shapes and relative positions in space by sharpness of outline, superposition, position of shadows, form of light and shade, lines of perspective, scale, and relative color. Anything that can be done to emphasize these factors will aid in achieving a heightened visibility. Where a low degree of seeing detail is desirable, the opposite of these examples must be utilized.

Movement involves any change in the other three qualities. Visibility increases with the time for observation. If the movement is accomplished slowly, visibility is maintained to a high degree. Rapid changes cause fatigue. There is a distinction between scientific visibility, which is physical and physiological, and dramatic visibility, which is psychological and emotional, and it is a combination of the two that must be considered in the theatre.

Locale—Locale is the expression of time and place as far as lighting is concerned. It is limited generally to the simulation to a greater or lesser degree of the conditions of the elements and the natural motivating sources of illumination. The lighting on the scenery, the costumes, and the make-up of the actor (generally fixed conditions) can give the changing effects that are experienced in nature. The term locale implies all of the more or less definite information owed the audience for its understanding of the play, that is, its intellectual response. The problem of indicating principles of procedure in regard to creating the effect of locale is so difficult that the simple method will be followed. By a process of induction, the principles will be evident from the following examples.

Suppose the play is a tragedy placed in a hut in the mountains of Kentucky. The time is the middle of the afternoon, and the play is realistic. These are the facts to be conveyed to the audience. The visibility level is low to medium, and the grays and blues are indicated. Consider, first, the motivating source, the sun. Too much sunlight will brighten the scene to a greater extent than is desirable; so only a small window is provided, and in order to prevent the warmth and romance of a sun about to set, it is quite white. Later in the play, as the tragedy increases, the sun sets behind an advantageous hill. The cold atmosphere of the mountain country grips the scene. For the present, the almost white sun is searching out the dark cluttered corners of the room. The hills seen through the window are a dim, gray blue. There is a dirty lantern hanging on a peg, which will be lighted later, and will give a smoky, furtive light. These very simple indications place the play and allow the remainder of the lighting to be determined by other functions.

If this same play were romantic and pleasing, it would require a warmer sunlight, and instead of dropping suddenly, enveloping the hut in darkness, the shadows would lengthen steadily, the color would become more and more rose tinted, with a glorious sunset sky and deep purple shadows in the mountains. The corners of the room would have, not gray cluttered jumbles of things discarded, but a warm reflection from the sunlight on the walls. The lamp, though simple, would be clean and attractive. The sunlight would be exaggerated with additional brightness, and probably supplemented with other light to brighten the scene. It would be directed to throw interesting shadows. In this instance, the criterion determining decisions is not realism but dramatic beauty.

From these two examples, it is seen that the sunlight is not the object of the expression, but a medium which may be utilized to convey to an audience not simply the time of day, but certain facts concerning the play, the people, their emotions and thoughts. This fundamental concept must be fully appreciated for an intelligent use of the factors of locale. First, analyze carefully the problem of locale for the particular play, to discover the essential or indicative elements that will convey the important facts to the audience. The many people will have different ideas as to what exactly constitutes, for example, moonlight. Some will see it as romantic and colorful, others will find it mysterious, still others will look upon it as peaceful and restful. Nevertheless, there is a common denominator of acceptance, a general recognition of certain basic characteristics. These will form a ground structure upon which may be built a convincing moonlight that will permit a wide variety of expression without ceasing to be moonlight. Adapt these features to the type and style of play under consideration by adhering to the realistic appearance or distorting away from it, and by emphasizing the gay or heavy qualities.

One of the dominant features of locale is the motivation of the lighting from the apparent sources of the illumination: the sun, moon, sky, and other natural sources of light, and artificial sources such as lamps, brackets, and fixtures. They are indispensable to the more realistic styles and help to make the less realistic forms more articulate. In the latter case, they need not be made realistic, but a distorted lamp will seem to give light quite as readily as a natural one and will, at the same time, contribute to the understanding of the necessary lighting.

Composition—This function is primarily the process of selection involved in providing dramatic visibility, locale, and mood. If there is any opportunity for individual æsthetic expression, it is in the composition of the intensities and colors in light. This function encompasses all of the principles of artistic composition: the use of line, color, and mass to attain balance and unity of expression. These are outlined in many text books of pictorial composition. It is best to follow them literally until the concept of good composition becomes cultivated. When this rightness of arrangement expresses itself without thought, these tenets will become a point of departure for a self-expression in the special possibilities of lighting.

In addition, the motivation behind the process of designing the arrangement of colors and forms, and the changes which they follow for pure dramatic picturization, is considered under composition. In this special sense it is not so much the application of the principles of abstract æsthetics as it is the expression of concrete visual images which are most *appropriate* for the type of play and the style of production. For example, the squalor and dinginess of the cellar in *The Lower Depths* may not present a beautiful picture, but if the lighting assists in creating the appropriate atmosphere, good dramatic composition has been provided. This is just as important a form of composition as the presentation of the ravishing, romantic beauty of a garden in moonlight for the balcony scene in *Romeo and Juliet,* or the compelling abstractions of color and form in movement that Thomas Wilfred is able to create with his color organ. Perhaps it is simpler to conceive of composition alone and separately in terms of this last example where the visual designs can be conceived as æsthetic abstractions of color and form in rhythmic movement. Broadly speaking, however, composition is the process of selecting the qualities of light which coördinate most appropriately with the idea of the play, and give the production a unified form or style.

Intensity is concerned with the range of brightness levels of the values selected from a pictorial and dramatic point of view to give the appropriate composition in the bright to dark scale in each scene of the play. Pictorially, lighting provides a far greater brightness range than painting, often as high as one thousand to one, so that considerable care must be taken to avoid glaring, bright areas and dead, dark spaces. A broader standard of values must be acquired before any subtlety of expression can be demonstrated. A study of black and white photographs of some of the old masters in painting will serve as a starting point in the analysis of the relation of values.

Color involves the selection of color tones æsthetically and dramatically to give an appropriate composition to the stage picture. The range of color does not provide greater choice than that available in pigment painting, but tints and shades, as the product of brightness variation, increase this range proportionally. The resultant effect of colored light on pigment complicates the approach from the standpoint of tone relations in painting, but by an allowance for the effect of light on pigment a wide range can be obtained.

Form includes the distribution of light on the sculptural architectural design of surfaces, areas, and space relationships of solid objects, creating a visual pattern of light and shade and color in the eye. The æsthetic principles of the relationship of forms, in position, measure, and shape have been developed upon the hypothesis of the fixed conditions of natural light.

With artificial illumination, the range of expression is considerably increased by the control over light distribution as well as the increased field presented by the intensity and color of light. The location of the light source and the direction of the rays determine the position and the size of the shadow of an object, and provide emphasis in the composition. The graded effect of tone on large areas is a natural characteristic of strip lighting. The arrangement of the parts of a setting in terms of harmony, sequence, and balance in accordance with the principles shown in masterpieces of the visual arts, related to the problems of the theatre, will serve as a solid background for design.

The conditioning to the theatre is the process of unifying manuscript and production. When formality is found in the manuscript, it must be followed in the lighting. This may be done with symmetry, dynamic color, monumental mass, and a sense of great space. Forms that are majestic should be used. If the play is free, let the composition appear to be accidentally fine. Let the balance be occult, the color harmonies delicate, the lines more sensuous. Depending on the action of the play, the focus will at one moment be at one point and at another at a different point. This must be allowed in the lighting composition. No one element of the production should be at odds with another. If the director is making a point with the composition of his actors, the lighting must emphasize it, for there must be a unity in the expression of a composition.

Movement considers the harmony, counterpoint, and sequence of musical composition interpreted in the form of visual changes in the foregoing qualities of light, which are distinguished by the eye, as music is detected by the ear. This is the basis for the design of movement in lighting composition. With immobile scenery, even with static lighting, the actors move from one grouping to another, changing the composition, but more obviously the distributions, colors, and intensities of light can vary the composition of the stage picture. They should be designed to follow the individual's desire for change suitable to the dramatic development of the plot of the play.

Consider the possibility of a mobile composition, the arrangement of the entire play in light so that each moment will bear a definite relationship to what has gone before and what is to come after; if this is done, there will be a unity of expression throughout the play as a whole, just as there is a unity in the characterization, idea, and plot of the play. This unity may express itself in harmony or contrast, in development or decline, or in any or all of the qualities of light that may make up this continuity of idea.

In the *Masse Mensch* of Ernest Toller, the real scenes would be contrasted with the dream scenes. This difference may be expressed principally as a contrast in color and form. The development of the real scenes, the idea of the growing spirit of revolution, should be emphasized with a strengthening of intensity and color and resolved with the defeat into a cold color. The dream scenes start on a strong emotional tone and become more and more poetic. This would be emphasized by an increasing sense of the ephemeral; strong colors would resolve into tints, form would progress from the more to the less real. This is an arbitrary symbolism of an acceptable kind. The intellectual plan is made articulate by its use in conjunction with the elements of the manuscript. The result is more likely to be a closely knit structure for the action of the play and will, therefore, have a tendency to sustain the interest of the audience.

Certain indications have been given for the transitions from scene to scene; now movement within a scene may be examined. It results in a more definite alteration in composition than in either visibility or locale. Movement should be used only if it contributes to the intellectual meaning or emotional content of the play. If the sun sets, it must set because it helps the plot in so doing; or because it is necessary to indicate a change of time; or to provide an emotional and romantic light for the leading character's line, "Sun Father, I come." There must be some reason for every movement in light if it is to aid the production, just as there is a reason for every aspect of the static lighting set-up.

Mood—In describing above the other functions of lighting, it has been necessary to qualify each in terms of dramatic content. This aspect of visual experience by which light creates an atmosphere or an emotional response for an audience, is called mood. The motivation is identical with the fundamental conception of the playwright and is inferred in the lines or described in the manuscript. Lighting should conform in each of its qualities so that the visual elements of production convey, even enhance, the emotional development of the plot, corresponding to the intent of the words and business of the actor. The method of arousing precise emotions or establishing a definite atmosphere by visual means for the majority of people in an audience is not yet, if ever, subject to rules or definition. Artificial lighting as a design element is too little understood to allow for a high degree of interpretive ability on the part of the designer, even if he is given an unhampered opportunity. Yet the awesome effect of an aurora borealis or the approach of a storm, and the pleasurable aspect of some of the more arbitrary uses of light often seen in musical productions, serve as sufficient proof that mood is a practical function of lighting. Mood is greatly abused in the theatre because it is too often the only objective in the mind of the director when he attempts more than intensity illumination. The scene of mystery in the inevitable green light, and the sickly sentiment of white draped figures in the pale blue light, and the host of other tricks to obtain "atmosphere" out of a hat are examples of the type. The proper feeling in a production must come from the essential correctness of every detail. If this is truly done, one will want to see a play again and again to catch the full significance of each of these elements, just as a symphony achieves its complete meaning and power only after it has been heard a great number of times. The creation of the proper mood, then, depends on all of the factors of production.

Intensity or brightness is generally associated with comedy, and darkness with tragedy, although an occasional reversal of the order may be used to promote contrast and emphasis.

Color, psychologically, is generally associated with various emotions; so that by changing the associational elements, the emotional effect is bound to be altered. Green is said to convey the feeling of gloom, sickness, and misery, but under other conditions it may represent spring, freshness, and joy. Cool colors may be sedative; warm, exciting. Beyond this, certain colors have a symbolic significance. Red stands for royalty, purple for sanctity, and white for purity. Utilize such obvious symbolism with the greatest care, or it will be uninteresting and trite. Generally, people prefer saturated colors to those which are neutralized, and tints instead of shades. Purples, blues, oranges, and reds are more appealing than yellows or greens. These facts may be used to influence the emotions of an audience in watching a scene.

Form in the light pattern or the size, shape, and position of objects in space, generally provides orientation by association with similar conditions in daily experience. Stone joints and steps often give the effect of scale. Contrasts in brightness, color, and form, always tend to increase the effect of difference. Straight lines may promote the feeling of strength;

curved lines, softness and beauty; jagged lines, unrest; horizontal lines, calmness; vertical lines, majesty; diagonal lines, movement; parallel lines, order; crossed lines, conflict. Large detail is heavy; small detail is delicate. Composition should create an emphasis that will convey an intelligibly emotional meaning.

Movement: changes from dim to bright, from cool to warm, from flat to solid, are usually cheerful and *vice versa*. Simultaneous and sequential contrasts promote understanding if thoughtfully done. The human being desires variety, but changes must be carefully handled and well timed. Rapid changes are exciting; subtle movement is quiet and satisfying. These suggestions must be treated with complete freedom by the designer. No rules are sufficiently flexible to be at the same time applicable to all types and styles of productions, and to have a concrete meaning. The above are general indications and must be treated as such.

SUMMARY

It is probably fortunate that it is impossible to determine the degree of application of each of the functions in the above outline for any particular production, because that would not allow for individual expression. However, Appendices II and III contain analyses of two plays as examples of the practical degree to which each function can be expressed. This method of approaching the visual picture assumes that there is nothing to interfere with its execution and that there is a complete and sympathetic understanding between the director, the designer, and the lighting designer. Needless to say, it also assumes that all of these people interpret the manuscript in the same terms. Such, however, is not always the case; so that some factors may be altered and a compromise effected. Since the designer and director usually consider the lighting as most facile, the correction is expected to be made in the lighting set-up. The inevitable compromises between a convincing expression of locale and the lighting necessary for visibility indicate that it is a problem of balancing the importance of each function.

If the playwright has considered these problems and either provided the situation, which is entirely flexible, or definitely predetermined the details to minimize the compromises, the final effect is bound to be more convincing. But he is not always careful in his selection of the place or the time of day for the action of his drama. In this event, it is usually wise to alter in accordance with an interpretation that will further the idea of the play rather than follow the stage direction. If the lighting is such that actors are required to be in particular positions for dramatic moments, it is well to have a complete understanding with the director so that his action will find them there. If the designer feels that he must have a large window where a small one is better for the lighting, the scheme may have to be altered to gain the same effect with the larger window. Since these differences have such a wide variety, it must be left for the inspiration of the moment and the ingenuity of the lighting designer to overcome them. They may be avoided by careful planning and coöperation, and this is the most desirable solution.

The foregoing analysis presupposes a high degree of control over lighting. Inasmuch as this is often wanting, because of the ignorance of the designer or technician, or the inadequacy of equipment and control apparatus, further adjustments of the plans must be made to allow for the effects that are obtainable practically under these conditions. In view of this situation, it has been found useful to establish an arbitrary method (see following chapter) for lighting the stage, which is sufficiently flexible to satisfy most of the plans made in view of the above analysis, but no description or explanation can supply the judgment or artistic sense of selection which is necessary to balance the intensities of colors and light so that they will give a thoroughly coördinated expression with the other elements of production.

Only through experience and the development of what might be called an artistic light sense can the designer hope to achieve this special taste for good lighting. A certain amount of taste can be cultivated, but sound ability is born in a person, and cannot be taught. It is in the interest of providing a designer with the simplest means of expression whereby, through experience, he may cultivate a taste for lighting, that this material has been prepared.

The technical aspects of lighting are so much more involved than any other means of expression perhaps, short of architecture itself, that until utterly flexible lighting equipment and control are provided, the designer must build his visual concept in very simple terms. If there are six spotlights, a set of floodlights, and four or five dimmers, the technician or designer or whoever is responsible for the actual lighting, will automatically proceed from the technical aspects to the æsthetic expression (the reverse of the process of the playwright or producer), and he will find it difficult to visualize any plans which have been made, discouraging this limited equipment. In the final analysis, the result depends upon the most expressive use of the equipment available.

THE APPLICATION OF LIGHTING
TO THE STAGE

by

S. R. McCandless and Louis Erhardt

THE APPLICATION OF LIGHTING TO THE STAGE

by

S. R. McCandless and Louis Erhardt

The visualized plans based on the material of the preceding chapter must be translated to the stage in terms of equipment and methods of staging. A photograph of a stage setting indicates the distribution of lighting from the various instruments, and by close study it is possible to determine to a degree the type of instruments and their positions. The ability of the designer to visualize almost photographically the details of equipment which are necessary to carry out his plans will facilitate the process of translating his concept into a finished picture. The usual methods of staging make it practical to consider the lighting instruments under four groups: (1) Those which light the *acting area;* (2) those used for a *toning and blending;* (3) those used to illuminate the various parts of the *background;* and (4) those *special instruments* which do not fit into any of the preceding divisions. (See Appendix IV: *Dictionary of Instruments* for description of each type that is used in these various groups.)

THE USE OF INSTRUMENTS

1. Spotlights are generally used to light the acting area. They can be mounted as illustrated in the diagrams (in the

Appendices) in a false beam in the ceiling of an auditorium, on the teaser or concert border, or on the tormenter battens. If the setting is an exterior and very deep, a second border and towers in the wings may be used. In some cases spotlights are mounted on the front of the balcony, and more rarely, in the footlight trough. For purposes of visibility, each area is lighted from two directions; and for purposes of plasticity and motivation, a cool color is used on one side and a warm color on the other. The usual arrangement of six areas is indicated in the diagram. Where the action is limited to a smaller section of the stage or where the setting restricts the acting area, the number of areas may be reduced.

The direction of light coming from the acting area spotlights mounted in various positions gives a variety of expression to the actor's face and figure. The direction of light from the bridge and the auditorium beam may be said to give the most realistic appearance to the actor, inasmuch as the diagonal direction from above creates a normal balance of highlight and shadow on the actor's face. Occasionally a back spot directed on the actor from above and behind can give a rather romantic halo or highlight. The tormenter position creates a more arbitrary and romantic effect. The balcony front tends to throw confusing shadows and to give a rather flat and startling appearance to the actor's face. Light directed from a footlight spot on the actor creates a definitely fantastic effect and is likely to give a large distracting shadow on the background.

Color mediums suggested for the acting area are those listed in the accompanying table as 1, 2, 3, 9, 16, 17, 18, 26, 29, 54, 57, 62, and 75; less often, numbers 6, 14, 25, and 41. These colors are tints and transmit a relatively high amount of light. Their use has been suggested from a careful analysis of facial illumination. Stronger and purer colors tend to cut

Color Medium

This tabulation includes a partial list of the new standard numbering for commercial gelatins. Those indicated by one asterisk are desirable for use in the acting area spotlights; those indicated with a double asterisk are the colors recommended for X-rays; and those indicated by the triple asterisk are the primary colors.

* 1—Frost
* 2—Light flesh pink
* 3—Flesh pink
* 6—Rose pink
* 9—DuBarry pink
**11—Medium magenta
*14—Rose purple
*16—Violet
*17—Special lavender
*18—Medium lavender

*25—Daylight blue
*26—Light sky blue
27—Light blue
*29—Special steel blue
32—Medium blue special
***36—Non-fade blue
**41—Moonlight blue
44—Medium blue green

48—Medium green
***49—Dark green
*54—Light straw
*57—Light amber
**58—Medium amber
60—Dark amber
61—Orange
*62—Light scarlet
***67—Fire red
*75—Neutral Gray

down the effect of visibility and to distort the make-up to a degree which is unsatisfactory. Normally speaking, all acting area spotlights directed along the same angle to the acting area should have the same tint and should be consistent in color tone with the motivating light from that general direction. Those from the opposite side should tend to give a contrasting effect of color to promote plasticity, the degree of contrast depending upon the vibrancy desired.

All acting area spotlights should be equipped with a diffusing medium so that the beam is soft-edged, if the play leans toward the realistic. In view of this, the instruments mounted in the auditorium ceiling or on the face of the balcony will require funnels to keep the spill light off the walls and ceiling. Where the arbitrary theatricality of a round or elliptically lighted area is desired, these precautions may be omitted. Soft-edged spotlighting can be achieved by the use of a frosted medium No. 1 (with an oiled center to permit greater directional transmission), or by scratching the edge of the color medium with a fine sand paper. The areas should overlap so that there are no low pockets in the illumination of the acting area. Mats (cutoffs) should be used where it is necessary to shape the beam or to keep it from falling on the proscenium or certain parts of the setting.

2. For blending these acting areas together, border striplights are used. They may be wired in three or four colors and should give a soft general illumination from above, over all the acting areas. They are usually hung on the concert (or No. 1) border or underneath the bridge. If the setting is exceptionally deep, a second borderlight halfway upstage may be found necessary. This is particularly true where cloth borders are used in place of a ceiling. In general, the colors to use are numbers 9, 41, and 58, or whatever particular colors will give the proper tone to the scene. By using these colors

in combination at varying intensities, it will be found that a wide range of flexibility is provided. In order to keep the light from this strip off the ceiling and the walls of the setting above the actor's head, it is often necessary to use a masking in the form of a shadow box. In most cases the light reflected from the floor will give a soft glow on the setting, but the primary purpose of the borderlight is to blend the acting areas together.

The most important instrument for toning the setting is the footlight strip. While it is very valuable in revues and musical shows to illuminate the chorus, the chief objection to it in a legitimate production lies more in its exceeding brightness and the resulting unnatural effect than from its careful use as a toning medium. The use of front (beam or balcony) lights has considerably lowered the value of footlights as a means of lighting the actors, but from no other source is it as easy to illuminate and tone the setting; and, where they are not necessary for this purpose, they serve to illuminate the act curtain when it is down. The position of the footlights is in a trough in front of the act curtain at the edge of the apron, extending across the width of the stage to within three or four feet of the proscenium arch. They are usually wired in three or four colors—red 67, green 49, and blue 36, and, if four, amber 58. The first three are the primaries of light which, when used in varying quantities, give the widest possible range of tonal effect. They should give a soft, even light over the scene, but should under no conditions fall on the proscenium itself. It is well to have them controlled in two or three sections so that they give a range in both color and distribution. The center section may be as long as the two ends combined.

3. Background lighting deals with the illumination of all parts of the setting which are not immediately surrounding

the acting area. The most important of these parts is the cyclo-rama, backdrop, or dome. The second group deals with ground rows, and the third with backings.

It has been found by practice that the best method for lighting the base of the cyclorama—and this holds for domes and backdrops—is a row of three-or-four-color base strips to give the horizon effects of sunset and to set the sky back from the ground rows in luminous intensity. These strips in conjunction with high-powered sources from overhead in the form of a three-colored striplight hung close to the drop itself or from a number of floods placed well downstage give an even illumination over the entire surface. The latter method is by all odds the best, because it tends to iron out any wrinkles which may appear in the cloth, but it eliminates the use of the flies between this position and the cyclorama.

Naturally, small backdrops can be lighted by a flood from each side and a strip overhead and below, but this practice tends to leave a dead spot in the center because of the distance from the light sources.

For greatest flexibility, the three primary colors should be used in the cyclorama footlights or horizon strips, with the addition of amber, but ordinarily—because of the demand for high intensity in the blue circuit—it is often wise to use a daylight 25, or dark steel blue 29, for daylight skies, a dark blue 36 for night skies, and an amber 58 for a simple simula-tion of sunset colors. Realistic sunset colors can best be pro-duced with the primaries. The same color selection holds for the overhead lights. Sectional control is often desirable be-cause the sky may be used to designate the direction of the rising or setting sun and for a formal composition in color or intensity with the more stylized type of play.

The lighting of ground rows is generally provided by the overhead cyclorama lights, but if there are a number of them, it is simple to get the sense of distance by putting a single color ground row strip (three-color for color changes) in front of each ground row at its base. Backings such as a screen or twofold, used to mask entrances in the box set, can be lighted by a backing strip mounted above the door, by a floodlight placed offstage and high so that the actor's shadow does not fall on the backing itself, or by a spotlight or highpowered flood directed against a large reflector which will give a soft glow in the entrance without danger of causing shadows. This lighting keeps the entrances from appearing as dark holes in the setting.

4. Many instruments which must be used in any lighting layout do not fall within these first three catagories. Those instruments which are used to emphasize certain bits of the acting area or bits of scenery, or those which represent the directional rays of the sun or the moon, or create the effect of fires of all kinds, fixtures, wall brackets, and all special effects such as projected patterns, fall within this group.

Entrances in any production are likely to be important. Therefore it is always wise to plan to have, in addition to the acting area lights, a special spotlight mounted on the bridge or first border to cover these entrances.

For sunlight and moonlight and all other phenomena requiring parallel rays of light, use projectors. These instruments may be placed at considerable distance from the acting area without undue loss of intensity.

Wall brackets and lamps on the stage should be kept sufficiently dim so as not to cause glare, but as far as possible in a realistic production, these motivating sources if masked on the audience side should give off as much light as possible in the opposite direction.

Fire logs, fireplaces, grate fires, and the like, when used on the stage, should be kept unobtrusive and should not display their artificiality any more than is necessary. If a pair of rotors (oppositely rotating transparent cylinders painted in strips of red, yellow, and black and turned by the heat of the lamps) can be mounted inside the fireplace, a very realistic effect of flicker is created. Otherwise, a judicious use of several lamps—red and amber—brought up and down on dimmers, will convey the impression of a flickering fire. Fire logs in fireplaces should be supplemented by a small floodlight placed just downstage and out of sight of the audience (if the fireplace is in the side wall) to give the luminous glow that would normally come from burning logs.

Projections are of two kinds. Those which have large detail and are not too sharply defined may be projected at a short distance by use of a Linnebach or shadow-projector—an instrument which uses a boldly painted slide of eighteen to thirty-six inches square. The second type is a lens projector similar to a stereopticon. The projection equipment for this instrument must be carefully figured on the basis of the distance of the instrument from the screen, and the size of the image desired. Equipment companies carry in stock a large number of moving effects which can be fitted to this instrument, such as rain, moving clouds, snow, and so on. Many of the books listed in the bibliography illustrate and explain these various effects in detail.

PROCEDURE

A plan of the layout should be prepared on paper showing the location of the instruments, their direction, and the areas which they illuminate (See Appendices II and III). Each of the preceding groups of instruments should be included in this plan. The thoroughness and accuracy of visualization will be more than amply repaid by the time saved and the nerves spared in the dress rehearsal period. It is not fair to hold up an entire company through having failed to specify the correct instrument, the right color, or some little detail which could have been foreseen. A system of notation should call all of these matters to attention and convey the plan to the crew in such a way that it will be understood. The layout should be accompanied by a schedule giving complete intelligence of the facts concerning each individual instrument such as type, wattage, color, mounting apparatus; special equipment such as mats, funnels, or cutoffs; connections; and the changes in these between scenes. Certain simplifications in this scheme are possible with an established crew.

In setting up the equipment for lighting, one person at the head of the crew can be designated as a floor man or electrician who is responsible for handling all of the crew except the switchboard operators. It is his duty to supervise the execution of the layout. He is responsible for the proper mounting of all instruments and must check the focus, connections, and accessories of each.

The customary mounting for spotlights, floodlights, and some special instruments, should allow for universal action. A mounting of this type is one which has two planes of rotation perpendicular to each other, and will allow the instrument to be turned in any direction. Every instrument should be mounted so that it will have the proper amount of directionality, and when it is mounted, the equipment should be clamped down tightly enough so that it will not be jarred or knocked out of position or permit the instrument to fall.

The usual procedure is to mount most of the instruments, then to lamp, connect, and test. After this is done, the instruments are focused as indicated on the layout sheet, and the color mediums and mats are put in. On the acting area, care must be taken in interpreting the meaning of the areas.

They should be considered as existing about five feet above the level of the floor. The face of an actor standing within the area should be lighted. After all focusing is completed, the floor man or electrician should check every instrument to see that it is firm, has the proper lamp, and a tight electrical connection. It is best to tie the ends of a cable connection together in a simple overhand knot so that it will not part accidentally. If the pin connection is loose, the prong should be spread with a knife.

During this process, the switchboard operators should connect each instrument to a feed circuit according to a predetermined plan and be in position to turn on each circuit as it is called for according to its connection, its use, or its number on the layout sheet. The switchboard should be sufficiently well marked to convey this information quickly, and the operators should eventually become familiar with every circuit and instrument by each designation. When the checking process is completed, such changes as have been necessary will have been made. Then the properties and all the details of the settings should be assembled and arranged. With this done, the setting is ready to be lighted.

The previous chapter deals with the relative importance and degree of application of each function of lighting in expressing the visual aspects of the style of production for each type of play. The degree of *visibility* for each part of the setting, particularly the acting areas, must be assured. For most realistic productions, *locale* is the dominant function, and the motivating light is the standard to which the rest of the lighting should be balanced. The aim to produce realism must be tempered with a constant selection of colors and distributions which give dramatic emphasis and *composition* to the stage picture. Finally, in this process of developing the lighting for a particular scene, the visual effect should convey the proper dramatic atmosphere or *mood*.

With these factors clearly in mind, the lighting designer can proceed with balancing the intensity, the color, and the form of distribution. After a preliminary set-up for each scene is worked out and recorded, cues and other light changes should be rehearsed to determine the sequence of operations on the switchboard and the appearance of the transitions from one set-up to another if they occur in the same scene.

Except when it is possible for the switchboard operator to see the effects he is producing, the designer or person in charge of the lighting should sit in the auditorium where during the lighting rehearsal and perhaps by means of a telephone (usually by shouting), he can give directions to the operator to regulate or balance the lighting. Considerable time should be allowed for this process even when the instruments are properly equipped and focused. The most serious weakness in the method lies in the loss of feeling when the designer must translate his ideas into mechanical terms so that they can be carried out at the switchboard by another person who ordinarily cannot see the stage. The process of balancing the intensities at the switchboard, adjusting the colors, correcting the distribution of light from the individual instruments, working out the various cues, and recording the readings, comprises what might be called a lighting rehearsal.

The following steps and precautions should be taken during the lighting rehearsal:

1. Exhibit the trial set-up if one has been prepared in advance. Otherwise start with all lights out and bring up the motivating lights on dimmer to approximately full intensity. Balance the intensity of the remaining instruments to create the proper visual picture.

2. Make corrections in positions of instruments, their di-

rection and equipment, such as color mediums and mats, before proceeding to the next step.

3. Check the distribution of the lighting on the acting areas in the important positions which have been determined during the acting rehearsals. The stage manager can be very helpful during the lighting rehearsal by moving through the various bits of acting business to determine whether the visibility on the acting area is adequate for all situations during the scene.

4. When the visual aspect is satisfactory from the standpoint of visibility, locale, composition, and mood, register the switchboard readings on the cue sheet.

5. Mark the position and direction of portable equipment, particularly if it has to be moved for another scene.

6. Record all instruments, colors, accessories, and connections on the light plot or plan.

7. If there are line or time cues, work out the sequence of operations on the switchboard and on the stage, and test the appearance of each step in the transition. Use a series of station points in time cues to guarantee the proper sequence of changes. Rehearse several times with the warning and dead cue to accustom the operator to the sequence, but record the set-up for each step before going on to the next.

8. Make a preliminary set-up for each scene following the above method.

9. If there is a curtain routine for light changes, they should be rehearsed some time before the dress rehearsal. Front lights and footlights adjusted for a particular scene do not always look well on the curtain, and under any conditions the footlights should come up as the house lights go down. The sequence is the opposite at the close of a scene or an act. Ordinarily there should be some light present at all times.

10. Correct the preliminary light plots and cue sheets so

that they may serve as a record of all the details of equipment and how it is used in the production.

Further adjustments will be necessary when the actors are brought on the stage for dress rehearsal. In the meantime a technical rehearsal and a costume parade will clear up many problems that are likely to arise to delay the final rehearsals. The technical rehearsal is held primarily to reduce the time for shifts and to work out the sequence of moving pieces of scenery, properties, and lighting instruments. It serves as a time also to make further corrections in the cue sheets and to rehearse cues and curtain routines. For a quick shift of scenery, movements have to be rehearsed as carefully as the lines of the play. The costume parade consists of the actors, generally completely dressed and made up, walking through their various bits of business. This gives the costume designer and the lighting designer an opportunity to see how their executed plans coördinate. Certain aspects of the color and the distribution of the lighting on the acting area often have to be adjusted and should be carried out and the changes recorded during this rehearsal. This procedure under ideal conditions should complete the assembling and correlation of all the visual elements in the production and should clear the way for uninterrupted dress rehearsals.

Ideal conditions in the theatre are seldom realized. The variables in the human equation make it almost impossible to anticipate completely the relation of all the means of expression in a production. This is primarily the reason for rehearsal. If the practical elements have been well planned and brought together, the dress rehearsal can be devoted to shaping up the less tangible means of expressing the idea of the play to an audience. In fact, the director should be free in these final stages to devote his time to fitting the actor into the scene, to building each scene, and to giving the proper dramatic emphasis to the whole performance. These rehearsals should be considered as performances without an audience. There should be as little interruption in the running of a scene as possible, and only those adjustments and corrections in the lighting that can be made without causing a disturbance should be attempted. Notes should be taken concerning all other matters, and the adjustments made before the next rehearsal. Every change in layout should be tested in rehearsal, and only very minor adjustments made after the last dress rehearsal. It is to be assumed at this stage that the production is ready for an audience.

From a technical point of view a performance should run like a well oiled machine. A smooth performance is an example of human and technical coördination such as is experienced in few other expressions. Actually there are many places where the machine may break down, and these vulnerable points must be carefully guarded. A lamp may fail, a fuse may "blow," or an instrument may be knocked out of focus. An audience can understand an actor's forgetting his lines or tripping over something, but it may be thoroughly distracted by a faulty light cue or a flickering caused by a loose connection. If the production is to be given a number of performances, precision must be maintained, equipment kept up to date, and even improvements made in the lighting. This is particularly true where the first performances are considered "tryouts" and the production is taken "on the road" before it settles down in its final home for a "run."

No written material on the practice of the theatre can serve the purpose of experience. The variety of conditions limits the value of detailed suggestions. The information contained in the preceding paragraphs should be used as a guide and serve as a stimulation to use light more extensively in dramatic production. Enthusiasm, however, should be tempered by a sincere respect for the more traditional means of expression in the theatre. Experimentation, visualization, and research should seek to extend the boundaries of the possible, but with limited equipment and relatively limited knowledge, the actual plans for a production should be simple, not too ambitious. It is far more satisfactory to plan an effect that is relatively sure of realization than to stake everything on a scheme that is likely to fail at the crucial moment. Lighting has great potentialities which can be realized when there is a profound knowledge of its uses, highly developed equipment and control, and a tradition which allows for its complete coördination with the other elements of expression in dramatic production.

COSTUME

by

ALINE BERNSTEIN

Aline Bernstein, one of America's foremost scenic and costume designers, began her career by designing costumes for the Neighborhood Playhouse's production of *The Little Clay Cart*, New York, 1924. Among the plays for which she has designed settings and costumes are: *Dybbuk*; *The Romantic Young Lady*; *Caprice*; *Ned McCobb's Daughter*; *The Game of Love and Death*; *Reunion in Vienna*; *To-morrow and To-morrow*; *Animal Kingdom*; *The Cherry Orchard*; *The Sea-Gull*; *Grand Hotel*; *Clear All Wires*; *Thunder on The Left*; *Mackerel Skies*; and *A Hat, a Coat, a Glove*. Mrs. Bernstein is also the author of *Three Blue Suits*.

COSTUME

by

ALINE BERNSTEIN

THE moment an actor comes upon the stage, he is in costume. He is no longer himself; he is the character he is representing, the character written by the author. His flesh is not his own nor his mind nor his temperament nor his clothes; whether he wears a suit belonging to himself or not, that suit must have something that marks him. This is the underlying principle of all costume design; it comes before any consideration of material or æsthetics. (I use the word actor to signify both male and female as the principle applies to both, and it is easier to use one word.)

The first point to be considered in designing or choosing a costume is a careful study of the text of the play, of the characters represented in their own channel, and of their relation to each other. A costume must in no way exceed itself but must aid an actor and help to establish in the mind of the audience the sort of man he is representing. In other words the dress must be suitable, whether a thing of great beauty or of rags or of all the scale between. Sometimes effects can be gained by subtle means barely noticeable to the eye, the under or over starching of a collar, the lengthening or shortening, or tightening or loosening, of a sleeve by so little as half an inch; and all theatre-goers know the effects that are

333

gained by comedians by the size of their hats, either too small or so large that their ears seem to hold them up.

In designing or selecting a costume there are four things to be considered, the character, the actor himself, the type of play, and the material. In the regular dramatic productions clothing is usually bought for the actors, and I have had struggles to make them wear what I considered proper. Many females of the species prefer to look either like a page from Vogue or Little Bo-Peep instead of the middle-aged matron that the author has written, or in any way to suggest the character itself. Above all things the actor must be comfortable and satisfied, as he is producing his effect with his own personality, flesh and blood. Actors are often desirous of impressing the audience rather with themselves than with the written characters. I believe this to be perfectly legitimate with certain plays known as society pieces where light entertainment and the personal appearance of the actor are pre-eminent and where audiences go for those alone. But in the more serious dramas—I will take as examples Chekov and Ibsen and Shaw—where men have written seriously of life and the relation of human beings to each other, their environment, and their social habitation, I believe that deep thought and care must be given to every detail of wearing apparel, not only clothes and hats but shoes, gloves, and jewelry.

Remember that the theatrical art differs from all other arts inasmuch as it is a product of many minds and people. Countless hands go to make a finished production, whereas a painter paints his picture and it is entirely his own, an author's book is his (the printing and binding make very little difference), and a composer's music, while it needs a good performer, exists in its entirety on paper.

The same principle holds good in designing costumes for period plays, but in period plays you have the aid of the style and the fact that the eye is more readily pleased, and there are countless sources from which to get your information. I rarely use what is known as a costume book but go to the direct sources from which the authors of costume books have drawn their information, that is paintings, sculptures, and art objects of the period itself. Many secrets of draping and making can be discovered from careful study of sculpture, particularly of the Greek and Egyptian, as the entire figure is there and the back and sides can be studied as well as the front. I often think what a pity it is that so few people are painting or modeling life as it exists today in all its interesting detail. The costume designer of two centuries from now will have to go to the fashion magazines or the stills of moving pictures for their information. There are no pictures of intimate social life as were painted in the early nineteenth century, no great portraits and conversation pictures such as were painted in the eighteenth century, no vast and rich store of portraits and groups of the Renaissance. Man in those times painted life as it was lived, formally and intimately, in all its detail, and those pictures are of the utmost value to the costume designer as well as to the scenic designer.

And here let me say that those two functions should be performed by the same person, with the possible exception of the musical revue. I will no longer design costumes for a play where I do not design the scenery as well, for the costumes on the actors have to move back and forth before the background and in and out of the light with perfect harmony.

As to the material used in period plays, that has to be determined by the money at hand for the production. Professional labor is expensive, and so, in these days, is material. Wonderful effects can be made with what I choose to call the translation of material. When the curtain goes up on a scene, a magic curtain rises with it, and through this magic curtain the spectators look with enchanted eyes. They are there to be amused or instructed or fooled according to the individual, maybe all three together. The illusion of the richest stuffs can be created with muslin, felt, oilcloth, velveteen, and a little paint applied judiciously. Sometimes far more beautiful effects are created by the artist in this way than by the use of real and expensive materials which often go flat under artificial light. Remember everything on the stage must be heightened, must be made more like itself than it really is, and selection must be made and used from things as they really are. That is the way good writing is done for the theatre; an absolute transcription of conversation among four or five people would be dull and uninteresting. The author selects the things for his characters to say that will point his story, the high spots of meaning, and so must the costume and scenic designer do with his material.

Color is so much a matter of personal taste that I can say little about it except that at the outset there must be a definite scheme. The way I proceed is to select the colors for the clothes of the principal actors, consult with them, and when we are settled, go on to the lesser characters and chorus or supernumeraries. I often take pieces of the colors and put them together, as the actors are grouped in a scene, to find if the effect is harmonious. This is a good practice but not necessary.

You will find that practically all actors, particularly females, have decided leanings toward certain colors and an absolute distaste for others; I have often had to remake an entire scheme on that account, to shift and change so that all are satisfied. It is a bad plan to have the actor dissatisfied with his clothes, for no matter how beautiful in design and color a costume may be, it is made into a fine and living thing by the actor, or it can be ruined by him. There are certain people who can carry their clothes on the stage with such dignity and beauty that the clothes themselves become finer than they really are, and others can make the most beautiful things appear tawdry.

The dye pot is a valuable adjunct to the designer, but it must be used with the utmost discretion. Color can be clear and it can be subtle, but it should not be muddy or arty. Color as well as line must be used to express your idea, but I should say that line, or style, is more important. And never forget how colors modify and change each other.

Cutting and fitting are both a matter of constant practice. If you are making a period costume, study carefully all the points of its style. Study the width and length of the skirts, the make of the trousers, how the sleeves are made, how they are set into the armholes, how the neck of the garment fits on the body, where the shoulder seams come, where on the human form the waistline is placed, where buttons are put, and how the garment was fastened at the time. There is nothing too great nor too small to be studied, and the sum total makes a complete and beautiful whole. There is no detail which should not be considered and worked over, and if you have enough interest in your subject, you will find the day will stretch so that there is time for everything. I do not mean that costume should be overloaded with small things and ornaments; I mean that certain fundamentals of style must be adhered to for a perfect whole.

In all matters connected with the theatre the finished product, or performance, is the only thing that counts. The start may be enthusiastic and good, but what matters is the picture that strikes the eye of the spectator when the curtain rises. The amateur must impose upon himself this discipline; on the professional the discipline is imposed by the nature of his contract if ever he is to have a second job.

The theatre is a fine place and should be treated with respect by all who work in it. Unfortunately at times the theatrical business is conducted by people of no integrity and no sympathy or understanding of its widespread power. It is a great source of fun, which we all need, and a wonderful medium for the dissemination of ideas.

There is not much money to be made designing costumes alone, certainly not much commensurate with the amount of work that goes into it. But there is a great deal of satisfaction in seeing one's ideas come alive as they do no where else so well as on the stage. A good living can be made by designing costumes for the films and for musical revues, but those are the only fields wherein, I believe, a decent living can be earned.

Everything that I have said I believe to apply to modern costume as well as to period. There is always the particular character as well as the general style, and above all things remember that the most important thing about a costume is the acting that takes place inside of it.

MAKE-UP FOR THE STAGE

by

Tamara Daykarkhanova

Tamara Daykarkhanova received invaluable training in acting under Nemirovitch-Dantchenko and Constantin S. Stanislavsky in the School of the Moscow Art Theatre. On her graduation from this school, she became a member of the permanent company. She has received instruction in dancing from Isadora Duncan and in singing from Madame Soia Lodi. In the Moscow Art Theatre, she played in Dostoievsky's *Brothers Karamazoff*; in Jushkevitch's *Miserere*; in Ibsen's *Brand*; and in Maeterlinck's *Blue Bird*. One summer she danced with Duncan's barefoot Russian troupe in London.

She left the Moscow Art Theatre in order to play ingénue parts in Petrograd at the Maly Theatre, in Theatre Krivoe Zerkalo under Nickolas Evreinoff, and in Pantomime Theatre under Vsevolod Meierhold. Leaving these stages to join Balieff's Chauve-Souris, she became the leading actress of that company and played all the first dramatic parts in short plays written or adapted from masterpieces of Pushkin, Lermontoff, Gogol, Turgeneff, Tolstoy, Tchekoff, and Gorki. Her tremendous versatility, her training in dancing and singing enabled her to appear in five or six different parts in a single evening. In the summer she would appear as guest artist in Kieff, Odessa, Tiflis, and other cities. Madame Daykarkhanova played with the Chauve-Souris in Paris, London, New York, and Berlin in addition to approximately twenty-five other cities in Europe and this country.

In 1931 she left the Chauve-Souris and made her home in New York. Here she founded the Studio of Stage Make-Up and more recently, Tamara Daykarkhanova's School for the Stage.

MAKE-UP FOR THE STAGE

by

Tamara Daykarkhanova

MAKE-UP IN THE PAST

Leo Tolstoy once observed that it would be perplexing to speculate on how greatly the history of mankind would have been altered if Cleopatra's nose had been a less provoking shape. It is safe to say, however, that the personal success of hundreds and hundreds of Cleopatras depends, to an enormous extent, upon the shape of the nose, on the shadows about the eyes, on the lines around the mouth, on the rouged, moulded outlines of the cheeks.

Actors of the past, as well as those performers who never realized that they were acting—the medicine men, the priests, the warriors dancing the ritual of glory, of conquest, of plunder—understood that in order to impress their audiences, to make an illusion come true before these audiences, they must alter their physical appearance. Hence, they applied paints to the body and face, or they wore a mask. In shoes with high heels, they further decorated themselves with such appurtenances as would immediately induce in the spectator the particular mood in which they desired him to be, equally receptive to a comedian's rendition of a phallic song or to a lofty interpretation of a noble tragedy.

The art of make-up is an old one. Excavations, revealing information of the Stone Age, prove beyond a doubt, that an extinct race of human beings covered their bodies with paints. Scientists are uncertain, however, of the underlying motive. It is difficult for them to say whether this was done to beautify the body or to protect it from the pernicious bites of insects. When and how make-up, or the painting and changing of the face, became a practice on the stage is not definitely known. It is generally assumed that the famous inventor of the second actor in Greek tragedy, Thespis, introduced the mask and make-up on the stage in the sixth century b. c. It is probable that the use of make-up on the stage originated among the worshipers of Bacchus, who smeared their faces with red wine. The make-up of the medieval actor in the mystery play is impressive for its realistic interpretation of the features of devils and saints, angels and animals, laymen and monks. The innumerable Feasts of Fools, Feasts of Asses, and other revels of the lower clergy, were enacted with faces painted strictly according to type. In the French morality play, *Bien Avisé et Mal Avisé*, for example, Fortune would wear a two-faced mask—one face kindly and smiling, the other grim and scowling.

In examining the illustrations of the commedia dell' arte, we find that the faces of the leading characters—Pantalone, Arlecchino, Capitano, Dottore—are made up effectively and convincingly. This is startling when we realize that the materials utilized in these make-ups were of the crudest. The celebrated Gros-Guillaume on the stage of the Hôtel de Bourgogne, would cover his face with a thick layer of flour. During the time of Elizabeth, the actor relied almost entirely upon the use of wigs and beards. Even in the days of David Garrick, little attention was paid to the realism of make-up. Garrick himself wore the white court wig of George III in nearly all his parts. Until the middle of the nineteenth century, when grease paint was invented, the make-up box consisted only of white chalk, carmine, burnt cork, and white lead with lard as a base.

With such meager equipment it is easy to understand why make-up fell into disrepute. The chemistry of paints was undeveloped and many coloring materials were injurious and even poisonous to the user. Little was accomplished in this art at the time of the maturity of Eleanora Duse's genius, and as a result, she renounced make-up completely. The actor today cannot renounce it. The very nature of the modern theatre and motion pictures, and their powerful lighting systems, make this art a necessity to the actor. He must be grateful to modern industry which has provided him with such an assortment of reliable paints and powders. He must be grateful, too, to the great artists who have evolved a scientific technique of stage make-up, helping him to equip himself to meet one of his major problems in the theatre.

STAGE MAKE-UP IN THE AMERICAN THEATRE

While the actor today may recognize how much has been accomplished in the art of make-up and in the materials and tools of this art, and while he may realize that modern lighting demands some knowledge on his part of the fundamental application of make-up, he has seldom been tempted to master its exacting technique. His own sad experience has taught him that the theatre, as he knows it in this country, operates under a system of type-casting, a system which, by its very nature, discourages the use of the make-up box. He has not learned to master this art because he has been forced to the realization that he will not be called upon to undertake a rôle unless he himself fulfils the physical qualifications of the characters he is to play. It seems to me that theatrical producers are beginning to see the absurdity of casting to type, and that this system may be forced to yield to another less pernicious to the growth and development of the actor. As the situation stands today, I feel I can safely say that no more than ten per cent of the American acting profession know very much about make-up.

I find this a highly deplorable condition, as make-up, more than costume or setting, conveys to the spectator the true essence of a great performance—the manifestation of a human soul in a human countenance. The nearer an actor comes to making his outward appearance correspond to the inner design of his part, the more brilliant and unforgettable will be the image he creates and the more surely will this image make the on-looker suffer and rejoice with him on the stage. In the words of a German author, "Make-up becomes the visiting card of the actor."

It is a comparatively simple operation to apply the conventional black face mask worn by an Al Jolson or a Moran and Mack. It is another thing to apply black paint to reveal the face of Emperor Jones. It is not difficult for an actor to apply a nose resembling that of Cyrano de Bergerac. But the problem of convincing an audience that behind this enormous and famous nose is a suffering and sensitive human being, may be solved only by a brilliant actor with an extensive knowledge of make-up.

I should like to emphasize at this point that the conception of make-up for a specific character must be simultaneous with the conception of the inner design of the rôle. A noted French actor and monologist, M. Signoret, once said to me,

Ce qui importe surtout, pour mettre convenablement un rôle en valeur, c'est de considérer que chaque être, réel ou imaginaire, porte le reflêt de son âme sur son visage et que sa

mentalité se retrouve jusque dans le moindre de ses gestes.[1]

This opinion is shared by the great contemporary Russian actors: Madame Knipper-Chekhova, Stanislavsky, Katchaloff, Moskvin, Michel Chekhov.

If this is true for the professional theatre, its importance is amplified many times for the actor in working in the Little or College theatre. There the actor must be even more meticulous about his make-up than he would be were he to appear in a Broadway playhouse. The majority of community theatres are comparatively small, intimate. The audience sits close to the stage. Obviously, on such a stage, make-up must be applied much more carefully than would be required in a metropolitan theatre. It is impossible, in dealing with a small stage, to use the same methods of applying grease paints, the same practice in preparing false, putty noses or chins, that might be employed in a large house. The application of wrinkles, the elevation of the frontal bone, all lines, all shadows, all blendings must be finer and less striking. This is as true in make-up as it is in the other plastic arts. Workmanship designed for close observation is fine and delicate, like the Persian prints or medieval miniatures. That designed for an audience which will view it from a distance is bolder in design and more daring in execution, like the cathedral gargoyles.

MAKE-UP AND STAGE LIGHTING

One must keep in mind the fact that the modern system of stage lighting entirely changes the physical appearance of the actor, fastening the attention of the on-looker on every detail of the performance. It is widely known that there are few,

[1] The most important thing, in order to give proper value to a rôle is to consider that every person, real or imaginary, bears on his face the reflection of his soul, and that his state of mind is found even in the least of his gestures.

if any, faces that can brave the revealing lights of the modern stage without the assistance of make-up. Nor is it an exaggeration to say that world-celebrated young beauties, under strong lights and without proper make-up, look like worn-out, faded women, wan, withered, yellowed. Make-up, therefore, becomes the restorer of beauty, of natural color.

Substantially, straight make-up is similar to the process of restoring paintings of old masters, or the icons of Russian artists. The original colors and outlines frequently disappear or are blurred by the pitiless grip of time or the barbarity of succeeding generations and must be retouched or restored. On the stage, the natural colors of the pigment are likewise falsified by the powerful, artificial lights, and it becomes the actor's problem to renew his natural colors and emphasize his good features by every means at his command. Thus, the actor's personality becomes distinctly the gainer.

Every actor must remember also the changes produced on his face by different systems of lighting. Consequently, he must alter and adjust his make-up in accordance with the quality and intensity of the lights which surround him on the stage. The ideal solution of the problem of lighting has been found in the combination of overhead, foot, and horizontal lights. If only overhead lights are available, or if the lights from above overbalance the foot and horizontal ones, then only the upper portion of the face and body is illuminated, producing an effect of deep shadows under all the protruding features. The forehead appears to have shiny spots, the eye sockets become dark holes, the cheek bones grow more prominent and the nose longer. If brilliant footlights alone are used, then the effect is reversed from that outlined above. Light from below throws a rather grotesque shadow on the upper part of the face. Light is thus thrown under the eyebrows, the eyes grow dull, and the forehead and the upper portion of the nose darker, shadowed, producing in turn, the effect of a fore-shortened head.

A one-sided horizontal lighting, for instance, may lend the face a convincing Rembrandtian appearance. Nemirovitch-Dantchenko, the famous director of the Moscow Art Theatre, during the "fortune-telling" scene in his production of *Carmencita and the Soldier*, illuminated Carmencita's face from below, thereby giving it a remarkable quality of mystery.

The selection of paints for good make-up and the method of their application, therefore, depends very much upon the coloring and intensity of the stage lights. Colored screens placed in front of the spots "kill" some of the paints. White, on the other hand, will always assume the color which illuminates it. Red, under a blue light, will become black or ashy purple. One frequently sees two young lovers on the stage under the blue of moonlight. Their faces almost invariably look like those of ghosts come to life. Red light brightens red; yellow light on red will make it a pale yellow, while green will darken it. The average blue under red light becomes black. The same is true for orange and yellow. Many blues become green under green lights, blue under blue lights. Thus, it becomes obligatory to equip the dressing rooms with lights corresponding to the general lighting scheme of the production. Many mistakes in make-up may thereby be easily avoided. The right scheme of lighting in addition to the proper application of make-up enhances the beauty of the face of the actor, making his features more or less prominent as the need may be, adding a spiritual or animated quality to his physiognomy.

ANALYSIS OF MAKE-UP

Make-up is the only means by which an actor can make his outward appearance reflect a character he is creating. The technique of make-up, like every phase of dramatic technique, requires definite preparatory work and definite routine practice. The problem, moreover, of a particular make-up must be attacked in the same manner, with the same psychological analysis as the character itself. The actor builds his make-up as he builds his character. If he does not understand and accept this fact, he materially decreases his chances of real success on the stage.

His first step is to establish the nationality of the character he is interpreting. Anthropology teaches us that races have their own characteristics and peculiar colorings. For the most part northern Europeans have fair complexions and broad, square faces. We find the Mediterranean peoples with olive skin, oval faces and well curved lips. The Slavic population of the great Russian and Baltic plains are readily known by their blonde hair and blue eyes, yet they differ enormously from the northern Europeans, although both belong to the Caucasian race. The Mongolian type is immediately brought to mind by the oblique eyes, slightly flat nose, and highly prominent cheek bones. In preparing make-up, we not only have to follow these generalizations, but we must adjust the racial features to the particular national traits. Albums of various races and nationalities are invaluable source books for the actor.

Once national traits are established, the next step is the adjustment of the make-up to the age of the part. Gray hair, wrinkles, sagging jaws, flabby skin are some of the obvious concomitants of old age. In addition, however, the actor must analyze the lines which life itself leaves on the faces of men and women. An old man who has passed through terrific suffering will carry the marks of his experiences in his face. Likewise, a man who has attained spiritual contentment will reflect his inner calm in his outward appearance.

The actor must remember that our emotions as well as the external circumstances of our lives, leave their marks upon our face. A sleepless night, a night of sorrow and tears, misery and distress, will leave dark shadows under the eye sockets, deep lines from the nostrils to the corners of the mouth, making it droop. Add a pale complexion to this weary countenance, and the audience will instantly sense the suffering of the character. Just so, a night of inebriation will result in inflamed eyes, underlined by reddish pouches. The so-called gay life is typified by an exaggerated redness of nose and cheeks. A life of disappointment will draw dark lines of sorrow at the corners of the mouth and cause heavy, vertical lines to appear on the bridge of the nose.

After the actor has established the nationality and age of the rôle, he must turn his attention to the analysis of the character. The traits, for example, of naïveté, trustfulness, and audacity must be indicated on the black face of Othello just as slyness, malice, and envy must be reflected on the white face of Iago.

Obviously, too, a man will often reflect his profession. A laborer on the highways will boast a face beaten by the sun and winds while the Russian bootmaker's face will be white and swollen, bringing to the audience a conception of his work —six days each week spent in a dark cellar, where sunlight never can penetrate, and the seventh, his day of rest, spent in hard drinking.

Then comes the adjustment of make-up to the particular epoch in which the character is functioning. History teaches us that each epoch has its own conception of beauty. Mona Lisa has no eyebrows; yet a quarter of a century ago, feminine beauty was measured by the abundance of the eyebrows. Today, our leaders of fashion again dictate plucking of eyebrows, returning once more to the Pre-Raphaelite conception of beauty. A fair lady of King Arthur's court, let us say Isolde, "la belle, la blonde," cannot resemble a coquette in the time of Molière. Venus de Milo or the frail, pale Infanta of Velasquez would be ridiculous in a flapper's dress with a cigarette between her lips and a flask in her pocket.

Up to this point, the discussion has been chiefly concerned with realistic make-up for realistic productions. Now we must approach a new problem, namely, the relationship of the face, the mask, the make-up, to the tempo and style of the production. The face of Hamlet, for instance, cannot be made until the director's aim in production is fully understood. Katchaloff's make-up for Hamlet in a Gordon Craig setting at the Moscow Art Theatre differed entirely from the same actor's make-up at the same theatre, when a realistic, historical setting was utilized. These two make-ups differed from each other as greatly as did Basil Sidney's in Arthur Hopkins' production of that play in modern, full evening dress, from that of the face of the Prince of Denmark himself. Abbie Putnam's face in *Desire Under the Elms,* under the direction of Kenneth Macgowan and in settings by Robert Edmond Jones, must differ completely from the face of O'Neill's heroine in Tairoff's interpretation in the Kamerny Theatre. An actress playing either Mary of Scotland or Queen Elizabeth in Schiller's thrilling and romantic conception of these rulers must have a vastly different make-up from what she would have were she portraying either of these ladies in Maxwell Anderson's version of the same theme.

Certain styles of production require the use of expressionistic or futuristic make-up in keeping with the lines of production. An excellent example of expressionistic make-up is the method which was employed occasionally by the Second Studio of the Moscow Art Theatre, when wigs were made of oilcloth, or of wool or velvet materials, eyebrows were pieces of fabric glued on to the face, and red cheeks likewise pieces of round red cloth. Yet the general effect was not absurd because all the details of make-up were in harmony with the setting and dramatic interpretation.

I would like to emphasize the fact that a futuristic make-up does not mean a ridiculous make-up. It does not mean that the eyes are placed where the nose should be or the nose on the back of the head. Futuristic make-up is done along abstract lines, but it is always cognizant of the specific problems of type, color, and character interpretation. In feeling, it is exactly the same as modern painting and sculpture.

THE TECHNIQUE OF MAKE-UP

In examining any human face, one will be able to distinguish one of two fundamental states or conditions. Either the facial expression will border on that of grief, of sorrow, or it will be that of gaiety, of cheerfulness. In analyzing the external factors producing these two major effects, we shall discover that the cheerful face finds its expression in facial lines going from down to up, giving it a more or less rounded aspect. In the melancholy face, all lines go down, lengthening it. If we will examine attentively the changes that occur on the face, we will notice immediately that when one laughs, one's face begins to grow larger, to approach a circle. Even the nose, the most immobile part of the mask, becomes larger and grows rounder. On the other hand, when we weep, the muscles of the face, particularly the corners of the mouth and eyes, droop. Old age produces similar changes, due to the fact that the bones protrude; the skin sags and drops, creating hollows in the cheeks. Youth is characterized by the rounded mask, with all facial lines tending upwards. These two fundamental laws aid us in conceiving a scientific make-up.

In preparing a make-up, we have to solve the problem of beauty and ugliness. Although there is no yardstick, no golden rule to govern our conception of beauty, a conception which is always personal and relative, we can say, nevertheless, that beauty lies in certain facial proportions, in the harmony of features, in the controlling influence of form, in the subordination of the parts to the whole. Ugliness, therefore, must lie in the disproportion, in the exaggeration of features. Thus, when one is going to prepare a beautiful face, one must give it the impression of harmony and proportion. In my own experience I have found certain criteria for beauty, which I attempt to give the face upon which I am working. The distance between the eyes should be the space of one eye. The proportional face should be divided into three parts: the first part consisting of the space from the hair line to the bridge of the nose; the second from the bridge to the end of the nose; the third from the end of the nose to the chin. The shape of a beautiful face should be an oval. Specimens of classic Greek sculpture supply us with excellent examples of a proportional, harmonious face.

It is of maximum importance that the actor playing a straight rôle should know his own face. Every face is asymmetric, a fact which often becomes too apparent on the stage. Every face is individual; each has its own merits and faults from a theatrical point of view. And the problem of straight make-up consists chiefly in emphasizing the merits of the face and concealing the defects. The results of improper make-up are immediately apparent on the stage, because the actor, not knowing the art of make-up, frequently emphasizes his defects. He may succeed in making a large mouth larger by the faulty application of rouge, or he may apply too little and the spectator will see no mouth at all.

The general principles of make-up are the same as those

in painting, which deals in light and shadow. Each lighted portion is projected, made prominent. Every darkened or shadowed portion is deepened, sunken, almost made to disappear. All parts of the face, therefore, that an actor wants to make prominent must be lightened; those that he wishes to conceal, darkened. As in painting he must know the answers to three questions: What paints should be used? Where should he apply them? How shall he blend them?

Modern industry offers us four types of paints: grease paints, dry paints, liquid paints, and greaseless paints. There are, furthermore, approximately ninety hues in the various kinds of paints, giving the actor a large range of choice. Among these various types I completely eliminate the use of dry paints, with the single exception of dry rouge. I find that dry paints usually produce an opaque effect and that they dry the skin. The grease paints I use are manufactured by Max Factor or Stein. I find that they are harmless to the skin and offer a satisfactory choice of shades and colors. Leichner's paints also are excellent, and I use many of them. It might be well, at this point, to emphasize the fact that a clearly defined application, well-blended, devised to give the natural effect of wrinkles, should be applied with "artistic brushes," according to the methods originated by experts of the Moscow Art Theatre.

Let us enumerate now the succession of operations in make-up. Then we shall be able to discuss and analyze each operation in turn. The order should always be as follows:

1. Application of cold cream.

2. Application of foundation or groundcoat on the entire face to the neck.

3. Moulding of cheeks and chin. (In case of old or character make-up, the application of wrinkles.)

4. Eyes.

5. Nose.
6. Forehead.
7. Powdering the face.
8. Lips.
9. Eyebrows and eyelines.
10. Additional retouching of cheeks.
11. Neck.

Cold cream cleanses the face. One must be lavish, therefore, in its application. After it is carefully and richly rubbed into the skin, it should be completely removed with a towel or tissue napkins, leaving a greaseless surface to the touch. Foundation is applied in order to give the face a base. The choice of color in this operation depends upon the type of rôle to be played as well as upon the age of the character. Each individual must make his own choice for each part. For straight make-up I find that grease paint, a shade darker than one's own complexion, is generally satisfactory. This is especially good for the American stage, usually lighted with straw or amber lights, which tend to blanche the grease paint slightly. One should never use too thick a foundation. The paint should be spread over the face to the neck until a smooth surface is achieved. It is important to remember that the modern stage is higher than the orchestra and that the chin does not conceal the neck, which must have proper treatment and attention. The foundation is blended with the fingers, always carefully working into the hair line. Otherwise a white line of demarcation will appear at the point where hair and forehead meet. If the foundation is poorly blended, high lights and shadows make an unexpected appearance upon the face of the actor.

Moulding, the third operation in the application of make-up, is designed to give the face the shape that is required for a particular characterization. As I mentioned elsewhere, it is almost always accomplished by the play of high lights and shadows. Occasionally, and for special purposes, the use of putty is employed to build up a nose, chin, temples, or forehead. This use of putty, however, requires highly specialized training, which it is impossible to discuss fully at the present time. The moulding of the face for straight make-up for actresses is accomplished by the use of rouge which is darker than the foundation and, therefore, sinks protruding parts of the face. A heavy chin, for instance, or too prominent cheek bones may be made less conspicuous by the use of rouge. A narrow or undersized chin, on the other hand, may be made to appear larger by high lighting the maxilla bone. For moulding the face for the young actor in straight make-up, I advise the use of grease paint of a slightly darker shade than the foundation. Should the face require a cleanly shaven appearance, the chin and cheek bones should be moulded with green-blue lining color. Let us emphasize at this point that the entire secret of moulding depends upon the actor's ability to blend the rouge or dark paint into the foundation so that the paints gradually disappear. The blending of the larger surfaces such as the cheeks is done by the tips of the fingers, while the blending of eye shadows must invariably be done with "artistic brushes." Perhaps one of the most essential operations of a proper make-up is the blending of the cheeks. Often one will find an actor placing the rouge only in the center of the cheeks without the proper blending, resulting in an unnatural doll-like quality.

At this point the ears should be covered with rouge.

In the case of a character, or an old make-up, the wrinkles are applied immediately after the moulding. In order to make the wrinkles appear natural, I recommend the use of a red-brown mixture. Only this shade, the same as is used for moulding faces depicting old age, corresponds to the pigments of our skin. Except in certain isolated instances, I do not suggest the use of black or blue lining colors for wrinkles. Wrinkles applied will look natural if the face is screwed up and the natural lines thus formed are deepened with the "artistic brush," or with a stick or pencil, if one feels a lack of facility in handling the brush. Once the wrinkles are drawn, they should be blended carefully with the tips of the fingers.

The make-up of the eyes is done in two operations; the first, prior to the application of powder, the second after. The latter operation will be explained in its place in the application of make-up. The proper make-up of the eyes is done in the following manner. The eyes are strengthened for a straight make-up by shadowing them on the upper and, more particularly, on the lower lids. With a fine brush lines are drawn close to the lashes. These lines must be blended until they gradually fade into the colors on the nose, on the cheeks, on the temples. Should an actress desire to make her eyes appear larger than they naturally are, she should prolong the lower line from the outer corner of the eye slightly beyond the eyelash and carry this end in an upward direction. By this method, deeply set, dull eyes may be made to flash and twinkle. If the upper lid is puffy, a dark color should be applied from the eyelash up and gradually blended with the tips of the fingers up to the eye socket bone. If the upper lid is hollow, it should be high lighted instead of shadowed. When the eyes are placed too closely together, the upper and lower shadows should be applied where the eye begins and extended a little beyond the eye in the direction of the temple. If the eyes are too far apart, shadows should be applied on the inner corner of the eye sockets. These operations are the same for men and women, with a single exception. In the case of the actor, the lower lid should be shadowed very slightly. In all cases one must always remember to rouge the upper eyelid, as this gives life to the eye.

This portion of the eye operation having been completed, work is begun on the nose. The modern stage, with its strong lighting system, often robs the nose of its true contours, turning it into a shapeless mass. For this reason it is necessary to place shadows on each side of the nose. If applied lightly, and blended properly into the foundation, these shadows will not only restore the shape of the nose under the footlights, but will correct its defects. Should the nose, for example, be too long, the application of the darker shadow color under the tip of the nose, will eliminate the tip as far as the audience can see. If, on the contrary, an actor wishes to elongate his nose, or to make it more prominent, the shadows should run from the bridge of the nose to the end of it and should be prolonged under the tip. Again the actor should remember that the blending of these shadows along each side of the nose must be thoroughly and expertly performed. When the actor decides on the use of nose putty to correct a snub nose or a sunken nose, he must remember, too, that nose putty will adhere only to the dry skin. Even the slightest trace of grease must be thoroughly removed, with a lotion or with alcohol.

The next portion of the face to be treated is the forehead. Here, one will generally meet one of two problems. Either the forehead is too high or broad or else it may be too narrow to meet the proportions of real beauty. The actress with a high forehead may cut part of it off with rouge while the actor may use the darker foundation. If, on the other hand, the forehead is too narrow, part of the hair may be blocked out. This may be accomplished effectively in the following manner: Cover the necessary portions of the hair completely with Pinaud's Pomade Hongroise, broadening or lengthening as much as is required. Allow the pomade to dry thoroughly. Then richly apply the grease paint foundation.

After all these operations have been completed, the face should be powdered. Cover the whole surface of grease paint, and apply the powder generously. Then with a soft baby brush, smooth or brush the face carefully and thoroughly. The superfluous powder will be removed in this way. In choosing the powder for a young make-up, the actor or actress should match the color of the powder to his individual grease paint foundation.

In coloring the lips, we must bear in mind that their size should be in proportion to the face. Porportion is particularly desirable for an actress's straight make-up. If the lower lips are much heavier than the upper ones, and if the space between the nose and lips permits, build up the upper lip. Should the distance between one's nose and lips be too short, however, the lower lip then may be narrowed with the use of the foundation of grease paint.

Again, we return to the eyes. I call this "retouching." The contours should be emphasized by a very thin line drawn with black lining, along the lower and upper eyelids, close to the eyelashes. If it is desirable to enlarge the eyes, the upper line may be prolonged a little in the direction of the temple and drawn with a downward stroke resembling a comma. This will give the effect of lengthened eyelashes. False eyelashes may, of course, be glued on; blonde ones may be darkened by painting. I will leave the application of mascara and cosmetics to actors' discretion, reminding them only that both mascara and cosmetics produce an effect only on about the first ten rows of the orchestra. The shape of the eyebrows may, of course, be altered. An eyebrow may be heightened by blocking out part of it. The method used to do this is the same as has been discussed in the treatment of the forehead.

Occasionally, at this point, an actress will observe that her cheeks are too pale. She may retouch them with dry rouge after, and only after, the face has been powdered. This will help her make-up, without having the dry rouge harm her skin.

The make-up now being completed, it may be necessary in some cases to cover the arms, neck, and hands with a special body liquid in a color corresponding to the foundation. This liquid is applied with a sponge and should be permitted to dry thoroughly.

In the treatment of the hair, it has been found that white powder, or white mascara, especially when applied on the temples, will make the hair appear gray or graying. The Broadway theatre seems to have an enormous prejudice against wigs. I feel this attitude due, largely, to a misunderstanding. Wigs, for contemporary characters, prepared by expert wig-makers, should be as effective as one's own hair. I have known many actors who have covered thinning hair, or completely bald heads, with transformations with such dexterity that the question of the naturalness of the hair has never arisen. The European practice is a vastly different one. There is scarcely a rôle in the repertory of the Moscow Art Theatre which is played without a wig.

The technique of applying artificial hair (crêpe hair) must be mastered thoroughly if it is to be employed satisfactorily. The actor must remember that beards and mustaches are glued to the lips and chin after the whole painting of the face is completed. It is obvious, of course, that those portions of the face on which the hair will be glued must be clean of all grease. The hair itself is applied with a strong spirit gum. The crêpe hair will be procured in braids which must be loosened and combed gently apart. As soon as enough hair is combed, the mustache and beard are glued on in small sections. They should never be glued on in a compact mass. Press the crêpe hair firmly to the face with a towel. When the hair is fixed in place, trim it into the desired shape or form with a pair of straight scissors.

In evolving a character make-up, an actor must be guided not only by the general principles and technique of straight make-up, but by the conception of the character to be played. The inner design of the character must be clearly understood before his outer appearance is planned.[2]

[2] Inasmuch as limited space prevents us from going into all the devious paths of character make-up, I have selected a few special examples which will explain how the technique of make-up is applicable to these cases. For analysis and illustrations see Appendix V.

APPENDICES

APPENDIX I

ILLUSTRATIONS OF THE FUNCTIONS OF LIGHTING

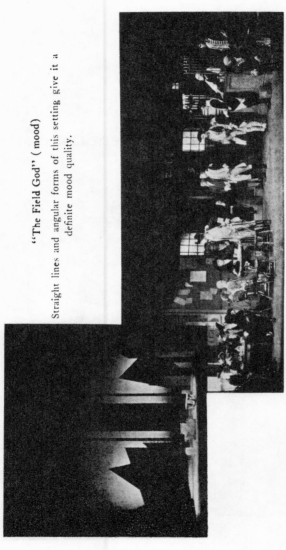

"The Field God" (mood)

Straight lines and angular forms of this setting give it a definite mood quality.

"The King's Coat" (visibility)

The amount of illumination on the acting area provided to show the actors' faces in a place which otherwise from a realistic point of view would be less bright, and the suppressing of the details of the setting, because of their relative unimportance, are examples of the use of light to obtain proper visibility. This illumination is only partially motivated by the sunlight coming in the window, but the effect is far more natural than that which would be given by the strong general illumination.

"Pueblo" (locale)

"Pueblo" (locale)

These two pictures illustrate the possibility of changing the time of day by means of lighting on the same setting.

"Berkeley Square" (composition)

"Berkeley Square" (composition)

These two pictures illustrate the ability of light to compose the picture, with the same setting. By keeping the light off the setting, or definitely on the acting area, the proper dramatic emphasis is given to the scene.

367

APPENDIX II

ANALYSIS OF THE PRODUCTION OF OTWAY'S
VENICE PRESERVED

Venice Preserved is heroic tragedy of the Restoration period. The style of production falls half-way between the classic and the romantic, the scenery being considerably more classic and the style of acting more romantic. The visibility is relatively high throughout; locale is only vaguely represented according to the demands of the manuscript. The composition of lighting is its most important function in this production. The demand for variety with the unit set calls for the use of definite area lighting as indicated in the accompanying cue sheets, and can be carried out as indicated in the plans of the lighting lay-out.

The colors are selected to give accent and pictorial composition to the costumes and at the same time to be consistent with the mood of the particular scene. The density of the color is somewhat exaggerated to convey the romantic style of the production.

The transition from scene to scene provides or creates the most difficult problem in lighting the production and is indicated in the cue sheets as a sequential operation. The business of the actor and the timing of the cues on the switchboard must be carefully coordinated so that the actor is constantly visible, and the movement of the lighting does not become distracting.

The mood element in the production is the result of the selection of colors and the control of the distribution of light to the important areas and details of the setting. The timing of the changes and the development of the pictorial composition in each scene to follow the action of the play enhance the mood quality considerably by virtue of the compelling arbitrary effect of lighting.

"Venice Preserved"

" Venice Preserved "

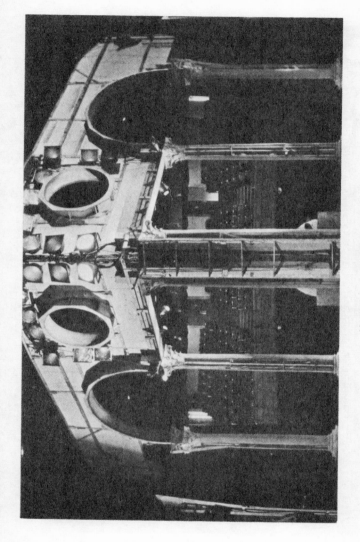

" Venice Preserved "

"Venice Preserved"

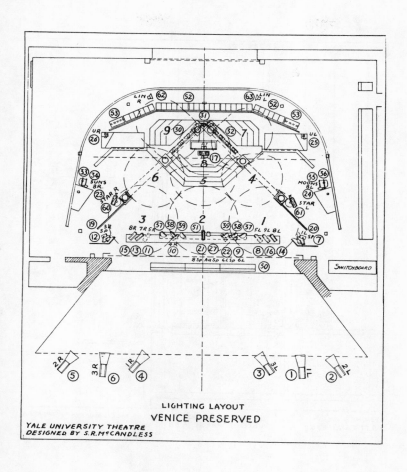

LIGHTING LAYOUT
VENICE PRESERVED

YALE UNIVERSITY THEATRE
DESIGNED BY S.R. McCANDLESS

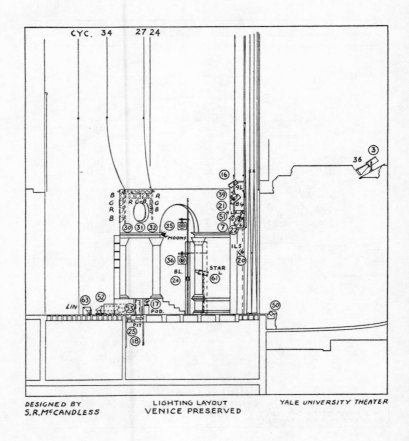

DESIGNED BY
S.R.McCANDLESS

LIGHTING LAYOUT
VENICE PRESERVED

YALE UNIVERSITY THEATER

MASTER SET-UP RECORD • • • MAIN BOARD

Production: Venice Preserved   Operator: Whitehill   Date: 12/20/33

Upper Section

CONTROL		D	13	14	15	16		E	17	18	19	20		F	21	22	23	24	Notes
CAPACITY		1000	250	250	250	250		2000	500	500	500	500		2000	500	500	500	500	Record of Plugging changes from scene to scene
TOTAL LOAD																			
POCKET	UP		1U1	2U1	1PL2	1PR3		3BL	1RL1	1PR1	1PR22PR1			3B2	2PL1	2PL2	2PR5	1B4	
	DN																		
USE	UP		Pod R	Pod L	1L3	3RS		XB	4L	6L	MS	BR		XA	BL	Mr/2	Mr/2	AgS	
	DN																		

CONTROL		H	H	43	44	45	46		47	48	49	50	51		52	53	54	55	56	
CAPACITY		2000	2000	1000	1000	1000	1000		1000	1000	1000	1000	1000		1000	1000	1000	1000	1000	
TOTAL LOAD																				
POCKET	UP	1B3S	TR1		2PL4	2PR4			1B1	4B2	4B1	1B2	XR1		X1	X22	X2	X3	2B4	
	DN																			
USE	UP	WK Lot.	Pt. Lt.		UL	UR			5L	5R	4R	6L	7R		8L	BR	9L	BS	6LS	
	DN																			

RIGHT SIDE
DIMMER READINGS & CUES ---- MAIN BOARD

Scene: Act I Sc-1-6   Production: Venice Preserved   Date: 12/20/33

M. Sw

D & S	D	13	14	15	16	E	17	18	19	20	F	21	22	23	24	Notes
Open				8												
Cue 1				F↑												When Area 1 is on. Slowly.
Sc. 2				0↓			5↑	5↑	5↑				10↑	10↑		② But that my doors…
" 3							0↓	0↓	0↓				0↓	0↓		
4															5↑	② S.M.
5a										①7↑			①6↑		0↓	① Before descend. St. ② After Stairs.
5b							9↑						4↑	F↑		④ Any that they love
6a							①0↓			①0↓			②0↓	②0↓		① Out of my bosom ② And liberty – Revenge
6b		F↑	F↑													③ Podium

M Sw

D & S	H	H	43	44	45	46		47	48	49	50	51					Notes
Open																	
Cue 1																	
Sc 2							①	5↑		5↑							② But that my doors…
" 3							②	0↓		0↓							① Keep me waking 5↑ ② Fill happiest man
4												F↑	F↑	F↑	F↑		① Circle from 3-6 0↓ ② S.M.
5a												0↓	0↓	0↓	0↓		Fast dim ② After stairs
5b								5↑	5↑	9↑	7↑						④ Any that they loved
6a								①0↓	①0↓	②0↓	②0↓						① Out of my bosom ② And liberty. Revenge
6b												④4↑		④4↑			③ Podium ④ Has the clock struck

Symbols: Interlock —   Uninterlock __   Up Throw ∧   Down Throw ∨

Dim Up ↑   Dim Down ↓   Sequence 1 2 3. etc.

"VENICE PRESERVED"

SPOTS

ITEM NO	MAKE	LENS	USE	LAMP	CUTOFF	MOUNTING POSITION	OUT-LET	DIM-MER THROW	COLOR Act I 1 2 3 4 5 6 7	II 1 2 3 4	III 1 2 3 4 5	NOTE
1	Kliegl	6" R	1L	1500WG40110V	Mat tr Pros	1st Beam	HLT	36∧ 26		28 PP	PP	
2	Pevear	8½"	2L	" " "	" " "	"	HL2	34∧	26	26 PA PA PA	26 26	
3	"	"	3L	" " "	" " "	"	HL3	32∧	26 26	PP PA PA PA	PP	
4	"	"	1R	" " "	" " "	"	HR1	35∧ PA		17 17 26 26	26	
5	"	"	2R	" " "	" " "	"	HR2	33∧ 57		17 17 26 26	26 26	
6	Kliegl	6"R	3R	" " "	" " "	"	HR3	31∧	17 17	17 17 26	26	
7	Torm Unit	6"8"	4L	400WG50.115V	Mat off Colm	Torm Pipe	1PL1	17∧ 26	26 26	PA PA PA 17 17		
8	Display	6x10"	5L	1000WG40.115V	"	Bridge	1B1	47∧ 17		PA 17 17 17 26 60		
9	"	"	6L	"	Mat off Colm	"	1B2	50∧ 17		17 17 PA PA PA 17		
10	"	"	4R	"	"	"	4B1	49∧		17 17 17 26 26	60	
11	"	"	5R	"	"	"	4B2	48∧		17 17 59 59 26 26 60		
12	Torm Unit	6"8"	6R	400WG50.115V	Mat off Colm	Torm Pipe	1PR1	18∧ PA	PA	17 17 26 26		
13	Display	6x10"	7R	1000WG40.115V	"	Bridge	XL1	51∧	PA PA	17 60		
14	"	"	8L	"	Mat off Cyc	"	X1	52∧	17 17	PP PP 58 57 57		
15	Kliegl	6"10"	8R	"	"	"	XR2	53∧	16 PA 58 17 58 57 57		
16	"	"	9L	"	Mat off Colm	"	X2	54∧	17 17 26 26 60		
17	Pevear	4½"5"	Medium	250WG30.115V		In Podium	See Notes		17		1
18	Century	5"8"	P.F	400WG40.115V		Ta Tarter Wharf	1PLS	15∧			
19	"	"	3RS	250WG30.115V		Torm Pipe	1PRS	16∧		61	
20	"	"	1LS	"		"	1PL2	15 N∆		27	
21	Display	6x10"	8S	1000WG40.115V	lens Shuttle	Bridge	X5	55∧	PA PA AA	47	
22	"	"	6LS	"		"	2B4	56∧	55		
23	Century	5"8"	8R	400WG30.115V		Tower	2PR1	20∧			
24	"	"	8L	"		"	2PL1	21∧			
25	Disp. Arc Hood	6"10"	1LF	1500WG40.115V		In Trap	2PL4	6 ∧		61	
26	Century	6x10"	UR	"		"	2PR4	6 ∧		61	
27	Torm Unit	6"8"	Aux-Sp	400WG30.115V	Mat off Cyc	Bridge	1B4	24∧	+1 AA	AA	

Notes: #1 2 Units 1U1-13∧ 2U1-14∧

FLOODS

ITEM NO	NO UNITS	MAKE	TYPE	LAMP	USE	MOUNTING POSITION	REFLECTOR	OUT-LET	DIM-MER THROW	COLOR	NOTE
30	6	Kliegl	Cyc Flood	500WPS40.115V	Cyc Floods	On Batten	Ellipsoidal Etched	3½∧ 35∧	40∧	C-R	1
31	6	"	"	"	"	"	"		42∧	C-GG	2
32	8	"	"	"	"	"	"		41∧	36	3
33	1	X-Ray Proj.	Sun	5 KWG40.115V	Sun Spot	Tower Pipe	Parabolic Mirror	2PR3	6∧	C-TT	
34	1	"	"	"	"	"	"	2PR3	5∧	C-TT	
35	1	"	"	"	"	"	"	2PL2	22∧	29	
36	1	Century Proj.	"	500WPS40.115V	"	"	"	2PL3	23∧	29	
37	2	Kliegl	Cyc Flood	"	Set Floods	Bridge	Ellipsoidal Etched	See Notes	48	C-R	4
38	2	"	"	"	"	"	"		49	5
39	2	"	"	"	"	"	"		36	6

Notes: #1 4U4-5U1 Gang #2 2U2-1U3 Gang #3 2U3-5U4 Gang #4 2B1-11∧ XL3-12∧ #5 2B2-9∧ X L4-10∧ #6 2B3-7∧ 3B4-8∧

STRIPS

ITEM NO	NO UNIT	MAKE	TYPE	LAMP	USE	MOUNTING POSITION	REFLECTOR	OUT-LET PER UNIT	OUT-LET	DIM-MER THROW	COLOR	NOTE
50	3	Century	Com'p't	60WA21.115V	Foots	Trough	Etched Al. Con'c't	4	FR3	27∧	C-R	
		"	"	100WA23.115V	"	"	"	"	FR2	28∧	C-G	
51	2	X-Ray	"	200WPS30.115V	1st Border	Bridge	"	3	FR1	30∧	BR1	
		"	"	"	"	"	"	"	3B1	E∧	41	
		"	"	"	"	"	"	"	3B2	F∧	61	
		"	"	"	"	"	"	"	3B3	B∧	11	
52	5	Pevear	Horizon	"	Flood bottom of Cyc	Floor	Parabolic Polish	2	5U3 55∧	38∧	C-R	1
		"	"	"	"	"	"	"		38∧	40	2
53	2	"	"	Dome Base	40W A21.115V	"	"	"	4		38∧	N.R.	3
		"	"	"	"	"	"	"	"		38∧	N.G.	5
		"	"	"	"	"	"	"	"		37∧	N.B.	6
		"	"	"	"	"	"	"	"		37∧	N.R.1	7

Notes: #1 4U1-3U1 Gang #2 4U2-5U2 Gang #3 4U1-5U1 Gang in Color Order #4 #7 Multiple Connect Red Horizon #4 #5 #6 Connect end Horizon strip

EFFECTS

ITEM NO	MAKE	TYPE	LAMP	USE	MOUNTING POSITION	ACCESSORIES	OUT-LET	DIM-MER	COLOR	NOTE
60	Century	Lens Proj	1500WG40.115V	Stars	On Stand	6" Objective	2PR3	G ∧	Stars	
61	Disp Arc Head	"	"	"	"	" "	2PL4	∧		
62	Linnebach	Linnebach	1000WG40.115V	Projection	Bottom Cyc	"	5U4	26∧	58 sprd	
	"	"	"	"	"		5U2	25∧		

INSTRUMENT SCHEDULE

Dec. 18, 1933

GH~WNA

APPENDIX III

ANALYSIS OF *IRISH LUCK* BY IRMA JONES

Although essentially devoted to comedy, this play cannot be so called since there is a goodly portion of eminently serious material. It is a drama of manners with tendencies toward the amusing. The production is realistic with a small degree of artificiality introduced to lighten the scene which is inherently more tragic than is desirable. The setting is described as the janitor's penthouse atop an apartment building.

The visibility indicated is medium with the exaggeration of intensity desirable to lighten the effect. This is limited by a rather necessary adherence to the time of day and the motivating sources.

Locale was important to the meaning of the play in regard to both time and place. A central fixture was added after the photographs were taken, which served to motivate the light around the table in the evening scenes. The careful treatment of the background aided in the placement of the setting.

The composition is casual. There is no attempt to increase the sense of design in the balance of the lighting. The acting areas are softly blended, accented where the sun or a lamp justifies and left diffuse where no special motivation demanded highlighting.

The sum total of the foregoing aspects is neither essentially heavy nor light, tragic nor comic; so it was left to color to pick up the mood of the scene. The selection of media was slightly exaggerated on the warm side and the level intensity increased. These two considerations tipped the balance in favor of comedy.

"Irish Luck"

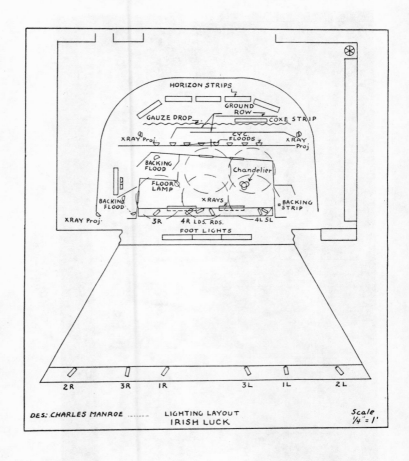

HORIZON STRIPS

GROUND ROW

GAUZE DROP — — COXE STRIP

XRAY Proj.

CYC. FLOODS

XRAY Proj.

BACKING FLOOD

Chandelier

FLOOR LAMP

XRAYS

BACKING STRIP

BACKING FLOOD

XRAY Proj.

3R   4R LDS. RDS.   4L 5L

FOOT LIGHTS

2R   3R   1R   3L   1L   2L

DES: CHARLES MANROE ....   LIGHTING LAYOUT
IRISH LUCK

Scale
¼" = 1'

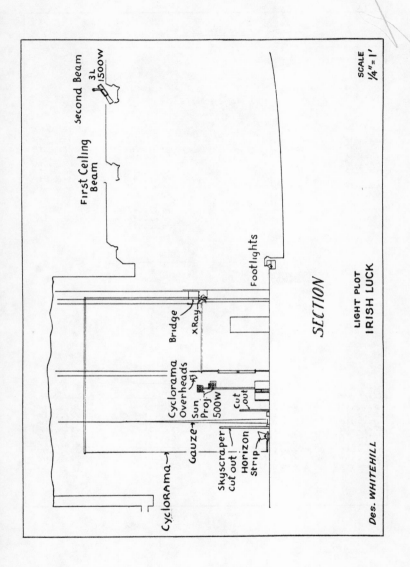

Cyclorama

First Ceiling Beam

second Beam

3L
1500W

Cyclorama Overheads

Sun Proj 500W

Gauze

Bridge

xRay

Skyscraper
cut out

Cut out

Horizon Strip

Footlights

SECTION

LIGHT PLOT
IRISH LUCK

Des. WHITEHILL

SCALE
¼" = 1'

381

IRISH LUCK

by

Irma R Jones

Act I. Set-up

Left Side   Right Side

Left Side			Right Side
5∧...↑F	27∧...↑//	D∧...↑6	15∧...↑F
6∧...↑F	28∧...↑7	F∧...↑//	17∧...↑8
7∧...↑F	29∧...↑/0	H∧...↑/2	18∧...↑8
9∧...↑8	31∧...↑4		19∧...↑/0
10∧...↑3	32∧...↑F	45∧...↑F	20∧...↑3
	33∧...↑6	46∧...↑F	21∧...↑F
40∧...↑4	34∧...↑6	47∧...↑F	7∧...↑6
41∧...↑F	35∧...↑F	53∧...↑9	
42∧...↑F	36∧...↑3		
37∧...↑F		13∧...↑F	
38∧...↑4		14∧...↑//	
39∧...↑F		16∧...↑3	

5∧...↑8 "So long young fellow"
   take a count of 50

Act II. Set-up

Left Side				Right Side
5∧...↑/3	34∧...↑5	D∧...↑8		21∧...↑4
8∧...↑F	35∧...↑F	F∧...↑8		22∧...↑4
10∧...↑2	36∧...↑7	H∧...↑/0		23∧...↑4
27∧...↑//	37∧...↑7	15∧...↑4		45∧...↑F
28∧...↑7	38∧...↑6	16∧...↑4		46∧...↑7
29∧...↑/0	39∧...↑4	17∧...↑9		47∧...↑7
31∧...↑F	40∧...↑9	18∧...↑7		53∧...↑/0
32∧...↑8	41∧...↑F	19∧...↑7		7∧...↑/2
33∧...↑5	42∧...↑7	20∧...↑8		

Begin dimming at the end of ten minutes

I. Station   I. Station

42∧...↓11   29∧...↓15   D∧...↓10
41∧...↓5   28∧...↓15   45∧...↓12
40∧...↓12   27∧...↓15   21∧...↓7
10∧...↓7   22∧...↓7
8∧...↓15

All acting areas down three points.

2. Station   2. Station

                "It's fair enough since you're asking for help"

                                                     23∧...↓6 on switch
                                                     D∧...↓4
                All acting areas up three points

29∧...↑11
28∧...↑7

3. Station   3. Station

4∧...↑6   9∧...↑11   D∧...↑7
37∧...↑7   4∧...↓15   H∧...↑9
36∧...↑4   35∧...↓3
34∧...↑7   39∧...↓8
40∧,41∧,42∧,   15↓

Act III. Set-up

Left side   Right side
8∧...↑F   D∧...↑5
9∧...↑8   F∧...↑8
10∧...↑F   H∧...↑8
31∧...↑3   15∧...↑F
32∧...↑2   16∧...↑F
33∧...↑4   17∧...↑12
34∧...↑4   18∧...↑7
35∧...↑F   19∧...↑5
36∧...↑F   20∧...↑3
37∧...↑F   21∧...↑3
38∧...↑6   22∧...↑5
39∧...↑F   43∧...↑8
40∧...↑6   45∧...↑6
41∧...↑F   46∧...↑F
42∧...↑F   47∧...↑F
                                                     53∧...↑3

383

IRISH LUCK

SPOTS

ITEM NO	MAKE	LENS	USE	LAMP	CUTOFF	MOUNTING POSITION	OUT-LET	DIM-MER Throw	COLOR Acts 1	2	3	NOTE
1	Kliegl	6x12	1 L	1500W/G40.115V	Mat to Pros	2nd Beam	HI 1	35 A	C 65-50	62	62	
2	Pevear	8x12	2 L	" "	" "	" "	HL2	33 A	"	"	"	
3	"	"	3 L	" "	" "	" "	HL 3	36 A				
4	"	"	1 R	" "	" "	" "	HR 1	36 A	57	C 65-50	C 65-50	
5	"	"	2 R	" "	" "	" "	HR2	34 A	"	"	"	
6	Kliegl	6x12	3 R	" "	" "	" "	HR 3	31 A				
7	Torm Unit	6x8	4 L	400W/G50.115V	Mat to Well	Bridge	2B1	17 A	C 65-50	62	62	
8	"	"	5 L	" "	" "	"	2B2	19 A	"	"	"	
9	"	"	4 R	" "	" "	"	4B1	18 A	57	C 65-50	C 65-50	
10	"	"	5 R	" "	" "	"	4B2	20 A	"	"	"	
11	Century	5x9	DSpL	250W/G50.115V	Mat to door	"	2B3	22 A	62+ oil frost	"	"	
12	"	"	DSpR	" "	" "	"	2B4	21 A	C 65-50	62+ oil frost	62+ oil frost	

FLOODS

ITEM NO	NO of UNITS	MAKE	TYPE	LAMP	USE	MOUNTING POSITION	REFLECTOR	OUT-LET	DIM-MER Throw	COLOR	NOTE
20	6	Kliegl	Cyc Flood	500W/PS40.115V	Cyclorama Floods	Batten	Ellipsoidal Etched	3K1	42 A	32	
21	6	"	"	" "	"	"	"	3x2	41 A	57	
22	6	"	"	" "	"	"	"	3x3	40 A	29	
23	1	X-Ray Proj	Sun	500W/G40.115V	Sun Spot	Port Tower	Parabolic Mirror	1PR4	5 A	None	
24	1	"	"	" "	"	"	"	4U1	6 A	"	1
25	1	"	"	" "	"	"	"	4U2	7 A	"	2
26	2	Kliegl	Cyc Flood	500W/PS40.115V	Cyc Floods DR	Stand	Ellipsoidal Etched	1PR1	55 A	F	
27	1	"	"	" "	Window backing DR	"	"	1PR2	9 A	57,32	
28	1	"	"	" "	Door backing R	"	"	2PR4	43 A	FF	

Notes 1+2: 24 + 25 Mounted on one tower · moved Stage Left for Act II - outlets 1U1 + 1U2 - Color 58

STRIPS

ITEM NO	NO of UNITS	MAKE	TYPE	LAMP	USE	MOUNTING POSITION	REFLECTOR	OUTLET per UNIT	OUT-LET	DIM-MER Throw	COLOR	NOTE
30	3	Century	Comp't	60W A21.115V	Foots	Trough	Etched Al Cont'd	4	FR1	27 A	C-R	
31	3	"	"	" "	"	"	"	"	FR2	28 A	57	
32	3	"	"	100W A23.115V	"	"	"	"	FR3	30 A	41	
33	2	X-Ray	"	200W PS30.110V	First Border	Bridge	"	3	3B1	"H" A	11	
34	2	"	"	" "	"	"	"	"	3B2	"F" A	29	
35	2	"	"	" "	"	"	"	"	3B3	"D" A	57	
36	6	Pevear	Horizon	" "	Flood bottom of Cyc	Floor	Parabolic Polished	2	5U1	39 A	25	1
37	6	"	"	" "	"	"	"	2	5U2	38 A	57	
38	6	"	"	" "	"	"	"	2	5U3	37 A	32	2
39	1	Coxe	Comp't	40W/T8.115V	Light ground row	"	White Painted	2	2U1	A A	None	
40	1	Century	Backing	40W A21.115V	Backing door left	Stand	White Painted	2	1PR1	15	B.G.A	

Note 1: 1 section DR for cyc thru window — Note 2: Change color to daylight lamps in Acts I + III

SPECIAL INSTRUMENTS

ITEM NO	MAKE	TYPE	LAMP	USE	MOUNTING POSITION	ACCESSORIES	OUT-LET	DIM-MER	SLIDE	NOTE
50	Chandelier	Gas	2-40W A21.115V	Ceiling Chandelier	Ceiling	None	3B4	5U3	None	1
51	Stand lamp	Property	2-40W A21.115V	Floor lamp	Floor	None	2PR2	5U3	"	2

Notes 1+2 Multiple at board with ghost load TL1

INSTRUMENT SCHEDULE

B.B.W., Jr

APPENDIX IV

A DICTIONARY OF INSTRUMENTS

Spotlights—There are three groups: the baby, using either a 250 or 400 watt G-30 lamp and having usually either a 4½″ x 7″ or a 5″ x 9″ lens; the standard spotlight, accommodating a 500, 1000, or 1500 watt G-40 lamp and having a 6″ x 10″ lens; and the large spotlight, using either a 1500 or 2000 watt lamp. (Note, only the largest of the standard class should be used with a 1500 watt lamp because the heat will shorten the life of the lamp and crack the lens.) The large spotlights ordinarily have an 8″ x 12″ lens.[1]

Spotlights give a sharp concentrated beam of light, which may be flooded and sharpened by moving the lamp closer to or farther from the lens. A falling off of intensity always accompanies flooding, and an increase in intensity results from sharpening. Color is given by the use of gelatin filters. The beam may be shaped by the use of black mat board.

A certain control over the light may be gained from the use of cutoffs such as funnels, flippers, mats, irises, *et cetera*. A control of intensity is obtained by the use of any of the standard stage dimmers. Further information concerning these instruments may be found in the texts mentioned in the bibliography.

---

[1] Recently a new form using an ellipsoidal reflector has been developed. It is from three to four times as efficient as the old spotlight within a limited range of spread of beam. It is made in 500 and 1500–2000 w sizes.

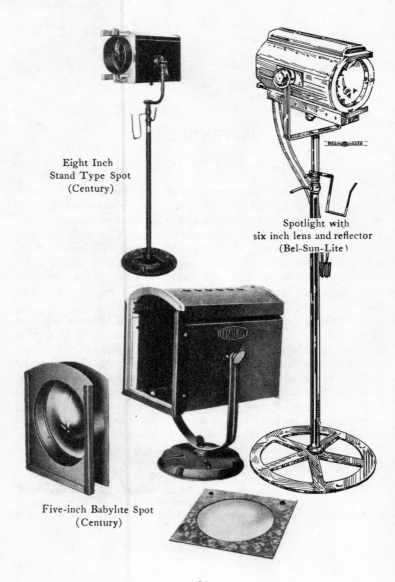

Eight Inch
Stand Type Spot
(Century)

Spotlight with
six inch lens and reflector
(Bel-Sun-Lite)

Five-inch Babylite Spot
(Century)

New Type Incandescent
Lekolite, Eight Inch Lens,
1000-2000 Watt (Century)

Lekolite, Six Inch
Lens, 100-500 Watt
(Century)

Lekolite, Eight Inch Lens
100-500 Watt (Century)

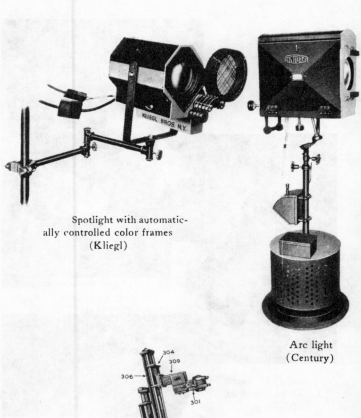

Spotlight with automatic-
ally controlled color frames
(Kliegl)

Arc light
(Century)

Arc Burner
(Century)

Elipsoidal Spotlight
500 Watt (Kliegl)

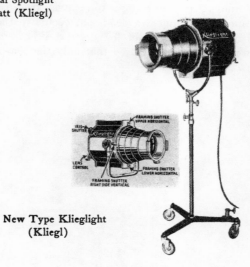

New Type Klieglight
(Kliegl)

Floodlights—There are two types: the wide angle beam or open faced flood; and the concentrated beam or projector. The open faced flood, sometimes called an Olivette, gives a broad spread of diffuse light; some have shaped reflectors which give a particular distribution, and these are preferable. The projector has a large parabolic reflector and concentric spill rings or louvers and is similar to the searchlights used on ships. This instrument gives a strong shaft of light of high intensity. The open faced type uses a 500, 1000, or 1500 watt P. S. type lamp. The projector uses either a 500 or 1000 watt G-40.

Color is obtained by the use of gelatin filters. Neither group can be matted very successfully. The projector can be varied in spread a little by moving the lamp closer to or away from the reflector, but if it is moved too much, a dead spot occurs in the center of the lighted area. By the use of louvers the direct emanation of the projector can be eliminated so that only the sharp beam of light remains.

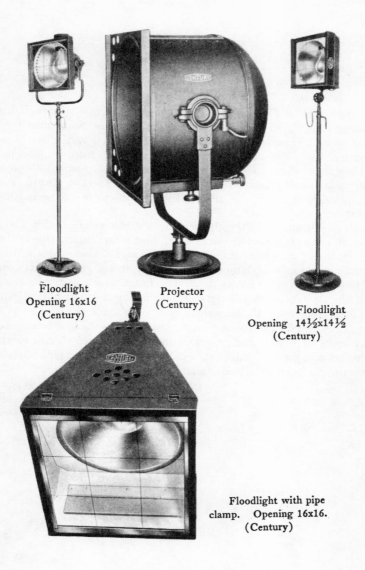

Floodlight
Opening 16x16
(Century)

Projector
(Century)

Floodlight
Opening 14½x14½
(Century)

Floodlight with pipe
clamp.   Opening 16x16.
(Century)

Striplights—These instruments consist of a row of floodlights wired for three or four colors in regular sequence. Sometimes they are an open trough with a line of sockets. The best variety are those having individual compartments with properly shaped reflectors. They all use P. S. type lamps varying from 50 to 500 watts. Portable strips are usually built in sections from 5 to 8 feet in length. Pin connectors at either end allow these sections to be connected together.

The distribution of the different types varies widely, and it is best to call in an expert before purchasing. This is particularly true of the strips used for lighting a cyclorama or dome. Color is obtained in three ways: colored lamps in the smaller strips, gelatin filters, or glass roundels in the larger strips. This instrument will cast shadows of objects parallel to its length, but if the object is perpendicular to a plane containing the strip there will be no shadows.

They can be controlled to a slight extent by shadow boxes and by series of fins. Color gradations may be obtained by the subtle variation of the individual circuits. A simple one-circuit type is made for the illumination of door backings.

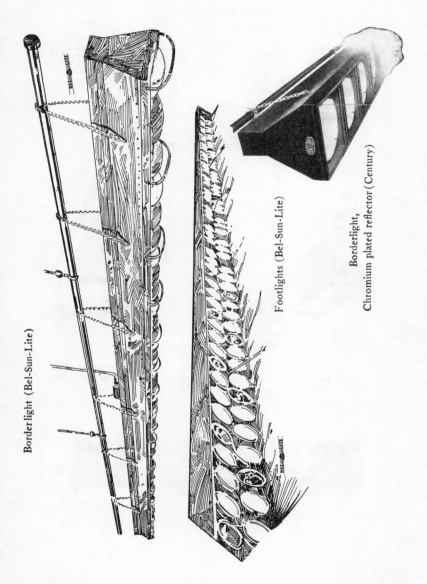

Borderlight (Bel-Sun-Lite)

Footlights (Bel-Sun-Lite)

Borderlight,
Chromium plated reflector (Century)

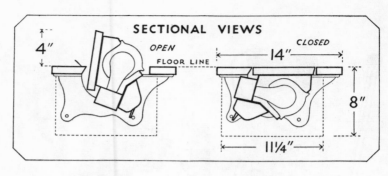

SECTIONAL VIEWS

4"

OPEN

FLOOR LINE

CLOSED

14"

8"

11¼"

Small size Borderlight,
Alzak reflectors
(Century)

Borderlight,
Rhodium reflector.
(Century)

Disappearing Footlights (Kliegl)

394

Cyclorama Footlights (Kliegl)

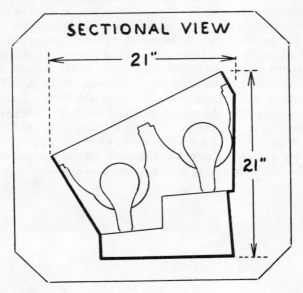

SECTIONAL VIEW

21"

21"

Linnebach Projector—This instrument is a shadow projector. It consists of a source, a dead black housing, and the slide to be projected. As long as the slide is parallel to the screen on which the projection is to be made, no distortion occurs. If it is not parallel, the distortion on the slide may be laid out mathematically by means of a plan and section and by squaring the design to be projected. It may also be done by the longer but no less certain trial and error method.

Lens Projections—Lens systems can be attached to the standard spotlight for this purpose. There must be a dutchman, which carries the second condensing lens, an effect head, or slide carrier, the objective funnel and the objective system including the two objective lenses. By means of this system a precise pattern can be projected a long distance. Here, again, if the projection is not made at right angles to the screen, distortion occurs, and in this case the trial and error correction will probably be the most satisfactory. The size of the image and the size of the slide have a definite relation to the focal length of the objective system and the distance between the instrument and the screen. The effect drums have either a clock work or an electric motor which drives the moving parts.

Other Effects—For many additional effects the reader is referred to the bibliography and instrument catalogues.

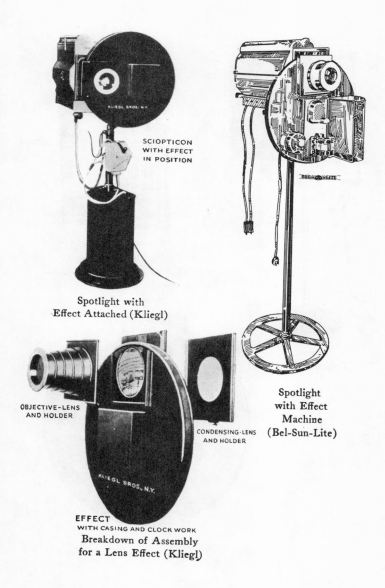

SCIOPTICON
WITH EFFECT
IN POSITION

Spotlight with
Effect Attached (Kliegl)

OBJECTIVE-LENS
AND HOLDER

CONDENSING-LENS
AND HOLDER

Spotlight
with Effect
Machine
(Bel-Sun-Lite)

EFFECT
WITH CASING AND CLOCK WORK
Breakdown of Assembly
for a Lens Effect (Kliegl)

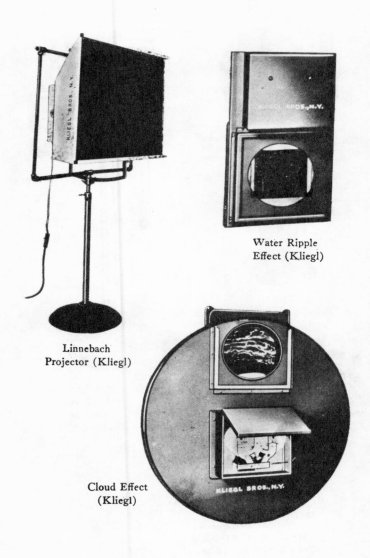

Linnebach
Projector (Kliegl)

Water Ripple
Effect (Kliegl)

Cloud Effect
(Kliegl)

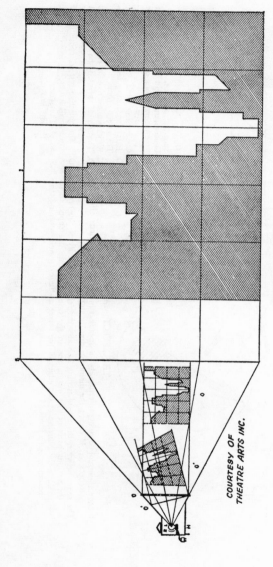

LINNEBACH LANTERN

A Linnebach lantern or projector, showing two slides for producing the same image.

O and O′. Plate glass on which the scene is painted. O′ slanted, O, parallel to the screen. When the slide is parallel to the screen, the image is not distorted. The fine lines indicate the plotted squares which serve as a guide in the construction of the slide. O′ shows the construction of the slide when it is used at an angle to the screen.

H. The hood which is painted dead black inside. R. Reflector. L. Light source, which is a high-powered concentrated filament lamp or an arc source (in the latter case, the reflector is not used.) S. Screen. Translucent if the projection is from behind, white if from the front. I. The image.

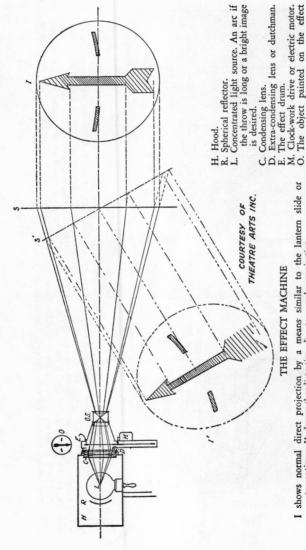

THE EFFECT MACHINE

I shows normal direct projection by a means similar to the lantern slide or stereopticon. I′ shows the distortion due to angular projection.

The space between the cross-hatching indicates the relative intensity of the rays of the various parts of the image, and in the case of I′, they are supposed to indicate the blurring of the edges of the image at the extremes, assuming that the center is in focus.

COURTESY OF
THEATRE ARTS INC.

H. Hood.
R. Spherical reflector.
L. Concentrated light source. An arc if the throw is long or a bright image is desired.
C. Condensing lens.
D. Extra-condensing lens or dutchman.
E. The effect drum.
M. Clock-work drive or electric motor.
O. The object painted on the effect drum.
O.S. The objective system, consisting of two small lenses.
S and S′. The screen.
I and I′. The image.

View of Snow Effect
Plate (Kliegl)

Hand Operated
Lightning Flash (Kliegl)

Rainbow Effect
Head (Kliegl)

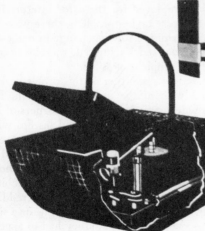

Electrically Operated
Lightning Flash (Kliegl)

APPENDIX V

ILLUSTRATIONS OF CHARACTER MAKE-UP

The illustration of Mr. Basil Sidney, one of the foremost American actors, shows him as he appeared in two rôles in his late success on Broadway, *The Dark Tower*. On the right of this photograph, Mr. Sidney is seen in straight make-up as Damon Wells. On the left is the same actor in the same play, in the rôle of Max Sarnoff, an avenging murderer. Here was a difficult task. The plot of the play depended entirely on the fact that no one in the audience should possibly know or guess, until it was disclosed at the climax of the play, that Wells and Sarnoff were one and the same person. In the program a fictitious name was employed for the actor interpreting Max Sarnoff. In addition to this very taxing problem, there was still another to be faced. The time permitted for the change in make-up from one character to another was strictly limited, thereby necessitating that both make-ups be as simple as possible.

Let us now examine Mr. Sidney's solution of this problem. His straight make-up was applied without the use of foundation. He covered his face only with powder, stressing the outer corners of his eyes and his eyebrows with a lead pencil. He outlined his lips with dark red rouge. Thus, he simplified his straight make-up. In devising his character make-up to suit the German Mr. Sarnoff, he had to find a means of providing himself with a ruddy complexion without using a grease paint foundation. For this, he substituted rubbing alcohol. This may be applied in a few seconds and holds the reddish hue on one's face for about twenty minutes—long enough for a single scene. At the end of that scene, when Mr. Sidney had to appear almost at once as Damon Wells, he had only to apply the powder to his face. To return once more to the operations for the character make-up, we find that he has ordered a wig made on a hair net. In order to change the shape of his nose, rubber rings were inserted in his nostrils. This device extends the nostrils without interfering with breathing or speech. This is frequently employed in make-up for the motion pictures. To change his diction and tone of voice enough to fool the audience and in order, furthermore, to make his upper lip more prominent, Mr. Sidney had a dentist create a set of false teeth made on a hook to fit over his own. The moulding of his face was done with dark lines under his chin. The photograph will clearly show that he has obtained, thereby, the effects of a heavy double chin. He applied false eyebrows, slightly high lighted his eyelids, and used a brown powder around the eyes in a circle into which the monocle fitted. This make-up was impressive and so adroit that no one in the audience discovered that Mr. Sidney played both Wells and Sarnoff until the end of the play when, as Sarnoff, in order to prove his point, he removed his wig and the rubber nostril rings on the stage, in front of the audience. Mr. Sidney was able to contrive this make-up through his complete understanding of the part as well as through his adeptness in the technique of make-up.

After this discussion it might perhaps be helpful to outline the colors and materials that I have used on myself in the photographs on these pages which portray me in a few of the rôles I have played in Balieff's *Chauve-Souris*.

For the straight make-up for the Madonna of the Italian Renaissance I have used the following chart. Foundation: Max Factor's grease paint #41/2; rouge: Stein's light moist; eye shadows and nose shadows: reddish brown mixture; powder: Max Factor's #7R; lips: Hudnut's Crimson #16; eyelines (applied with "artistic brush"): Stein's lining color #17; eyebrows (black): Max Factor's Dermatography dark brown pencil. Slight retouching after the application of powder with Stein's orange dry rouge.

The chart of paints for the decrepit ballerina of de Maupassant's *The Minuet* is as follows: Foundation: Stein's Grease Paint #11; high lights: Stein's #27; wrinkles: reddish brown mixture; eyebrows: grease paint #27, in order to give them a bushy appearance.

For the make-up for the part of Merry Wife, a gossip and tale bearer in *The Moscow Fiancées*, I used the following: dark complexion: Stein's grease paint #10; wrinkles: reddish brown mixture; high lights on nose, cheek, and chin: Stein's grease paint #5; eyebrows: blocked out with Pinaud's Pomade Hongroise.

Basil Sidney in "The Dark Tower"

Tamara Daykarkhanova

As the decrepit ballerina of
de Maupassant's "The Minuet"

As she appeared in
"The Moscow Fiancees"

Tamara Daykarkhanova

As a Madonna of the Italian Renaissance

406

BIBLIOGRAPHY AND INDEX

BIBLIOGRAPHY

I. Bibliographical Sources

Baker, Blanch M.—Dramatic Bibliography. Wilson 1933
Gilder, Rosamond—A Theatre Library. Theatre Arts 1932
Smith, Milton—Guide to Play Selection. Appleton-Century 1934
Tucker, S. Marion—Theatre Books for the School Library.
Theatre Arts 1932

II. History, Drama, and Books of General Interest

Allen, J. T.—Stage Antiquities of the Greeks and Romans. Long-
mans 1927
Arlington, L. C.—Chinese Drama; from the earliest times until
today. Kelley and Walsh, Shanghai, China, 1930
Arliss, George—Up the Years from Bloomsbury: an Autobiog-
raphy. Little 1927
Arvold, A. G.—The Little Country Theatre. Macmillan 1922
Baker, George Pierce—Dramatic Technique. Houghton 1919
Balmforth, Ramsden—The Problem Play and Its Influence on
Modern Thought and Life. Holt 1929
Barrymore, John—Confessions of an Actor. Bobbs 1929
Bellinger, Martha F.—A Short History of the Drama. Holt 1927
Bernhardt, Sarah—Art of the Theatre. Dial Press 1925
Bernheim, Alfred L., and others—The Business of the Theatre.
Actors' Equity Association 1932
Brown, John Mason—The Modern Theatre in Revolt. Norton
1929
————, Upstage. Norton 1930
Campbell, T. M.—German Plays of the 19th Century. Crofts
1930
Carter, Huntley—The New Spirit in the European Theatre.
Doubleday 1926

Chambers, E. K.—The Medieval Stage. Oxford 1903

Chandler, Frank W.—The Contemporary Drama of France. Little 1920

Cheney, Sheldon—The Theatre. Longmans 1929

———, The Art Theatre. Knopf 1925

———, The Open-Air Theatre. Kennerley 1918

Clark, Barrett H.—Study of the Modern Drama. Appleton-Century 1928

———, Contemporary French Dramatists. Appleton-Century 1915

———, Eugene O'Neill: the Man and His Plays. McBride 1929

Crawford, Mary Caroline—The Romance of the American Theatre. Little 1913, new ed. 1925

Crawford, P. Wickersham—Spanish Drama before Lope de Vega. Univ. of Pa. Press 1922

Dickinson, Thomas Hubert—Contemporary Drama of England. Little 1925, new ed. 1931

———, Outline of Contemporary Drama. Houghton 1927

Drinkwater, John—The Gentle Art of Theatre Going. Houghton 1927

Eaton, Walter Prichard—The Actor's Heritage. Little 1924

Ervine, St. John—The Organized Theatre. Macmillan 1924

Fiske, Minnie Maddern—Mrs. Fiske. Appleton-Century 1917

Fitzmaurice—Kelley, James—Lope de Vega and the Spanish Drama. Gowans and Gray, London, 1902

Flickinger, Roy C.—The Greek Theatre and Its Drama. Univ. of Chicago Press 1918

Gilder, Rosamond—Enter the Actress. Houghton 1931

Granville-Barker, Harley—The Exemplary Theatre. Little 1922

———, On Dramatic Method. Sidgwick 1931

Gregory, Lady Isabella Augusta—Our Irish Theatre. Putnam 1913

Guhathakurta, P. G.—Bengali Drama. Routledge 1930

Haigh, A. E.—The Attic Theatre. Clarendon Press, Oxford, 1898

Hammerton, John Alexander—Barrie; the story of a genius. Dodd 1929

Harding, Alfred—Revolt of the Actors. Morrow 1929

Henderson, Archibald—European Dramatists. Appleton-Century 1926

Hornblow, Arthur—A History of the Theatre in America. Lippincott 1919

Hughes, Glenn—The Story of the Theatre. French 1928

Jastrow, Joseph—Character and Temperament. (Conduct of Mind ser.) Appleton-Century 1916

Kennard, Joseph Spencer—The Italian Theatre. Rudge 1932

Koht, Halvdan—Life of Ibsen. Norton 1931

LeGallienne, Eva—At 33. Longmans 1934

Lombard, Frank A.—An Outline History of the Japanese Drama. Houghton 1929

Lord, Louis E.—Aristophanes, His Plays and His Influence. Longmans 1925

MacClintock, Lander—Contemporary Drama of Italy. Little 1920

Macgowan, Kenneth—Footlights Across America. Harcourt 1929

Mackay, Constance D'Arcy—The Little Theatre in the United States. Holt 1917

Malone, Andrew E.—Irish Drama. Scribner's 1929

Mantle, Burns—American Playwrights of Today. Dodd 1929

Mantzius, Karl—A History of Theatrical Art. Duckworth, London, 1903

Martinovitch, Nicholas N.—The Turkish Theatre. Theatre Arts 1933

Moses, Montrose J.—The American Dramatist. Little 1925

Moulton, Richard Green—Ancient Classical Drama. Oxford 2nd ed. 1898

Nicoll, Allardyce—British Drama. Crowell 1925

————, The Development of the Theatre. Harcourt 1927

————, Masks, Mimes, and Miracles. Harcourt 1931

————, A History of Late Eighteenth Century Drama, 1750–1800. Macmillan 1927

————, A History of Early Eighteenth Century Drama, 1700–1750. Macmillan 1925

————, A History of Early Nineteenth Century Drama, 1800–1850. Macmillan 1930

————, A History of Restoration Drama, 1650–1700. Macmillan 1923

Palmer, John Leslie—Molière. Brewer 1930

Pichel, Irving—Modern Theatres. Harcourt 1925
————, On Building a Theatre. Harcourt 1920
Quinn, Arthur Hobson—History of American Drama from the Beginning to the Civil War. Harper's 1923
————, History of the American Drama from Civil War to Present Day. Harper's 1927
Russell, Charles Edward—Julia Marlowe, Her Life and Art. Appleton-Century 1926
Sayler, Oliver M.—Inside the Moscow Art Theatre. Bretano's 1925
Sheppard, John Tresidder—Aeschylus and Sophocles; their Work and Influence. Longmans 1927
Stanton, Sanford E.—Theatre Management. Appleton-Century 1929
Starkie, Walter Fitzwilliam—Luigi Pirandello. Dutton 1927
Stevens, Thomas Wood—The Theatre; From Athens to Broadway. Appleton-Century 1932
Stratton, Clarence—Theatron: An Illustrated Record. Holt 1928
Stuart, Donald Clive—The Development of Dramatic Art. Appleton-Century 1928
Symons, Arthur—Eleonora Duse. Duffield 1927
Tchekhov, Anton—Literary and Theatrical Reminiscences. Translated and edited by S. S. Roteliorsky. Doubleday 1927
Urban, Joseph—Theatres. Theatre Arts 1929
Van Klenze, Camillo—From Goethe to Hauptmann; studies in a changing culture. Viking Press 1926
Wiener, Leo—Contemporary Drama of Russia. Little 1924

III. Play Production

Clark, Barrett H.—How To Produce Amateur Plays. Little 1917, new ed. 1925
Dean, Alexander—Little Theatre Organization and Management. Appleton-Century 1926
Dolman, John—The Art of Play Production. Harper's 1928
Hopkins, Arthur—How's Your Second Act? French 1931
Issacs, Edith J. R.—Theatre: Essays on the Arts of the Theatre. Little 1927
Krows, Arthur Edwin—Play Production in America. Holt 1916

Smith, Milton—The Book of Play Production. Appleton-Century 1926

Stratton, Clarence—Producing in Little Theatres. Holt 1923

IV. Scenic Art and Designing (see Stage Lighting)

Barber, Phillip—Scene Technician's Handbook. Whitlocks, New Haven, 1927

Binstead, Herbert Ernest—Furniture Styles. Pitman 1929

Browne, Van Dyke—Secrets of Scene Painting and Stage Effects. Dutton 1913

Clifford, Chandler Robbins—Period Furnishings. Clifford and Lawton 1927

Harker, Joseph—Studio and Stage. Nisbet, England, 1924

Helvenston, Harold—Scenery: A Manual of Scene Design for the Amateur Producer. Stanford Univ. Press 1931

Issacs, Edith J. R.—Theatre Arts Prints (Introduction by John Mason Brown). Theatre Arts 1929

Jones, Robert Edmond—Drawings for the Theatre. Theatre Arts 1925

Luckiesh, Matthew—Color and Its Application. Van Nostrand 1921

Polunin, Vladimir—Continental Method of Scene Painting (Edited by C. W. Beaumont). Beaumont, London, 1927

Simonson, Lee—The Stage Is Set. Harcourt 1932

————, Theatre Art; Its Progress Through Four Centuries. Norton 1934

V. Stage Lighting (Compiled by S. R. McCandless)

GROUP I.—INSTRUMENTS, CONTROL, AND METHOD

Fuchs, Theodore—Stage Lighting. Little 1929. An excellent book on all the technical aspects of stage lighting, which contains a far more complete bibliography than is found here.

Fuerst, Walter R., and Hume, Samuel J.—Twentieth Century Stage Decoration. Knopf 1927. A thoroughly illustrated survey of the methods of staging in the modern theatre.

Kranich, Friedrich—Buhnentechnik der Gegenwart. Vol. II. A profusely illustrated and comprehensive survey of continental equipment and methods. In German.

McCandless, S. R.—A Method of Lighting the Stage. Theatre Arts 1932. A more complete survey of the methods described in these pages.

Nelms, Henning—Lighting the Amateur Stage. Theatre Arts 1931. A good analysis of a simplified layout and control board.

Powell, A. L., and Rodgers, A.—Lighting for the Non-professional Stage Production. Krieger publications 1931. A profusely illustrated handbook of a practical nature.

Selden, S. and Sellman, H. D.—Stage Scenery and Lighting. Crofts 1930. A good elementary text book of the technical aspects of lighting.

GROUP II.—APPROACH TO STYLE AND DESIGN
WITH LIGHTING

Appia, Adolphe—Die Musik und die Inscenierung. F. Bruckman, Munich, 1899

Cheney, Sheldon—Stage Decoration. Day 1928

Macgowan, Kenneth, and Jones, Robert Edmond—Continental Stagecraft. Harcourt 1922

Moderwell, H. K.—The Theatre of To-Day. Dodd 1927

VI. Costuming

Brummell, Beau—Male and Female Costume. Doubleday 1932

Calthrop, Dion—English Costume. Macmillan, new ed. 1923

Chalmers, Helena—Clothes, On and Off the Stage. Appleton-Century 1930

Diez, W., and others—Zurugeschiechte der kostume. Braun and Schneider n.d.

Evans, Mary—Costume Throughout the Ages. Lippincott 1930

Giafferri, P. L.—L'histoire du costume feminin français de l'an 1037 à l'an 1870. Nilsson, Paris, 1925

Grimball, Elizabeth G., and Wells, Rhea—Costuming a Play. Appleton-Century 1925

Haire, Frances—The Folk Costume Book. A. S. Barnes 1927

Kelly, F. M. and Schwabe, R.—Historic Costume 1490–1790. Scribner's 1925

Komisarjevsky, Theodore—The Costume of the Theatre. Holt 1931

Mann, Kathleen—Peasant Costume in Europe. Macmillan 1931
Morse, H. K.—Elizabethan Pageantry. The Studio Publications Inc. 1934
Norris, Herbert—Costume and Fashion. Dutton 1927
Tilke, Max—The Costumes of Eastern Europe. Weyhe 1925
———, Oriental Costumes, Their Designs and Colors. Bretano's 1924
Young, Agnes Brooks—Stage Costuming. Macmillan 1927

VII. Stage Make-Up

Holland, Cecil—The Art of Stage Make-Up for Stage and Screen. Cinematex Publishing Company 1927

VIII. Acting

Alberti, Madame Eva—A Handbook of Acting. French 1932
Bosworth, H.—Technique in Dramatic Art. Macmillan 1926, rev. ed. 1934
Calvert, Louis—Problems of the Actor. Holt 1918
Crafton, A., and Royer, J.—Acting: A Book for the Beginner. Crofts 1928
Crauford, Lane—Acting: Its Theory and Practice. Smith 1930
Hornblow, Arthur—Training for the Stage. Lippincott 1916
Pardoe, T. Earl—Pantomimes for Stage and Study. Appleton-Century 1931
Stanislavsky, Constantin—My Life in Art. Little 1927

INDEX

Acting, Intuitive School of, 95
Actors' Contracts, 225, 226
Actors' Equity Association, The, xvi, 132-139, 191, 225
Actors' Fidelity League, 135
Actors, 29-30, 88-89, 208
Actors' Salaries, 127, 131, 133
Actors' Society of America, 122, 133
Adams, Maude, 146
Addison, Joseph, 90
Aeschylus, 7-9, 14, 24, 73
Aesopus, 27
Afer, Publius Terentius (see Terence), 21-22
After Dark, 272
Ah! Wilderness, 148
Ajax, 9
Alaric the Goth, 28
Albee, E. F., 123, 128
Alchemist, The, 82
Alexander the Great, 17, 18, 28
All for Love, 86
Alzire, 70
Amaco, 175
American Company, The, 101
American Federation of Labor, 133
Ames, Winthrop, 146, 161
Anderson, Max, 121
Anderson, Maxwell, 173, 175, 350
Andreini, Francesco, 39-40
Andreini, Isabella, 39-40
Andrew Jackson, 175
Androcles and the Lion, 97
Andromaque, 52
Anglin, Margaret, 121, 146

Antigone, 9
Antoine, André, 64-66, 174
Appia, Adolph, 146, 147
Aretino, Pietro, 37, 41
Ariosto, Ludovico, 37
Aristophanes, 16-17
Aristotle, 128
Aristotle's Poetics, 24, 35-36
Arms and the Man, 97
Arouet, François Marie (see Voltaire), 48
A Short View of the Immorality and Profaneness of the English Stage, 90
As Husbands Go, 246
Associated Actors and Artistes of America, 134
Atellan Verses, 22
Athalie, 52
August, Karl, 72
Augustus, Romulus, 29

Bab Ballads, 16
Bacchae, The, 14
Bajazet, 52
Baker, George Pierce, 145, 152-153
Baron, Michel, 55
Barrie, Sir James Matthew, 96
Barry, Philip, 165, 173
Barrymore family, The, 146
Barrymore, John, 147
Barrymore, Lionel, 147
Bartholomew Fair, 82
Basic Agreement, 137

417

Bates, Blanche, 121
Beaumarchais, de, 55
Beaumont, Francis, 80
Beaux' Stratagem, The, 87
Beck, Martin, 124
Behn, Aphra, 89
Bein, Albert, 175
Béjart, Armande, 50
Belasco, David, 116, 119, 123, 146, 151
Berkeley Square, 231
Bernhardt, Sarah, 64, 120
Bernstein, Aline, xvii, 332
Betterton, William, 89
Bien Avisé et Mal Avisé, 342
Billings, Josh, 261
Björnson, Björnstjerne, 66
Blumenthal, Oscar, 67
Booth, Edwin, 110
Booth, Junius Brutus, 105
Boucicault, Dion, 109
Bracegirdle, Anne, 89
Brady, William A., 232
Brahm, Otto, 67
Bride of Messina, The, 73
Brieux, Eugène, 66
Broun, Heywood, 274
Browne, Maurice, 146
Bruning, Albert, 133
Bühne, Freie, 67
Burbage Company, The, 79
Burbage, James, 79
Burgoyne, General John, 101
Burke, Melville, xvi, 198

Calderón de la Barca, Pedro, 44
Caligula, 22
Campbell, Maurice, 117
Campbell, Mrs. Pat, 121
Candida, 97
Carmencita and the Soldier, 347
Carnival, 232

Caron, Pierre Augustin (Beaumarchais), 55
Carter, Huntley, 145
Carter, Mrs. Leslie, 121
Casting (reference to), 189, 200, 202, 218, 224, 249
Castro, Guillen de, 47
Cercle Gaulois, 65
Cervantes Saavedra, de, 44
Chapman, George, 80
Charlemagne, 31
Charles I, 83
Charles II, 85
Charles V, 43, 68
Charles IX, 56-57
Charles X, 62
Charlie's Aunt, 223
Chekhov, Anton Pavlovich, 166, 334
Chekhov, Michel, 345
Chénier, Marie-Joseph, 55
Cibber, Colley, 90
Cicero, Marcus Tullius, 26
City Dionysia, The (see Dionysia), 7
Clark, Barrett H., xvi, 158
Claudius I, 22
Clavigo, 72
Cléopatre Captive, 45
Cleveland Playhouse, 151
Clinton, General Henry, 101
Clouds, The, 16
Coburn, Charles D., 133
Cohan, George M., 265
Coleman, Mrs. Edward, 85
Coleridge, Samuel Taylor, 95
Collier, Jeremy, 89
Columbia Amusement and Burlesque Interests of America, 135
Comédie Française, 53, 58, 59
Commedia dell' arte, 38, 43, 45, 68, 342
Company of Comedians from London, The, 100
Congreve, William, 87, 88

Conkle, E. P., 175
Connelly, Marc, 231
Conquest of Granada, The, 86
Conspiracy and Love, 73
Constant Prince, The, 44
Continental Playhouse, The (reference to), 88
Cooke, George Frederick, 95, 104
Corneille, Pierre, 45-50, 53, 86
Cornell, Katharine, 146
Costume (reference to), 12, 54, 108, 133; Parade, 193, 327; Plots, 248; Principle of Design, 333-335; Sources of information, 335
Country Wife, The, 87
Cox, George B., 120, 123
Craig, Gordon, 147, 271, 350
Critic, The, 92, 254
Cromwell, Oliver, 84
Crosman, Henrietta, 117
Cushman, Charlotte, 105, 110

Daguerre, Louis Jacques Mandé, 129
Daly, Arnold, 121
Dante, Alighieri, 37
D'Avenant, Sir William, 84, 85, 89
Davenport, Fanny, 117
Davis, Owen, 173, 175
Davis, Richard Harding, 234
Daykarkhanova, Tamara, xvii, 340
De Angelis, Jefferson, 121
De Architectura, 36
Decline of the West, The, 295
Dekker, Thomas, 80
Desire Under the Elms, 350
Deutsches Theater, 66
Dionysos, 6, 7, 10, 11, 12, 15, 26
Direction: Character Description, 226; Characterization, 204, 207, 255; Climaxes, 201; First Reading of the Play, The, 191, 203, 241, 251-252; Ground Plans, 190, 221, 243-247; Interpretative Direction, 189; Laugh Lines, 228; Methods of Direction, 187-265; Play Manuscript, 79, 200, 220, 243-244; Play Production (reference to), 239; Rhythm, 201; Scene Plot, The, 245; Schools of Direction, 189; Stage Business, 205, 243, 245; Stage Direction (reference to), 75, 239, 311; Stage Pictures, 206; Tempo, 201, 221; Theatre Craftsmanship (reference to), 200; Timing, 229
Director, The, 146, 187, 327; And Actors, 194-195, 205-207, 209-211, 212, 230, 231, 259-262; And the Playwright, 179-181, 188-189, 202, 218, 219, 240-241; And the Script, 188, 191, 202, 220; Manuscript of the, The, 203; Practice and procedure for the, 258; Preparatory Work, 188-191, 194, 202-203, 220-225, 240-251; Qualifications of the, 200-201, 212, 217; Style of the, 212
Dixey, Henry E., 121
Douglass, David, 100
Dramatic Clubs, 172
Dramatic Criticism, 179, 187
Dramatic Schools, 199-200
Dramatist Guild of America, 168, 188
Drew, John, 146
Dryden, John, 86
Ducis, Jean François, 54
Dugazon, 57
Duse, Eleanora, 42, 343

Eastman, George, 129
Edison, Thomas A., 129
Edward II, 79
Egmont, 72
Ekhof, Konrad, 74

Electra, 9, 12
Emperor Jones, The, 274
Engaged, 111
English, Conover, 123
Erhardt, Louis, xvi, 288
Erlanger, A. L., 123, 137
Escape, 97
Esther, 52
Euripides, 13, 14, 15, 24, 73
Everyman in His Humor, 82

Fall and Conversion of Theophilus, The, 31
Farquahar, George, 86, 87, 89
Faust, 31, 72, 74
Felix, Elisabeth Rachel, 64
Fescennine Verses, 19, 22
Fiske, Harrison Grey, 117
Fiske, Minnie Maddern, 116, 121, 146
Fiskes, The, 123
Flavin, Martin, 165, 173, 175
Fletcher, John, 80
Fontanne, Lynn, 146
Footlights Across America, xix, 150
Ford, John, 80
Forrest, Edwin, 96, 105, 110
Foy, Eddie, 121
Frederick the Great, 73
Frohman, Charles, 115
Frohman, Daniel, 115

Gale, Mrs. Lyman, 146
Gallus, Quintus Roscius (see Roscius), 26-27
Galsworthy, John, 96
Gammer Gurton's Needle, 77
Garrick, David, 90-91, 342
Geddes, Norman Bel, 146, 273
Geddes, Virgil, 175
Gelosi, I., 40
George, Grace, 232
Getting Married, 97

Gilbert, W. S., 16, 111
Gillmore, Frank, 134
Gilpin, Charles, 274
Gladiatorial Combats of the Romans, The, 27
Godfrey, Jr., Thomas, 101
Goethe, Johann Wolfgang von, 72-74
Golden, John, 161
Goldoni, Carlo, 41-42
Goldsmith, Oliver, 90-93
Goodman, Mr., 101
Goodwin, Nat, 116
Gorboduc, 78
Gottsched, Johann Christoph, 69
Götz von Berlichingen, 72
Gozzi, Carlos, 41
Great Divide, The, 234
Great Train Robbery, The, 130
Greek Comedy, 16-18
Greek Tragedy, End of Vital Period of, 13-15
Green, Paul, 173, 175
Greene, Robert, 78
Grein, J. T., 66
Gros-Guillaume, 342
Group Theatre, 171
Gwyn, Nell, 89

Hackett, James K., 117
Hadrian, 15
Hallam Company, The, 99-104
Hallam, Lewis, 100
Hallam, William, 99
Hamburgische Dramaturgie, 71
Hamlet, 54, 102, 273
Hammond, Percy, 263
Harbor Light, 175
Harcourt, William, 133
Harding, Alfred, xvi, 4
Hardy, Alexandre, 45, 46, 49
Harrison, Bertram, xvi, 216
Hastings, Warren, 92

Hauptmann, Gerhart, 66, 75
Hayman, Al, 123, 126
Hayman and Frohman, 115
Heavenly Express, 175
Henry III, 40
Henry, John, 102
Hernani, 62
Heywood, Thomas, 80
Hiss! Boom! Blah!!!, 175
Histrio-Mastix, 84
Hitler, Adolf, 75
Homer, 19
Home Sweet Home, 110
Hopkins, Arthur, xvi, 146, 147, 176, 350
Hopper, De Wolf, 121
Hopwood, Avery, 223
Horace, Quintus Horatius Flaccus, Quotation from, 25
Howard, Leslie, 231
Howard, Sidney, 162, 166
Howe, Gen. William, 101
Hoyt, Charles H., 118
Hrotsvitha, playwright, 31
Hugo, Victor, 62
Hurtig and Seamon, 18

Ibsen, Henrik, 66, 334
Iffland, August Wilhelm, 74
Independent Booking Office, 117
Independent Theatre, The, 66
Iphigenia, 72
Iphigénie, 52
Iris, 95
Irving, Henry, 97
Italia Liberata, 37

James I, 83
James II, 90
Jefferson, Joseph, 109, 110, 117, 263
Jew of Malta, The, 79
Jodelle, Stephen, 45
Johnson, Dr. Samuel, 91

Jolson, Al, 344
Jones, Henry Arthur, 95, 96
Jones, Robert Edmond, 146, 275, 350
Jones, Inigo, 88
Jonson, Ben, 81, 82-83, 87
Journey's End, 98
Justice, 96

Kalich, Bertha, 121
Katchaloff, Vassily Ivanovitch, 345, 350
Kean, Edmund, 95, 105
Keith, B. F., 123, 128
Keith-Orpheum, 123
Kemble, Charles, 105
Kemble, John Philip, 93-94
Killigrew, Thomas, 85
King's Company, The, 89
Kircher, Athanasius, 129
Klaw and Erlanger, 115, 116, 119, 126, 134
Klaw, Marc, 123, 125, 137
Knipper-Cheknova, Olga, 345
Krutch, Joseph Wood, 293
Kyd, Thomas, 78
Kynaston, Edward, 88

Labussière, 59
L'Arronge, Adolf, 67
Latham, Major, 130
Lauder, Harry, 124
L'Avare, 50
Lazarus Laughed, 175
Le Barbier de Séville, 54
Le Bourgeois Gentilhomme, 50
Le Cid, 47, 53
L'Ecole des Maris, 50
Le Docteur Amoreux, 50
Left Bank, The, 168
LeGallienne, Eva, xxvi
Lenaea, The, 15
Le Thebaïde, 51

Les Femmes Savantes, 50
Les Précieuses Ridicules, 50
Lessing, Gotthold Ephraim, 70
Liars, The, 96
Lighting (reference to), 75, 146, 193, 203, 245, 248, 272, 283; Background Lighting, 319; Classicism, 296; Color, 292, 300, 305, 309; Color Mediums, 316-322; Comedy, 294; Composition, 291, 298, 304, 324; Contrasts in, 294; Expressionism, 296, 298; Form, 292, 301, 305, 309; Formalism, 296; Functions of, 290; Instruments, Classification of, 315; Instruments, The use of, 315-322; Intensity, 292, 300, 305, 309; Interpretation of a Mental Picture in terms of, The, 299; Locale, 291, 293, 295, 296, 297, 299, 301, 324; Mood, 290, 291, 308, 325; Motivation, 298, 308; Movement, 292, 298, 301, 306, 310; Naturalism, 297; Plans for, 290; Procedure, 289-312, 322-327; Qualities of Light, 292, 299; Realism, 296, 297; Rehearsal, Steps and Precautions, 325; Romanticism, 296, 297; Setting Up Equipment, 323; Style of Production, The, 295; Switchboard, 324; Tragedy, 293; Type of Play, The, 292; Visibility, 291, 293, 294, 299, 324
L'Imposteur, 50
Little Minister, The, 96
Lodge, Thomas, 78
Louis XIV, 50
Louis XVI, 55
Louis XVIII, 60
Love for Love, 87
Lower Depths, The, 304
Loyalties, 97
Lucilius Junior, 265

Lunt, Alfred, 146
Luther, Martin, 68
Lyceum Stock Company, 115
Lyly, John, 78
Lysistrata, 16

Macbeth, 94, 105
Macgowan, Kenneth, xix, 146, 147, 150, 275, 350
Machiavelli, Niccolo, 37, 41
Mack, Julian W., 137
Mackenzie, Compton, 232
Macklin, Charles, 90
Macready, William Charles, 95, 105
Maid of Orleans, The, 73
Maistre Pierre Pathelin, 45
Make-Up (reference to), 6, 54; Actors' Approach to, 348; Analysis of, 347; Futuristic, 350-351; History of, 341; Lighting, 343, 345; Paints, 353; Successions of operations in, 353-360; Technique of, 351
Malade Imaginaire, La, 50
Man and Superman, 97
Mann, Louis, 121
Mansfield, Richard, 117
Mantle, Burns, 162
Marriage de Figaro, Le, 55
Marlowe, Christopher, 78-80
Marlowe, Julia, 146
Mary Stuart, 73
Massemensch, 307
Massinger, Philip, 80
Masters, Edgar Lee, 175
Matisse, Henri, xxi
Matthews, Brander, Quotation from, 87
Maude, Cyril, 121
Mayor of Sherm Center, 175
Mayor of Zalamea, The, 44
McCandless, S. R., xvi, 288

McClintic, Guthrie, 146
McConnell, Frederic, 151
McCullough, John, 110
McGovern, J. P., 123
Medea, 14
Médicin Malgré Lui, Le, 50
Menander, 17, 18, 21
Men in White, 172
Merchant of Venice, The, 100
Method of presentation, The origin of a new, 33
Metternich-Winneburg, Clemens Wenzel Lothar, 60
Michael Angelo, 277
Middleton, George, 175
Middleton, Thomas, 80
Mielziner, Jo, 146
Miller, Gilbert, 231
Miller, Henry, 121, 234
Mimes (reference to), 22, 27
Minna von Barnhelm, 71
Minsky Brothers, 18
Miracle Plays, The origin of, 32, 45
Miss Sarah Sampson, 71
Modern Temper, The, 293
Molière, 41, 49-52, 87, 167, 350
Mondori, 46
Moody, William Vaughn, 234
Moran and Mack, 344
Morrison, Priestly, 238
Moscow Art Theatre, 145, 350
Moskvin, Ivan Mihailovitch, 345
Moss, B. S., 123
Motion Pictures, 128-132, 139; Kinetoscope, 129; Picture Companies, 148-149, 164, 190; Vitagraph, 129; Zoetrope, 128
Mourning Becomes Electra, 291
Mrs. Dane's Defence, 95
Mud on the Hoofs, 175
Musical Comedy, 233
My Life in Art, xxii
Mystery plays, The origin of, 32, 45

Napoleon Bonaparte, 60, 71, 74, 75
Nashe, Thomas, 78
National Association of the Motion Picture Industry, 135
Nemirovitch-Dantchenko, Vladimar Ivanovitch, 347
Nero, 22
Neuber, Frederika Carolina, 69
Neuber, Johann, 69
New Spirit in the Theatre, The, 145
Nicholson, Kenyon, 173
Nicomède, 50
Niépce, Joseph Nicephore, 129
Nixon and Zimmerman, 115, 125
Norton, Thomas, 78

Odéon, The, 66
Odyssey, 19
Oedipus at Colonus, 9
Oedipus the King, 9, 13
Oenslager, Donald, xvi
Oldfield, Anne, 90
O'Neil, George, 175
O'Neill, Eugene, 146, 148, 162, 165, 166, 170, 173, 174, 175, 291, 350
O'Neill, James, 117
Oresteia, 8
Orlando Furioso, 38
Orphan, The, 86
Othello, 100
Otto II, of Saxony, 31
Otway, Thomas, 86

Paderewski, Ignace, xxi
Palmer, A. M., 111
Pantomimes (reference to), 22, 27
Paphnutius, 31
Pasadena Community Playhouse, The, 151
Payne, John Howard, 110
Peele, George, 78
Pemberton, Brock, xvi, 146, 186
Persistence of Vision, The, 128

Peter Pan, 96
Petit Bourbon Théâtre, The, 50
Petrarch, Francesco, 37
Philip of Macedon, 15
Phillipe, Louis, 62
Physician of His Own Honor, The, 44
Pichel, Irving, xvi, 144
Pinero, Arthur Wing, 96
Plain Dealer, The, 88
Plautus, Titus Maccius, 21-22, 27, 36, 37, 77
Plays (in reference to), 32, 95, 160, 173
Play Readers, 160
Play Revision, 179, 188, 202, 240
Playwright, The (see director), 159-168, 179
Playwrights' Excuses, 159
Poetaster, The, 82
Pope Paul II, 36
Porter, Edwin S., 130
Prince of Parthia, The, 101
Proctor, F. F., 123
Producer (reference to), 179, 194, 218, 225
Producing Managers' Association, The, 135, 137, 138
Production, Definition of, 289
Provincetown Players, 146, 163, 174
Provok'd Wife, The, 87
Prynne, William, 83
Putnam, Abbie, 350

Queen Elizabeth, 75
Queen Henrietta Maria, 84
Quin, James, 91

Rachel, 64
Racine, Jean Baptiste, 51-52
Radio Broadcasting (reference to), 98, 139

Rain, 291
Raleigh, Sir Walter, 81
Ralph Roister Doister, 77
Realistic School of Thought, The, 63
Recruiting Officer, The, 87
Reformation, The, 82
Rehan, Ada, 121
Rehearsal Period (reference to), 132; Dress Rehearsal, 193, 209, 211, 230, 257, 272; First Rehearsal, 191, 203, 251; Length of, 225; Mechanical, 227, 229, 240
Reinhardt, Max, xxi, 145
Reis, Moses, 123
Religious Festival, The, 14
Renaissance, 34, 40-41
Restoration, The, 82
Reynolds, Sir Joshua, 93
Rhinock, Joseph L., 120, 123
Rice, Elmer, 165, 168, 171, 173, 174
Richelieu, de Cardinal Armand Jean du Plessis, 46
Riggs, Lynn, 173
Ristori, Adelaid, 42
Rivals, The, 91
Road, The, 104, 126-128, 131, 147, 150
Roar China, 273
Robbers, The, 73
Rôget, Peter Mark, 128
Romanticism, 60-63
Romeo and Juliet, 304
Roosevelt, Theodore, 120
Roscius, 26, 55
Round Robins, 138
Rowley, Samuel, 80
Royal Polish and Electoral Saxon Court Comedians, The, 69

Sachs, Hans, 67
Sackville, Thomas, 78
Saint Joan, 97

Salvini, Tommaso, 42
Sanderson, Julia, 121
Sardou, Victorien, 63
Saunderson, Mary (Mrs. Betterton), 89
Savage, Col. Henry W., 233
Savoy Operas (reference to), 16
Scenic Art: Backdrop, 272; Color (reference to), 190, 336; Color Sketches, 282; Designing, Creative Ideas in, 281; Exteriors, 223-224, 282; Furniture, 190, 221; History of Scenic Art, 271, 276; Methods of Producing Scenery, 281; Perspective, 36, 147; Physical Accessories of the Stage, 187; Properties (reference to), 108, 190, 221, 229, 245; Property Men, 192; Property Plot, 246; Scenery (reference to), 25, 32, 36-37, 75, 108, 127, 190, 193, 202, 229, 245; Scenery Building, 282; Scenery Painting, 283; Scenery Shifting, 284; Stagecraft (reference to), 145; Stage Designing, 147; Stage Setting, Design for a, 146, 222-223; Stages, Types of, 32-33, 284
Scenic Designer, The, 190, 202, 205, 245, 273
Schiller, Christoph Friedrich von, 73-74, 350
School for Scandal, The, 92
Schroder, Frederich Ludwig, 74
Scott, Cyril, 121
Scott, Sir Walter, 93
Scribe, Eugène, 63
Sears, Zelda, 233
Seawife, 175
Second Mrs. Tanqueray, The, 95
Selling Plays, 159-168
Seneca, Lucius Annaeus, 22, 24-25, 27, 265
Separate Maintenance, 175

Shakespeare, William, 71, 73, 79-82, 83, 129, 261
Shaw, George Bernard, 96, 162, 167, 334
Sheridan, Richard Brinsley, 92-94, 254
Sheriff, R. C., 98
She Stoops to Conquer, 91
Shirley, James, 80
Shubert, J. J., 118, 123
Shubert, Lee, 118, 123
Shubert, Sam S., 118, 119
Shuberts, The, 124, 134, 151
Siddons, Sarah, 93
Sidney, Basil, 350
Signoret, 344
Sills, Milton, 133
Silver Box, The, 96
Simonson, Lee, 146, 273
Sixtus IV, 37
Skene, The, 11, 25
Skinner, Otis, 146
Socrates, 16
Something To Live For, 175
Sophocles, 9, 13, 14, 24, 73
Sophonisba, 37
Sothern, Edward H., 146
Spanish Tragedy, The, 78
Spectator Papers, The, 90
Spengler, Oswald, 295
Stair and Havlin, 117
Stanislavsky, Constantine, xxii, 345
Star System, The, 104-111
Steele, Sir Richard, 89
Stern, Ernst, 146, 147
Stewart, Grant, 133
Still, John, 78
Stock, 106-111, 150, 172
Strange Gods, 243
Street Scene, 168
Strife, 97
Strindberg, August, 66
Sudermann, Hermann, 74

Sulla, Lucius Cornelius, 26
Sunday, 175
Suppliants, The, 8
Synge, J. M., 174

Tairoff, Alexander Yakovlevitch, 350
Talma, François Joseph, 56-58
Tamurlaine the Great, 78
Tartuffe, 50
Tasso, 72
Television, 139
Terence, 21-22, 27, 31, 36, 37
Terry, Ellen, 97
Texas Steer, A, 118
Thais, The origin of, 31
Theatre: Agents, 167; American Theatre, The, 98-141; Backers, 163-164, 169; Booking Offices, 114; Christianity in, 27, 30; Community Theatres, 172; Depression in the (reference to), 138, 145, 199; Drama Departments, 173; English Theatre, The, 75-98; Exile of the Theatre in England, 27-29, 85; French Theatre, 45-67; German Theatre, The, 67-75; Greek Theatre, The, 5-29; Italian Theatre, The, 34-42; Little Theatres, 66, 146, 147, 150, 172; Managers, 80, 90, 107, 123, 160, 174, 225; National Theatre, The (German), 71; New Theatre, A (reference to), 139; New York Theatre, 169; Organization, 111-138; Roman Theatre, The, 18-30, 36-37; Spanish Theatre, The, 42-44; Summer Theatre, The, 172; University Theatres (reference to), 148, 152-154; World War, The, 75, 87, 88, 98, 127, 135
Théâtre du Marais, 46

Théâtre Français (reference to), 42, 52, 54, 55, 59, 62, 65
Theatre-goers (reference to), xv. xix, 170, 212, 213
Theatre Guild, 146, 151, 163
Théâtre Illustre of Molière, 49
Théâtre-Libre, 65
Theatre Union, 171
Theatrical Syndicate, The, 114, 125
Thespis of Icaria, 7, 342
Three Oranges, The, 41
Trissino, Gian Giorgio, 38
Throckmorton, Cleon, xvi, 146, 270
Toller, Ernest, 307
Tolstoy, Leo, 341
Tolstoy, Lev Nikolaevich, 66
Toy Theatre, The, 146
Tragedy of Cato, The, 90
Tragical History of Dr. Faustus, The, 79
Tragic Muse, The, 94
Trajan, 28
Tread the Green Grass, 175
Tree, Beerbohm, 97
Trojan Women, The, 14
Troupe of Monsieur, The, 50
Turgenev, Ivan Sergyeevich, 66
Turn to the Right, 162
Twelve Pound Look, The, 96

Udall, Nicholas, 77
Uncle Tom's Cabin, 291
United Booking Office, 123, 128
United Managers' Protective Association, 134
United States Amusement Company, 124
Unities, 24, 48, 61

Valasquez, Jeronimo, 350
Vanbrugh, Sir John, 87, 88, 90
Vaudeville Managers' Protective Association, 135

Vega Carpio, de, Lope Félix, 43-44
Venice Preserved, 86
Vestris, Eliza, 95
Victoria, Vesta, 124
Vitruvius Pollio, Marcus, 36
Volpone, 82
Voltaire, 48, 53, 54, 70

Wagner, Richard, 67, 167
Wallenstein Trilogy, The, 73
Warfield, David, 121
Washington Square Theatre, The, 146
Way of the World, The, 87
Weber and Fields, 117
Webster, John, 80

Wedekind, Frank, 74
What Every Woman Knows, 96
White Rats, 130, 134
Wild Duck, The, 66
Wilfred, Thomas, 304
William of Orange, 90
William Tell, 73
Wilson, Francis, 116, 134
Woffington, Peg, 90
Woods, Albert Herman, 151
Wurst, Hans, 68-69
Wycherley, William, 87

Ye Bare and Ye Cubb, 99

Zealous Players, 40